Queen Victoria

Queen Victoria

Walter L. Arnstein

First published 2003 by
PALGRAVE MACMILLAN
Houndmills, Basingstoke, Hampshire RG21 6XS and
175 Fifth Avenue, New York, N.Y. 10010
Companies and representatives throughout the world

PALGRAVE MACMILLAN is the global academic imprint of the Palgrave Macmillan division of St. Martin's Press, LLC and of Palgrave Macmillan Ltd. Macmillan® is a registered trademark in the United States, United Kingdom and other countries. Palgrave is a registered trademark in the European Union and other countries.

ISBN 13: 978-0-333-63806-4   hardback
ISBN 10: 0-333–63806-9   hardback
ISBN 13: 978-0-333-63807-1   paperback
ISBN 10: 0-333–63807–7   paperback

This book is printed on paper suitable for recycling and made from fully managed and sustained forest sources.

A catalogue record for this book is available from the British Library.

Library of Congress Catalogue Card Number: 2003042978

10   9   8   7   6   5   4   3   2
12   11 10 09 08 07 06 05 01

Typeset by Cambrian Typesetters, Frimley, Surrey
Printed and bound in Great Britain by
Creative Print & Design (Wales), Ebbw Vale

To Katharine and Julianne

Contents

List of Illustrations

Acknowledgments

The author and publishers wish to thank the following for permission to use copyright material:

Tate Enterprises, for the painting *Victoria Receiving News of Her Accession* by Henry Tanworth Wells. Reproduced by permission of Tate Enterprises, © Tate, London 2002.

V&A Picture Library, for the image *Princess Victoria Visits a Cotton Mill*, from *Pictures and Stories of Queen Victoria's Life* by Mrs O. F. Walton. Reproduced by permission of V&A Picture Library, © V&A Picture Library 2003.

Royal Collection Enterprises for the following images: *Her Majesty the Queen, the King of the Belgians, Lord Hill and the Duke of Wellington proceeding to the Royal Review*, after J. F. Taylor (RCIN 630524); and *To the Queen's Private Apartments, Prince Albert on knees carrying a royal child on top, wreathed in garland, two other children, Queen Victoria standing behind*, by Dean & Co. (RCIN 605909). Both images reproduced by permission of the Royal Collection Enterprises, the Royal Collection, © 2002, Her Majesty Queen Elizabeth II.

The Royal Collection Trust for the following photographs: *Queen Victoria, the Prince and Princess of Wales, and the Bust of the Prince Consort, 1863* (photographer uncredited); *Queen Victoria, Diamond Jubilee portrait, 1897*, signed and dated 'Victoria R 1837–1897,' by W & D. Downey; and *Effigy of Queen Victoria, c. 1860s* (photographer unknown). All photographs reproduced by permission of the Royal Collection Trust, the Royal Archives, © Her Majesty Queen Elizabeth II, and the photographer.

Every effort has been made to trace the copyright holders but if any have been inadvertently overlooked the publishers will be pleased to make the necessary arrangements at the first opportunity.

Preface

This book is based in part on many years of teaching British history at the University of Illinois at Urbana–Champaign and on the encouragement derived from a number of undergraduate and graduate seminars that focused on the queen and her world. It is also based on wide reading in relevant secondary works and in published collections of relevant letters as well as on numerous visits to the Royal Archives at Windsor Castle to consult unpublished journal entries and letters to, by, and about Queen Victoria. Much of the research at Windsor was incorporated into a series of topical conference papers and published articles – all of them cited in the bibliography – that enabled me to discuss some of my conclusions with numerous historians of modern Britain, including Michael Thompson (University of London), Roland Quinault (University of North London), Paul Smith (University of Southampton), Wm. Roger Louis (University of Texas), and Fred Leventhal (Boston University).

At Windsor I was given much fruitful assistance by Sheila de Bellaigue, the enviably well-informed Registrar, and her associates. Most generously, Sheila de Bellaigue also consented to review the entire text of this book prior to publication, saving me thereby from a number of historical *faux pas*. I am grateful to Professor Jeremy Black of the University of Exeter for first inviting me to undertake this project, and to an outside reader asked by Palgrave Macmillan to review the typescript; I have followed the recommendations of that reader in clarifying numerous statements. I am also in debt to my friend Dr Michael Shirley of the Department of History at Eastern Illinois University for reading the entire typescript with care, for making numerous helpful suggestions, and for assisting me with my word-processing program. I am indebted not least of all to my wife who, in this book as in its predecessors, has alerted me to typographical errors, awkward transitions, and stylistic infelicities. Inasmuch as I do not subscribe to the literary theory that has proclaimed the death of the author – at least not yet – I should add that any errors that may yet be found in these pages are the fault of the author and of no one else.

W. L. A.

1 *Victoria Receiving News of Her Accession* by Henry Tanworth Wells

The late-Victorian painter Henry Tanworth Wells provides a romanticised depiction of the early morning visit to Kensington Palace on June 22, 1837, by the Lord Chamberlain and the Archbishop of Canterbury. (Oil on canvas; Tate Britain, Museum, London; © Tate, London, 2002.)

1 Introduction

'Another damned, thick, square book! Always scribble, scribble, scribble! Eh, Mr Gibbon?!' Those, we are told, were the words of a brother of King George III when he was presented with the second volume of Gibbon's multi-volume *Decline and Fall of the Roman Empire*. Historians and biographers have continued to 'scribble' since the 1770s, and very few women have been the subject of more biographies than has King George III's best-known granddaughter. In order to justify the appearance of yet another life of that monarch, this introductory chapter will first provide a brief overview of some of the major works about the queen that have appeared and how the utilisation of newly available manuscript sources and the reassessment of published materials have led to reinterpretations of her life. The final pages of the chapter will outline the precise purposes that this book is intended to fulfill.

Queen Victoria has been dead for little more than one hundred years, and she has already been the subject of more biographies than any other woman born since 1800. More than five hundred distinct books about her have been published; in addition, there have been hundreds of essays and articles, both popular and academic. According to a recent survey of holdings in the United States Library of Congress, the world's largest, among women subjects, only the Virgin Mary, Joan of Arc, and Jane Austen ranked ahead of the queen. The Virgin Mary, Joan of Arc, and Jane Austen share one distinction: relatively little primary source material is available for any of them, and the discovery of hitherto unknown sources seems unlikely. Paucity is certainly not the word, however, that applies to the vast corpus of primary source information, printed and manuscript, that has become accessible about Queen Victoria. It is only during this past generation that many of the hitherto unpublished materials have become available to biographers.

Numerous lives of the queen were written while she was yet alive, among them inspirational works such as *Victoria's Golden Reign: A Record of Sixty Years as Maid, Mother, and Ruler* (1899). The first major biography to appear after her death was that by Sidney Lee. It was an outgrowth of a monumental late-Victorian publishing venture, the sixty-three-volume series entitled *The Dictionary of National Biography*, a collection of 36,000 mini-biographies spanning a millennium of English and British life. One of the original co-editors was that prestigious 'man of letters' Leslie Stephen, the father of Virginia Woolf. The other co-editor and later sole editor was Sidney Lee, the brilliant and upwardly mobile Oxford-educated son of a London merchant. Lee selected many of the 653 contributors to the *Dictionary of National Biography*, and he wrote an extraordinarily large number of the sketches himself. He was 'methodical and exceptionally accurate, a fanatical worker without being a pedant.'[1] The first printed volume appeared in 1882, and the project was just reaching its conclusion when Queen Victoria died. A month later Sidney Lee undertook the challenge of writing an essay on that monarch for the final supplementary volume. Within a year, he ended up with a life 93,785 words long, making it the longest contribution of all to the *Dictionary of National Biography*. Half a year later, that essay, slightly revised, was also published as a separate book, a book 632 pages long.

Lee had much printed material to work with, if only because a great many Victorian politicians and diplomats and European statesmen had by 1901 left memoirs, or had been the subject of biographies that included letters to and from the queen. Twice in her lifetime the queen had, herself, authorised the publication of long excerpts from her diaries, and she had become the *de facto* co-author of Theodore Martin's five-volume biography of her husband, Prince Albert. Yet Lee was keenly conscious of the difficulty of the task he faced. He was writing the story of an honored and lamented monarch immediately after her death. At the same time, he was setting down the facts as accurately as he knew how. He proved quite willing, therefore, to censure Victoria for her prolonged absence from Britain's public life during the years after Albert's death in 1861. As he gently reminded his readers, back in the 1860s and early 1870s, some statesmen and journalists had written about the revered queen with 'remarkable frankness', thereby interpreting 'very liberally the principle of the freedom of the press.'[2] He also assured those readers that, although he would take note of the queen's family life and her symbolic roles, it was the 'circumstance of politics [that] is to a large extent the scenery of every sovereign's biography.'[3] Lee's is obviously not the final word on Queen Victoria, and his book has been out of print for eight decades; yet it remains a remarkable example of skillful century-old scholarship – clear, precise, judicious, sympathetic and yet in no sense hagiographical.

The queen's next major biographer was Lytton Strachey, a member of London's intellectual Bloomsbury group, who at the time of the First World War was looking back on – and turning his back on – the Victorian era in which he had grown up. In *Eminent Victorians* (1918), Strachey announced dramatically: 'The history of the Victorian Age will never be written: we know too much about it.' All that a prospective biographer could do was

> to row out over that great ocean of material, and lower down into it, here and there, a little bucket, which will bring up to the light of day some characteristic specimen, from those far depths, to be examined with a careful curiosity.[4]

The subjects – or victims – of this experiment in mini-biography were the convert Cardinal Henry Edward Manning, nursing pioneer Florence Nightingale, educator Dr Thomas Arnold, and soldier–adventurer General Charles 'Chinese' Gordon. None of the four ever entirely recovered from the subtle skewering that Strachey inflicted, in large part because Strachey skewered with such enormous skill. When word came a few years later that Strachey was now willing to tackle the queen herself in a full-length life, people wondered whether Victoria too was about to suffer trial by biographical ordeal.

The answer turned out to be far more complex. Strachey had certainly not lost the art of writing with an ironic edge, but – in a curious fashion – the personality of the queen cast her spell over the Bloomsbury littérateur. 'He analysed, he dissected, he derided, but at the end he could not help admiring. . . . His book enhance[d] the Queen's reputation'.[5] The result was that Victoria's life emerged as a kind of fairy tale: the cloistered young princess growing up in Kensington Palace; the royal teenager exulting in her new position while tutored by the prime minister Lord Melbourne, who 'became, in the twinkling of an eye, the intimate adviser and the daily companion of a young girl who had stepped all at once from a nursery to a throne';[6] then the bride of Albert and in due course the mother of nine children, as Albert became first her husband, then her private secretary, and then in all but name her co-monarch. There came the tribulations, such as the behind-the-scenes quarrels with Lord Palmerston, the foreign secretary, and there came the triumphs, such as Albert's personal project, the Great Exhibition of the Works of All Nations of 1851, the first true World's Fair. Ten years later came Albert's death, the wound that would not heal.

Strachey's biography reads like a novel, but the specific quotations from letters and speeches and the descriptions are all accurate. Strachey's artistry is achieved by the manner in which he juxtaposes the historical bricks that make up his edifice. For the most part, he does not feel compelled to make things up. The result was what in 1921 one American reviewer called a 'classic in English literature,'[7] a book that sold more copies than any other biography ever of Victoria. Strachey had available to him at least two major sources that had not been available to Sidney Lee. One was a two-volume set of excerpts from the detailed diaries of Victoria as a princess and as a young monarch. The other was a set of three long volumes of hitherto unpublished letters by (and sometimes to) Victoria during the first third of her reign – all the way to the death of Albert. And therein lies one significant limitation to the value of Strachey's work. Three-quarters of the work focuses on the first half of the queen's life, and the final eighty pages merely skim over the final four decades.

During the middle years of the Victorian era, Walter Bagehot, an admired journalist and political scientist, had written a provocative book to which he had given a prosaic title, *The English Constitution*. People still talked about Britain's government, he pointed out, as they had one hundred years earlier – as if it were primarily made up of King, Lords, and Commons. In reality, Bagehot suggested, 'A Republic has insinuated itself beneath the folds of a monarchy.'[8] The *efficient* part of Britain's government in the 1860s, Bagehot argued,

was made up of the House of Commons and, even more important-
ly, of the prime minister and his cabinet, those members of the legislature who exercised administrative responsibility in the name of the
monarch. That monarch retained important *dignified* functions, however, as a focus of obedience, as the head of society, as a model of
morality, and as an exemplar of governmental continuity, while the
actual governors switched places from time to time.

Bagehot by no means dismissed these *dignified* functions as unimportant: they gave sanctity and legitimacy to the British state, but the
monarch did not administer that state. Indeed, if a single party possessed an overall majority of seats in the House of Commons and if
that party was agreed on a single leader, the prime minister, then,
argued Bagehot, the monarch was left with only three *efficient* functions: 'the right to be consulted, the right to encourage, and the right
to warn.'[9]

Walter Bagehot had a great many late Victorian and twentieth-
century readers, but – as we now know – Queen Victoria was not
among them. Her grandson George V, who reigned from 1910 to
1936, was such a reader, however; indeed he came to look at
Bagehot's work as a bible for twentieth-century constitutional monarchs.[10] And it was while George V was king in the 1920s and early
1930s that six big books of additional hitherto unpublished letters
were brought out that would make it possible for future biographers
of the queen to write about the last two-thirds of her reign in as well-
informed a fashion as Strachey had written about her youth and
about the first third of her reign. These books were supplemented by
a two-volume set of letters exchanged between Queen Victoria and
the prime minister whom she ultimately came to appreciate least,
William Ewart Gladstone.

A youthful Oxford graduate named Frank Hardie pounced on
those newly published letters, and they made him furious! They
demonstrated, in his eyes, that the distinction that Bagehot had
drawn between the *dignified* and the *efficient* powers of the Crown was
a highly porous one. Instead, he bluntly concluded, they completely
'invalidated'[11] Bagehot's interpretation. Rather than acting as a retired
widow during the years after Albert's death, Victoria demonstrated a
behind-the-scenes influence that became ever more pervasive – over

issues of foreign policy, over important appointments in Church and State, and over legislation. As Hardie grudgingly conceded, the queen proved to be as influential as she was because she was extraordinarily industrious and because she possessed a superb memory for detail. Hardie admitted that the queen may not have seen her actions as unconstitutional, but he thought it right 'to emphasize to what depths of unconstitutionality she sank.'[12] In her later years, he pointed out, she gave a decided preference to Conservative ministries over Liberal ministries – because, in her judgment, Conservative ministries were generally sensible and reliable and Liberal ministries were not. Hardie's own conclusion was succinct: 'All the accumulated evidence goes to show that between 1861 and 1901 Queen Victoria ruled as well as reigned.'[13] Subsequent biographers of the queen were to show far less interest in her political role.

During the later 1930s and 1940s, some of the letters exchanged by Albert and his brother were published for the first time, as was much of the correspondence between Queen Victoria and the Prussian royal family and some of the queen's notes to her private secretary, Sir Henry Ponsonby. In the meantime, the unpublished materials in the Royal Archives were being organised and made available to scholars. In 1964, Elizabeth Longford took advantage of such sources by bringing out the one-volume biography of Queen Victoria that set the standard for such books for the next generation and even for our own time. Although not an academic, she was a well-trained and eminently readable historian and biographer who has written other books such as a valuable two-volume biography of the Duke of Wellington. In preparing her portrait of the queen, Lady Longford had at her disposal at least two additional major sources that her predecessors had lacked. The first of these was Princess Beatrice's transcription of Queen Victoria's diary or journal, a document that the monarch faithfully kept from the age of fourteen to the age of eighty-one. One hundred and twelve sizable bound volumes remain, and if comments on topics such as the queen's relations with her children have been severely bowdlerised, this is far less true of her appraisals of ministers of state, of foreign rulers, and of particular political controversies.

A yet more important primary source to which Elizabeth

Longford and more recent biographers have had access is the correspondence that began in 1858 when Queen Victoria's eldest daughter, Princess Victoria (or 'Vicky'), married the heir to the Prussian (and later the German) throne and went off to live in Berlin. That daughter became the closest confidante of the queen, who wrote to her daughter happily and impetuously and often: on the average of twice a week for the next forty years. It is in these letters – almost 3,800 of them by Queen Victoria – that, as Elizabeth Longford has noted, we can truly discover Victoria in 'all her passions, obsessions, contrariness, practicality, immaturity, wisdom and irresistible charm.'[14] Both correspondents expected that the letters would be burned after their deaths, but happily the letters survived all manner of vicissitudes including World War II bombs, and between 1964 and 1990 a significant portion of that correspondence was published. It is in these letters that many biographers have found Queen Victoria at her most candid and her most quotable.

It was with these and other archival materials at her disposal that Elizabeth Longford wrote her lively but carefully documented biography. The only significant limitation to that work is that topics such as the queen's constitutional role are never systematically discussed. We are told that Queen Victoria often spoke of ministers and servants in the same breath, and the biography tends to deal with them in a comparable fashion. In the process, Lady Longford became the first of several biographers to track down and to treat with great sensitivity the story of John Brown and of the manner in which that Scottish servant came in the years after 1864 to play so central a role in the life of his royal mistress as she gradually came to terms with life after Albert.

A number of other lengthy one-volume biographies of Queen Victoria have been published since 1964, but as Giles St Aubyn concedes – and he is the author of one of them – Lady Longford's work remains 'the envy and despair of those who venture to follow her.'[15] Cecil Woodham-Smith's biography of 1972 takes the story up to the death of Prince Albert, in 555 pages, and more recently Monica Charlot's *Victoria: The Young Queen* has done the same in 432 pages. Both necessarily devote more space to the queen's earlier years than does Lady Longford, and Monica Charlot makes the most meticulous use of what remains of the queen's journal. It is interesting to note that although Prince Albert became the subject of a five-volume biography and although many other eminent Victorians ended up with posthumous triple-deckers, no twentieth- or twenty-first-century biographer has, as of 2002, succeeded in completing a multi-volume life of the great queen herself.

In 1987, Stanley Weintraub, a prolific Professor of Arts and Humanities at Pennsylvania State University, became the first American to try his hand at a full-scale scholarly biography of the queen. He subtitled it 'an intimate biography' and it became a bestseller. Although Weintraub made use of no important cache of new or unknown papers, he did seem to be inspired by one major purpose, to take the queen off her pedestal and to remind his readers that the monarch's feet were fashioned of clay rather than of marble. Weintraub's book, in turn, inspired one of his reviewers, David Cannadine, a distinguished historian of modern Britain, to sketch a pen-portrait of the monarch that reminds us that not all twentieth-century scholars have been admirers. By the last phase of her reign, Cannadine writes, 'the Queen had become very fat, rather ugly, semi-invalid and half-blind. . . . In general she was callous, insensitive, obstinate, outspoken, capricious and bigoted' and 'quite extraordinarily selfish.' A 'long unchecked habit of self-indulgence effectively transformed the monarch into a monster and her courtiers into sycophantic cyphers. . . . The result was a court regimen at once tyrannical and tedious, unbearable and unreal.'[16]

The difficulty with this assessment as with hagiographic obituary appraisals such as Marie Corelli's,[17] which described the monarch as a brave, benign, and beneficent heroine, is what has been called 'selective Victorianism.'[18] So much primary source material for the era and for the major figures who lived in it remains, that some plausible evidence is at hand for almost any generalisation that we may venture to put forward so long as the countervailing evidence is ignored.

Since Weintraub's book, there have appeared three other lengthy biographies of the queen. Giles St Aubyn's portrait has the great virtue of balance. It is distorted neither 'by idolatry' nor 'by malice.'[19] Its chief limitation is its lack of either footnotes or endnotes. The chief limitation of Carolly Erickson's *Her Little Majesty* is a lack of concern with historical context and an overly active imagination when it comes to telling us precisely what people long dead were thinking. In the words of one critic: 'Whereas the historical novel traditionally offers history in the form of fiction, the historical biography too often offers fiction in the form of history.'[20] The best of the lengthy post-Longford biographies of the queen is the most recent, Christopher Hibbert's 504-page *Queen Victoria: A Personal History.*[21] It does not pretend to provide a brand new interpretation, and it is unconcerned with historiographical disputes. At the same time, it is balanced in approach, it is fully documented, and like Christopher Hibbert's many other biographies – of George III and George IV, of Wellington and of Nelson – it is eminently readable.

If, through the eyes of a literary scholar such as Weintraub, Victoria appears a flawed figure at best, then how does she fare at the hands of contemporary theoretically inclined feminists who pursue the approach known as Culture Studies? For twentieth-century feminists, it is clear, Victoria has always served as an ambiguous role model. On the one hand, she was the best known and the most influential female ruler in the world, and thus she could hardly be ignored. On the other hand, Queen Victoria observed every now and then that 'We women . . . are *not fitted to reign*'[22] and she privately protested against 'this mad wicked folly of "Women's rights" with all its attendant horrors.'[23]

Dorothy Thompson is a feminist but not part of the 'theoretical culture studies' movement; rather she is a historian specialising in social 'history from the bottom up.' The most surprising aspect of her brief biography, published in Britain as *Queen Victoria: Gender and Power*, is how sympathetic she is to the queen. Whatever Victoria's attitudes about the legal and social roles of women, argues Thompson, her career strengthened the role of the monarchy as an institution, and the very presence of a woman on the throne served the cause of gender equality. The book is not so much a life as a series of linked interpretive essays of which the most provocative is chapter 4, 'Victoria and John Brown.'[24]

One of several culture studies theorists of our day who have written about Victoria is Adrienne Munich, the Director of the Women's

Studies Program at the State University of New York at Stonybrook, where she teaches courses in Art, English, and Comparative Literature. In her book *Queen Victoria's Secrets*, Munich's professed purpose is not to 'engage in a further effort to discover a real Victoria' but rather to examine 'malicious as well as pious distortions, cultural fantasies as well as literature, painting, memoirs, and letters to explore some of the ways in which Victorian culture accommodated ideas to represent its self-interested moment.'[25] The author provides us with seven largely distinct topical essays on such subjects as death, domesticity, motherhood, and empire, framed by a largely theoretical introduction and epilogue. The strength of the work lies in the numerous nineteenth-century sketches and verses that she includes. Its weakness lies both in its opacity and in the dizzying web of symbolism and metaphorical excess that envelop her conclusions.[26]

Margaret Homans' *Royal Representations: Queen Victoria and British Culture, 1837–1876* is another work specifically intended, we are told, 'to address the limitations of traditional forms of history and biography.'[27] The author sets the queen in the context of British literature, and provides the reader with revelations as mysterious as the following: during the early years of her widowhood, 'the Queen's retreat from embodied self-representation (which is also a disguise) into a doubly displaced literary form of representation . . . complements the movement towards greater popular political representation' embodied in the Reform Bill of 1867.[28]

Although some of the contributions that culture studies specialists have thus far made to our understanding of Queen Victoria and her world may be viewed with a skeptical eye, numerous books and articles of the past decade have proved more valuable. In *Democratic Royalism: The Transformation of the British Monarchy, 1861–1914*,[29] Professor William Kuhn has called helpful attention to the manner in which a number of important late Victorian Liberals played a significant role in adapting that institution to an increasingly democratic, meritocratic, and socially egalitarian society. In *A Royal Conflict*,[30] Katherine Hudson has brought to life both the family and the curious mental world of Sir John Conroy, the courtier who envisaged himself as creating and elevating the very 'People's Queen' who came to despise him. In *Becoming Victoria*,[31] Lynne Vallone has made the fullest use ever of surviving (and often hitherto unpublished) letters, stories, drawings, journals, and educational materials in order to provide a persuasive account of the upbringing of the future queen.

An often helpful way to understand the queen is to learn more about her children. Recent books that have proved particularly revealing in that respect are the biographies of her eldest daughter Vicky, *An Uncommon Woman* by Hannah Pakula,[32] her third son Arthur, *Witness of a Century* by Noble Frankland, and her youngest son, *Prince Leopold* by Charlotte Zeepvat.[33] In analogous fashion, Michaela Reid's *Ask Sir James*[34] tells us a great deal about the queen's life and state of health during her final two decades. That readily available but little-explored sources can provide new understanding is the implication of Richard Williams' monograph, *The Contentious Crown.*[35] Williams reminds us that widespread republican sentiment in Victorian Britain was not limited to a few years of Victoria's widowhood. The proponents of Britain's monarchy may have outnumbered the critics, but the critics never disappeared for long.

A yet more significant example of historical revisionism has been provided by Frank Prochaska. He demonstrates that a vast subject had been virtually ignored by biographers of Queen Victoria and her descendants. In *Royal Bounty: The Making of the Welfare Monarchy,*[36] he points out that one of the chief links between Victoria and her people involved neither her opening of Parliament nor her correspondence with her ministers but her role as royal patron and philanthropist. Prochaska concludes that Queen Victoria may well have 'contributed more to the nation's health and happiness through her charitable administration than through her political one.'[37]

Even a biographer who makes use of all such recent research may find it virtually impossible to write a completely satisfactory life of Queen Victoria. By the time of her death, she had become the most famous woman in the world; her face appeared on every coin and every postage stamp used by her subjects in the United Kingdom and, to a large degree, throughout her empire. Not least of all, she had been transmuted into an adjective that we continue to encounter in every-day as well as in academic life. The biographer concerned with her surroundings as well as her life must keep in mind the dramatic changes that coincided with that life:

An 'age of aristocracy' gave way to something close to universal manhood suffrage at the municipal, the county, and the national level.

The world of the sailing vessel and the stage coach gave way to that of the steamship and steam locomotive.

The whale-oil lamp gave way to the electric light.

The goose-quill pen gave way to the typewriter.

The messenger boy gave way first to the telegraph and then to the telephone. When Sir Robert Peel was named prime minister in the year 1834, he was traveling in Italy. It took eight days for the invitation to creep from London to Rome. When the news of the queen's death was released to waiting journalists outside Osborne House shortly before 7 p.m. on the evening of January 22, 1901, that news reached the major capitals of the world within half an hour. By nightfall, in Washington, DC, President William McKinley had already sent to the new king a telegram of condolence on behalf of the people of the United States.[38]

In Britain itself, Queen Victoria's reign coincided with the tenure of eleven Lord Chancellors, of ten prime ministers, of six army commanders-in-chief, and of five Archbishops of Canterbury. It also coincided with the tenure of ten governors-general of Canada and sixteen viceroys of India. In France there had ruled one king, one emperor, and seven presidents of the Third Republic, and in the United States eighteen different men had served as president. At the time of her birth, she was the niece of at least a score of living aunts and uncles with their various spouses and children – legitimate and illegitimate. At the time of her death, she had six living children and thirty-nine grandchildren, and she had become 'the Grandmother of Europe.'

When one thinks therefore about all the transformations that took place and about all the changing personal and institutional contexts in which the monarch lived and reigned, one begins to understand how difficult it must be to write a truly satisfactory biography of Queen Victoria. If the work does justice to all facets of her life and reign and world, it is bound to seem far too long. Yet if it is short, it is almost certain to leave out something vital. Perhaps, like Dr

Johnson's famous dog standing on his hind legs, one should not expect to see it done well; one should be surprised to see it done at all. Taking into account the difficulties enumerated above, how can this new biography be justified? It seeks to accomplish five purposes:

(1) To incorporate into a relatively short and fundamentally chronological narrative some of the insights and assessments provided by the numerous new books and articles of the past two decades, including eight topical articles of my own. Special attention is therefore given to such neglected subjects as Victoria's religious views, her constitutional role, and her connections with Britain's army and with Ireland.

(2) To provide a reminder of the fact that the queen was not only a personality and a symbol and an adjective but also a multidimensional human being and an active player in the domestic politics and the international relations of the nineteenth century. Some biographers have become so eager to provide an 'intimate portrait' and retrospectively to psychoanalyse the private personality that they have neglected not only the public face that Victoria presented both to her people and to her fellow monarchs but also the influence that she exercised on both people and events.

(3) To provide enough of the economic, social, cultural, and political context so as to make the queen's life intelligible even to readers who do not possess a broad background knowledge of the nineteenth century.

(4) Whenever possible, to cite the queen's own words as a key to understanding both her character and the manner in which she understood the world in which she lived. The queen is often worth quoting.

(5) While acknowledging that no brief life can do full justice to all facets of Victoria's life and world, to whet the reader's appetite for more and to alert that same reader to the books and the articles in which additional historical nourishment may be found.

2 *Princess Victoria Visits a Cotton Mill*

An episode from one of her tours with her mother during the early 1830s.
(Mrs O. F. Walton, *Pictures and Stories from Queen Victoria's Life*, 1901; V&A
Picture Library; © V&A Picture Library 2003.)

2 The Cloistered Princess

King George III, whose formal reign lasted from 1760 until 1820, and his wife Queen Charlotte, were the parents of fifteen children, an all-time record for an English or Scottish monarch. Inasmuch as all but two of those children grew to adulthood, there seemed to be no danger thereafter that the Hanoverian dynasty, that had begun back in 1714 with the monarch's great-grandfather King George I, would soon die out.[1] And yet there was. Under the rigid provisions of the Royal Marriage Act of 1772, the marriages of all of George III's children required the personal approval of the king.[2] In order to avoid domestic political favoritism, he insisted that none of those children marry a commoner, and, according to the Act of Settlement of 1701, Roman Catholics were excluded from the rank of royal consort. In order to find eligible brides, royal sons therefore had to look to either one of the Protestant German kingdoms and principalities or to one of the Scandinavian kingdoms.

The king's eldest son, the Prince of Wales, was legally married in 1795 to his first cousin Caroline of Brunswick, but that marriage proved a stormy one that resulted in the birth of only one child; she was named Charlotte after her paternal grandmother. After the birth of the princess, the Prince of Wales and Caroline lived apart. Because of the insanity of King George III during his last years, the Prince of Wales was formally proclaimed Prince Regent in 1811. The Regency era (1811–20) proved to be a troubled era for Britain's royal family, however, because the Prince Regent and his brothers impressed many Britons as a generation of aging debauched reprobates. Most of them lived with mistresses rather than with wives, and their expenses perennially exceeded the monetary allowances that Parliament had allotted them. A decline in the political influence of the Prince Regent and of his royal brothers accompanied the decline in their public reputation.

An exception was made for the Prince Regent's daughter, the Princess Charlotte. During the years of economic depression that followed the British triumph in 1815 over Napoleonic France, young Charlotte, the heiress presumptive, appeared as a royal breath of fresh air. In May 1816 she married Prince Leopold of Saxe-Coburg, the younger son of the Duke of Saxe-Coburg-Saalfeld, a miniature German state. One of his elder sisters had married into Russia's imperial family; that connection had gained him a commission in the Russian army during the Napoleonic Wars. He was therefore a member of the entourage of Czar Alexander when in 1814 that ruler paid a historic state visit to London. Leopold appeared handsome and charming and cosmopolitan, and young Princess Charlotte preferred him to all other suitors. The wedding was a lavish one, and the two settled down happily at Claremont, a country house in Surrey purchased for the new couple. Tragedy followed less than a year and a half later, however, when Princess Charlotte died immediately after delivering a still-born son. The Prince Regent was devastated, and the doctor in charge of the birth committed suicide.[3] Even those who had sharply criticised the Prince Regent in cartoons and lampoons, for his self-indulgence and his extravagance, mourned the lively young princess. In Lord Byron's words,

> Those who weep not for kings shall weep for thee. . . .
> Of sackcloth was thy wedding garment made;
> Thy bridal fruit was ashes; in the dust
> The fair-haired daughter of the Isles is laid,
> The love of millions . . .[4]

The Prince Regent and Parliament were so moved by this outpouring of affection that they gave Leopold the titles of Royal Highness and Field Marshal and permitted him to keep for life both Claremont and a remarkably generous income of £50,000 a year.[5]

The episode provided a ready reminder that even if the popular reputation of Britain's monarchy had reached a nadir during the later 1810s, sentiment favorable to the royal family could readily be reawakened if an appropriate heir could be found. But who was next in line for the British throne?

With the death of King George III early in 1820, the Prince Regent was transformed into King George IV. He had had no legitimate children other than Charlotte, and even though his estranged wife, the Princess Caroline, died in 1821, the corpulent and ailing monarch did not marry again. His next younger brother, the Duke of York, had been married for many years to a Prussian princess, but they were childless. The third son, the Duke of Clarence, had a great many children, ten in all by the same woman, an actress named Dorothy Jordan. Although they lived together as a family for two decades, the duke made no effort to wed the actress legally; all his children were therefore illegitimate.

In the aftermath of the deaths of both Dorothy Jordan and Princess Charlotte, the fifty-two-year-old Duke of Clarence went about the process of searching for a legitimate bride. He was turned down by several candidates, but in 1818 he found one in Princess Adelaide of the German state of Saxe-Meiningen. In the meantime the fifth son, the Duke of Cumberland, had already found a wife, but he was thus far childless,[6] and the sixth son, the Duke of Cambridge, found one in yet another princess from a small German state, Augusta of Hesse-Cassel. Only three of King George III's six daughters had ever married, and none of their children survived infancy.

In the aftermath of the death of Princess Charlotte, no one was more eager to find a legitimate bride in order to produce a legitimate heir than was the fourth son of King George III, Prince Edward the Duke of Kent. He felt inwardly certain that destiny was calling him. After all, a gypsy in Gibraltar had once prophesied that his life would involve numerous setbacks but that his only child would grow up to become a great queen. During the wars with France, the duke had proved himself to be a courageous soldier but also a cruel one. In 1803 his severity had provoked an army mutiny in Gibraltar, an incident that brought his military career to an abrupt end. Back in England, he annoyed his royal father by associating with a number of political and religious radicals including Robert Owen, the paternalistic factory owner who is often described as 'the Father of British Socialism.' He also served as the patron of dozens of charities such as the Westminster Infirmary and the Literary Fund for Distressed Authors. Like most of his brothers, however, he found it impossible to live within his income, and in 1816 he escaped his creditors by

moving to Brussels, where the cost of living was far cheaper than it
was in London. There he lived with Madame Julie de St Laurent, a
vivacious middle-class French woman who served as his loyal companion for a quarter of a century.

After the death of Princess Charlotte, the fifty-year-old Duke of
Kent assumed that Parliament would gladly wish to pay off his debts
and boost his income if he pensioned off his long-time companion
and agreed to contract a legal marriage. Parliament initially refused,
but eventually it did add £6,000 to that annual income. In the meantime, the duke courted a prospective bride in the person of Victoire,
the widowed Princess Regent of Leiningen, another small German
state. One of her brothers ruled the Duchy of Saxe-Coburg; another
was the wealthy widower Prince Leopold. She already had two children, Feodora and Charles, but she was only thirty-two years old, and
she could presumably have more.

After initial hesitation, she accepted the duke's proposal, and in
May 1818 they were married, first in a Lutheran ceremony in
Germany, then six weeks later as part of a dual Anglican wedding in
England along with his older brother, the Duke of Clarence, who
married Princess Adelaide. For reasons of economy the Duke of Kent
and his bride returned to Germany to live, but in March and April of
the following year, with Victoire more than seven months pregnant,
they journeyed some 427 miles in a caravan of horse-drawn coaches
from Amorbach in Germany to Calais in France. Because he could
not afford an extra coachman, the duke drove the largest coach himself. They settled in Kensington Palace on the outskirts of London in
order to make certain that their child would be born on British soil.
She appeared on May 24, 1819, 'a pretty little Princess, as plump as a
partridge'.[7] In defiance of contemporary aristocratic custom, the
baby was brought into the world by a female obstetrician, Charlotte
von Siebold; she was breast-fed by her mother, and she became the
first member of Britain's royal family to be vaccinated against smallpox.[8]

A month later the little girl was christened with the names
'Alexandrina Victoria.' Her father would have preferred one or more
of the names then common in Britain's royal family – Charlotte,
Augusta, Elizabeth, and even Georgiana – but the Prince Regent, the

duke's resentful brother, was in charge of the ceremony, and he rejected them all. And so the baby was named Alexandrina after the czar of Russia, one of her godfathers and Britain's ally during the Napoleonic Wars, and Victoria after her mother, who was usually known as Victoire. When one considers the tens of thousands of Victorias and Vickys that were to dot the British, European, and American world during the century that followed, it is astonishing to realise that in the Britain of 1819 the name Victoria was virtually unknown. Both of the princess's names impressed the English people as distinctly foreign, and during the 1830s several Members of Parliament introduced bills to change the legal name of the young princess. Those efforts failed.

As a soldier, the Duke of Kent may have been a martinet, but he doted on his new wife and on his baby daughter. He also prided himself on his personal fitness; indeed he expected to outlive all his brothers. In order to save money, he moved his family to Sidmouth on the English Channel coast for the winter. There he caught cold and contracted pneumonia. Available medical remedies, including extensive blood-letting, proved unavailing, and on January 23, 1820 he died. His baby daughter was scarcely eight months old.

His widow was left alone with a mountain of her husband's unpaid bills, in a new country whose language she scarcely spoke and would never completely master. She had few friends in England, and she was tempted to return to Germany. Her brother, Prince Leopold, persuaded her, however, to bring up her baby in England, and the Prince Regent, now King George IV, grudgingly allotted her a suite of rooms in Kensington Palace. Her brother also provided her with £3,000 a year to add to her royal widow's pension of £6,000. A middle-class merchant family would have considered such a sum the height of luxury, but by the standards of Britain's great aristocratic households it was not. When the second of the Duke of Clarence's infant daughters died later in 1820, plump little Victoria came to be third in line for the throne – after her father's elder brothers. By contemporary royal and aristocratic standards, however, Victoria's upbringing was both simple and spare. As a child the princess did not have a room of her own; the furnishings in the palace rooms were second-hand, and the carpets threadbare. The meals were frugal; they so often included mutton, the cheapest meat available, that the young princess determined that if she ever became queen, she would never have mutton served again.[9]

The household of the infant princess was also a relatively isolated one. Little Victoria was surrounded by the German-speaking ladies that made up the household of the Duchess of Kent, but her mother sought to make English the princess's first language. In due course, Victoria became almost equally proficient in speaking and writing German and French, and to a lesser degree, Italian. Most observers agreed, however, that she spoke English clearly, carefully, and without an accent.[10] The writer and poet Arthur Benson, who met Victoria for the first time less than two years before her death, was very much surprised by her voice: 'It was so slow and sweet. – some extraordinary *simplicity* about it – much higher than I imagined it & with nothing cracked or imperious or . . . wobbly. It was like the voice of a very young tranquil woman.'[11]

Although the princess's governess, Baroness Louise Lehzen, was German by birth and upbringing, the series of private tutors who began to educate her even before she turned five were not. The most important of those tutors was a Church of England clergyman, the Reverend George Davys, who taught her the alphabet and who afterwards became her prime instructor in history, geography, Latin, and religion. Queen Victoria was later to describe herself as a slow learner, but contemporary evidence contradicts that appraisal. She could be rebellious on occasion, but by the age of six little Victoria could read readily and do simple arithmetic; in due course individual tutors were engaged to teach her writing, arithmetic, natural history, French, and German. As was true of other upper-class girls, she also had teachers for riding, dancing, drawing and painting, and music. In addition to five hours of lessons six days a week, Monday through Saturday, she was allotted time for walks and for play. One of her favorite activities with Baroness Lehzen was to dress up her collection of 130 Dutch peg dolls.[12] Every Sunday her mother took her to a Church of England service.

In 1830, the Duchess of Kent formally asked two senior Anglican bishops to judge the appropriateness of the schooling to which the princess had been exposed thus far. After subjecting Victoria to a lengthy oral examination, the bishops awarded high marks to both the mother and the daughter. 'In answering a great variety of questions proposed to her,' they reported,

> the Princess displayed an accurate knowledge of the most important features of Scripture History, and of the leading truths and precepts of the Christian Religion as taught by the Church of England, as well as an acquaintance with the Chronology and principal facts of English History remarkable in so young a person. To questions in Geography, the use of the Globes, Arithmetic, and Latin Grammar, the answers which the Princess returned were equally satisfactory.

The Archbishop of Canterbury, Dr William Howley, was consulted as well, and he concurred that 'Her Highness's education in regard to cultivation of intellect, improvement of talent, and religious and moral principle, is conducted with so much success as to render any alteration of the system undesirable.'[13]

The female servants at Kensington Palace would curtsey and address little Victoria as 'Your Royal Highness,' and the predominantly male tutors provided her with comprehensive teaching in a greater variety of subjects than was received by upper-class boys at public schools such as Eton and Harrow. By early Victorian standards, the little princess was therefore well educated, and she made commendable progress in all subjects except Latin. At the same time, Victoria's childhood was often a lonely one, one that she came to feel as a form of imprisonment, and one that included very few children her own age. Even her half-sister Feodora, of whom Victoria was very fond, was eleven years older. She scarcely knew most members of her father's family – including the monarch himself, King George IV. On the single occasion on which he invited her and her mother for a visit, however, he impressed her favorably. 'He was large and gouty,' Victoria was to recall, 'but with a wonderful dignity and charm of manner.'[14] When the king escorted his niece into a drawing room where an orchestra was playing, he asked her which piece of music the group should perform. 'God Save the King,' was Victoria's quick response.[15]

The uncle whom Victoria came to know best was her mother's brother Leopold, and her visits to his home at Claremont came to be among the happiest memories of her childhood. He was the most immediate and the most affectionate father figure in her close circle. As a teenager, she reminded him of 'the happy time when I could see you and be with you, *every* day!' There was no one, she assured him, who loved or admired him more than did his favorite niece. 'From my earliest years the name *Uncle* was the dearest I knew, the word *Uncle, alone,* meant no other but you!'[16]

Princess Victoria still had a number of other uncles, however, whose actions and longevity impinged directly on her own life. In June 1830 came the death of King George IV after a long period of illness and seclusion. He was little lamented by most of his subjects. The streets of London, indeed, had 'more the appearance of rejoicing than of mourning.'[17] Since the brother next in line, the Duke of York, had predeceased him, the throne went to the Duke of Clarence, who took the name of King William IV. William was somewhat eccentric, but he was in several respects also a good-natured and likable man, and his wife, now Queen Adelaide, served as an admirable consort. He was, however, already sixty-five years old, and he could hardly be expected to have a long reign. Adelaide and he were, moreover, increasingly unlikely to have children who might survive him. In 1830, the eleven-year-old Victoria therefore became heiress presumptive to the British throne.

At about the same time, Victoria's life experienced two other changes. Her affectionate half-sister Feodora was married off to a German princeling; thereafter she was able to visit Kensington Palace only at rare intervals. And her Uncle Leopold, who had lived in England most of the time during the 1820s, was offered not one kingship but two. In the 1830s, except for anomalous small states such as Switzerland, the European continent was made up solely of kingdoms and empires, and when a new country emerged – such as Greece (after its war of independence against the Ottoman Empire) – it seemed natural for its leaders to choose as ruler a respected prince with ties to other European royal families. Greece was a distant land, however, afflicted by bandits, by disease, and by financial problems, and ultimately Prince Leopold turned the offer down.

In 1831 came a similar offer from a land far closer to Britain, Belgium. Back in the seventeenth century it had been known as the

Spanish Netherlands. During the eighteenth century it had come to be known first as the Austrian Netherlands and then as a province of Napoleonic France. The Congress of Vienna of 1815 had assigned it to the King of the Netherlands, but in 1830 the predominantly Roman Catholic Belgians rebelled against the rule of the Protestant Dutch. In due course the Great Powers of the day recognized Belgium as a separate kingdom with Leopold as monarch. He had been brought up as a Lutheran, but he soon married a Roman Catholic daughter of King Louis-Philippe of France. Such an alliance seemed most likely to ensure the continued security of independent Belgium, a country that had adopted (according to Leopold) a 'very liberal Constitution.' The seventeen-year-old Princess Victoria felt sure that, under her uncle's care and guidance, Belgium had become 'the happiest country in the world.'[18]

These events gave new emphasis to what came to be known as the 'Kensington System,' an arrangement whereby the young Victoria was to be kept completely under the control of her mother and of her mother's household manager, Sir John Conroy, a British soldier of Irish ancestry who had become the Duke of Kent's equerry and who, after the latter's death, made himself indispensable to the widowed duchess as financial adviser and personal secretary. Conroy, who was married and the father of six children, possessed a swashbuckling charm, and – although they may never have been lovers – the duchess became deeply devoted to him. Her brother Leopold was later to suggest that Conroy's influence over the duchess became 'so strong that it would once have been called witchcraft.'[19] Conroy had an exalted opinion of his own social position and of his ability to mould Victoria into a model queen through whom he would exert a beneficent social and political influence over Britain's people.[20] He therefore persuaded the duchess that the brothers of her late husband were intent on gaining illegitimate authority over her daughter and that the Duke of Cumberland (the fifth son of George III) was indeed plotting against the life of Victoria – because he was next in line for the throne.[21] For such reasons, Conroy and the Duchess of Kent did their best to keep Victoria secluded also from the new royal couple, even though William and Adelaide made a number of friendly overtures. The duchess even found an excuse to prevent Victoria from attending the new king's coronation.

Instead the Duchess of Kent and Conroy insisted on an immediate rise in status and a vast increase in annual income for the duchess. Their demands were so brazen that the Duke of Wellington, prime minister at the time, thought it best not to lay the actual letter before King William IV. The Duchess of Kent was not granted the title that she sought, Dowager Princess of Wales, but in due course, the newly-elected Parliament did designate the duchess as regent in case Victoria should inherit the throne before the age of eighteen. The duchess's annual income was also increased by £10,000 a year in order to further the education of her daughter.[22] Far from satisfying the duchess, these arrangements made her yet more arrogant and insistent on proclaiming her rights and privileges as future regent. In the process she gradually alienated her daughter.

In Kensington Palace, the young princess remained under minute-by-minute surveillance. Not only did she lack friends of her own age (except for one of Conroy's daughters), but never was she left in a room without a servant. Never was she allowed to go downstairs without someone holding her hand. At night she slept in her mother's bedroom. As Victoria was (privately) to recall a generation later:

> I had led a very unhappy life as a child – had no scope for my very violent feelings of affection – had no brothers and sisters to live with – never had had a father – from my unfortunate circumstances was not on a comfortable or at all intimate or confidential feeling with my mother . . . and did not know what a happy domestic life was![23]

The princess's partial salvation lay in her governess, Louise Lehzen. She had been born the humble daughter of a Lutheran pastor and had come from Germany to England as the governess of Feodora; because she spoke English well, she was a logical choice to perform the same role with Victoria. In his position as King of Hanover, George IV had created her a baroness. It was Baroness Lehzen who gave the little princess her undivided love and devotion and who helped preserve her individuality and equanimity within the Kensington Palace prison. 'Lehzen taught her to control her moods and tantrums. Lehzen taught her to wear a mask of dignity in a potentially dangerous world.'[24]

It was under Baroness Lehzen's guidance that the princess

absorbed the moral strictures of evangelical authors such as Hannah More and Maria Edgeworth: they emphasised the importance of truth-telling and of curbing the willfulness of the young; they also encouraged the utilitarian pursuit of knowledge about the real world – such as textile machines and coalmines and historic sites and dates – as opposed to fairy tales and exotic adventures. Under Lehzen's supervision, at age thirteen the princess also began the custom that she was to continue, with only rare intermissions, until her final days: to keep a daily journal in which she described each day's activities. It was under her governess's guidance also that the princess began to read some of the classic French plays and memoirs in the original language. It was the intention of her chief tutor, the Reverend George Davys, that Victoria pursue a course of study 'more fitting to the character of a Prince than a Princess.'[25] Feminine accomplishments were to be balanced by a careful perusal of William Blackstone's four-volume *Commentaries on the Laws of England* and of Lord Clarendon's history of the great Civil War that the British Isles had experienced during the middle decades of the seventeenth century. 'Reading history is one of my greatest delights,' she announced when she was fifteen. 'I like reading different authors, of different opinions, by which means I learn not to lean on one particular side.'[26] She also enjoyed the poems of Sir Walter Scott and the works of two American authors, James Fenimore Cooper's *Last of the Mohicans* and Washington Irving's *Conquest of Granada*.[27]

Not that her school days were confined to reading alone. She reacted against her utilitarian education by finding melodrama, romance, and delight at the theatre and at the opera house. The Italian composers Vincenzo Bellini and Gaetano Donizetti were in their heyday, and Victoria doted on the performances of the beautiful Giulia Grisi, one of the operatic superstars of the day. Returning home from a night at the opera in 1834, she wrote in her journal in bold capital letters, 'I was VERY MUCH AMUSED INDEED.'[28] The princess became a stagestruck and starstruck teenager, who at the age of thirty-three estimated that in the course of the previous twenty years she had spent 350 evenings at productions of Italian opera. She was so delighted by the performances of one the most remarkable bass-baritones of the day, Luigi Lablache, that she embarked on singing lessons with him in 1836, lessons that were to continue at intervals for the next two decades. The son of an Irish mother and a French father, who grew up in Italy, Lablache proved to be 'a very patient and excellent master, and so merry too.'[29] In the meantime, Lucy Philpot Anderson, one of the most distinguished English pianists of the day, had become the princess's piano teacher. Back in 1822 she had been the first woman to appear as soloist with London's Philharmonic Society, the first modern orchestra in England, and during the decades that followed she would appear nineteen times more, even as she served as teacher to six of Victoria's children.[30] The princess therefore learned to sing and to play the piano with a high degree of competence. At the same time, Richard Westall, for nine years her drawing master, taught her how to sketch the people around her in a few deft strokes. She also completed numerous watercolor paintings – both of people and of landscapes.[31]

It was in 1832 that, at Sir John Conroy's urging, the Duchess of Kent and her daughter began a series of annual carriage tours to different parts of England and Wales. Their purpose was to display the heiress to the throne to her future subjects. They also had the effect of seeming to establish a rival court to that of King William IV. Conroy encouraged the city fathers of the municipalities through which such 'Royal Progresses' passed to present 'loyal addresses' to the duchess, to arrange processions and parades and to have the local soldiery provide formal salutes in honor of the princess. Late in 1832, Oxford University enhanced Conroy's own self-esteem by awarding him the honorary degree of Doctor of Civil Law on the same day that the Corporation of Oxford granted him the 'Freedom of the City.'[32]

Although the king was understandably deeply annoyed by the manner in which such tours were organised without his consent, they did enable Victoria to learn much about the land over which she was destined to reign. She became acquainted not only with Oxford's ancient Gothic buildings but also with the stately homes in which lived the land's leading aristocrats. She was driven as well through Birmingham, with its blazing iron furnaces, its heaps of coal, and its ragged children, and through the great naval base at Portsmouth.[33] These travels could involve dramatic adventures, such as the time when the mast on their ship broke as they approached Plymouth harbor. On another occasion, the princess's party was involved in a carriage accident near St Leonard's; Victoria helped rescue her mother and her little dog Dash from the overturned landau and the horses struggling on the ground.[34] Eventually Victoria grew weary of such travels, however. As she wrote in 1835, 'Though I liked some of the places very well, I was much tired by the long journeys & the great crowds we had to encounter. We cannot travel like other people, quietly and pleasantly.'[35]

During these same years, she engaged in a lengthy correspondence with Uncle Leopold, in the course of which the King of the Belgians provided his niece with maxims to follow once she became queen:

- 'Persons in high situations must particularly guard themselves against selfishness and vanity.'
- One's 'character should be so formed as not to be intoxicated by greatness and success, nor cast down by misfortune.'
- 'Health is the first and most important gift of Providence; without it we are poor, miserable creatures.'
- 'Our times resemble most those of the Protestant reformation; then people were moved by religious opinions, as they now undoubtedly are by political passions.'
- 'Hypocrisy is the besetting sin of all times, but *particularly of the present*, and many are the wolves in sheep's clothes.'
- 'You know that in England the Sovereign is the head of the Church. . . . In times like the present, when the Crown is already a good deal weakened . . . , I believe that you will do well, whenever an occasion offers itself to do so . . . , to express your sincere interest for the Church, and that you comprehend its position and count on its good-will.'
- 'One must not mind what newspapers say. Their power is a fiction of the worst description, and their efforts marked by the worst faith and the greatest untruths.'
- 'People are far from acting generally on the dictates of their interests, but oftener in consequence of their passions, though it may even prove injurious to their interests.'
- 'As a fundamental rule, . . . be courageous, firm and honest, as you have been till now.'[36]

King Leopold could sometimes sound pompous, but he treated his niece with great earnestness as a future fellow-monarch. It was with Uncle Leopold that, to an increasing degree, the princess discussed the political situation in Britain as well as in France, in Spain (where a civil war was unfolding), and in Portugal (where one of her Coburg cousins had married a queen of her own age). Leopold's observations on events impressed his niece as being ever to the point. As she confided to her diary, 'To hear dear Uncle speak on any subject is like reading a highly instructive book; his conversation is so enlightened, so clear.'[37]

Her feelings toward Sir John Conroy and at times toward her mother were, however, increasingly less favorable. During the autumn of 1835, Victoria contracted a severe illness, and we remain uncertain of its precise causes. They may have been psychological as well as physiological. It was at this very time that Conroy demanded that the princess sign a document naming him as her official private secretary. She refused.[38] In the meantime, relations between King William IV and the Duchess of Kent grew ever more frosty. When he learned that, in defiance of his commands, she had taken possession of seventeen additional rooms in Kensington Palace, he publicly upbraided her at a dinner at Windsor Castle. It was his greatest wish, the monarch declared, to live long enough to enable Princess Victoria to inherit the crown directly. He deeply disliked the prospect of having his sister-in-law, a lady who had 'grossly and continually insulted' him, reigning as Princess Regent. She was a person 'surrounded by evil advisers and . . . is herself incompetent to act with propriety.'[39]

It may have been grossly discourteous of the king to insult a guest publicly in his own castle, but he had good cause. As Princess Victoria approached her eighteenth birthday in May 1837, the king, who presented her with an elegant grand piano as a gift, was quite willing to enable her to set up her own establishment, independent of her mother. The duchess and Conroy put enormous pressure on the princess to sign a letter refusing the offer and insisting that, although legally of age, she was still far too young to reign in her own right. 'Victoria did not write that letter,' growled the king when he saw it. He was correct.[40] At Kensington Palace, the behind-the-scenes battle for supremacy continued. Conroy insisted that he *had* to become

Victoria's private secretary, because – he implied – the princess was mentally retarded. In the meantime, her mother reminded her that all of Victoria's success 'so far has been due to your *Mother's* reputation. Do not be *too sanguine* in *your* own *talents* and *understanding.*'[41] All of these desperate machinations to keep the eighteen-year-old princess in her place crumbled on the morning of June 20, 1837. The Archbishop of Canterbury and the Lord Chamberlain sped to Kensington Palace at 5 a.m. The mid-summer sun had already risen when, in her dressing-gown, the princess descended from her mother's bedroom to meet the two emissaries *alone.* They ceremonially informed her that her uncle was dead, and they fell on their knees to kiss the hand of the teenager who had just become their new queen. These are the words that she wrote in her journal that night:

> Since it has pleased Providence to place me in this station, I shall do my utmost to fulfil my duty towards my country; I am very young and perhaps in many, though not in all things, inexperienced, but I am sure, that very few have more real good will and more real desire to do what is fit and right than I have.[42]

3 *Queen Victoria on Horseback* (1837)

Her Majesty the Queen, the King [Leopold] of the Belgians [*left*], Lord Hill [*behind the Queen*] and the Duke of Wellington [*right*] proceeding to the Royal Review. (Lithograph after J. F. Taylor – RCIN 630524; the Royal Collection © 2002, courtesy of Her Majesty Queen Elizabeth II).

3 The Royal Teenager

Most human lives can be divided into chapters of a book, but seldom can the opening of a new chapter have involved a more dramatic transformation than the one undergone by Princess Victoria on June 20, 1837. A good many of the people of Great Britain had seen her at a distance, and leading politicians had exchanged a remark or two with her at a reception, but thus far she had remained in her mother's shadow, and for the broader British public her personality was opaque. And then at one stroke the Lord Chamberlain and the Archbishop of Canterbury set her free from her Kensington Palace 'prison.' Within a month, her court had moved to a location far closer to the center of metropolitan London, Buckingham Palace, and within two months she had transformed ancient Windsor Castle, some thirty miles up the river Thames, into her alternate home. On occasion, too, she visited the Royal Pavilion at Brighton, the Arabian Nights extravaganza that architect John Nash had fashioned for her uncle, the Prince Regent, and that had transformed this channel coast community into the favorite seaside resort for Londoners.

In the meantime, on that same June day, the heralds at St James's Palace had formally proclaimed her as the new sovereign. They were prepared to hail her as 'Queen Alexandrina Victoria,' but she insisted that the 'Alexandrina' be dropped from her formal title once and for all. She had also been introduced to her government at a meeting of the Privy Council. Of that large ceremonial body of men, almost one hundred were present. They included not only the members of the Whig cabinet in office in 1837 but also all the surviving members of the (elected) House of Commons and the (largely hereditary) House of Lords who had held cabinet office at an earlier time or who had been granted privy councillor status as a special honor. Two of

Victoria's paternal uncles, the Duke of Cumberland and the Duke of Sussex, were among those present, and they knelt before their young niece to kiss her hand and to swear formal homage. The other privy councillors followed suit. They had been surprised to see their new queen enter the chamber entirely alone, accompanied neither by Sir John Conroy nor by her mother nor by any female attendant. As she noted in her journal that night, it was her firm intention to meet her ministers *quite alone*.[1] In size, young Victoria appeared like a child less than five feet tall. She wore a black mourning dress (for the deceased king); she carried herself with rare grace; and she read the required declaration that transferred formal royal power into her hands in a clear, dignified, and self-assured manner. 'She not merely filled her chair,' marveled the Duke of Wellington, 'she filled the room.'[2]

That night she moved out of her mother's bedroom forever. Her mother did, indeed, accompany Victoria in due course to both Buckingham Palace and Windsor Castle, but the Duchess of Kent and her ladies were allotted suites in a quite separate portion of each palace. Despite the Duchess's pleas, no place in Queen Victoria's household was found for Sir John Conroy. He remained in the vicinity for another two years, however, as the Duchess of Kent's extravagant and irresponsible financial manager; only then did he leave both her employ and the country. He was granted a substantial pension, but he was to die in 1854 still pleading in vain for the hereditary Irish peerage that he felt he merited as a reward for all his services to the royal family.[3]

During her first three years as queen, Victoria and her mother often sat at the same dinner table, but she spoke to her mother as seldom as possible. In reciprocity, on Victoria's nineteenth birthday her mother presented her daughter with a copy of Shakespeare's *King Lear*.[4] In the meantime, Baroness Lehzen remained Victoria's prime female companion, although the queen also appointed a mistress of the robes (the elegant Duchess of Sutherland), eight ladies of the bedchamber, eight women of the bedchamber, and eight maids of honor to make up her formal entourage. Most of these women were recommended by Lord Melbourne and were therefore the wives and daughters of important Whig politicians.[5]

During the summer of 1837, the young queen gloried in her new position. Almost every day there was a ceremonial reception at which the kingdom's leading politicians, clergymen, landed gentlemen, army officers, and occasional bankers and merchants – and their wives – gained an opportunity to be presented to their new monarch. At dinner parties, the palace band would play, and professional musicians were often invited. Maids of honor were all chosen on the basis of their musical as well as their linguistic talents, and many evening meals at court were followed by singing and piano music; on occasion the queen herself would participate. Even more often than before, Victoria attended either the theatre or the opera, and on six distinct occasions she watched the remarkably handsome young American animal trainer Isaac van Amburg successfully keep wild lions and leopards at bay with a stick of rhinoceros hide.[6] Except for the time of Princess Charlotte's courtship and marriage, for half a century the royal family had been identified with madness, with eccentricity, with profligacy, and with old age. Suddenly royalty came to mean youth and energy, a firm sense of duty juxtaposed with palace dances that lasted into the early morning hours. As Lord John Russell, the Home Secretary, observed, 'We have had glorious female reigns. Those of Elizabeth and Anne led us to great victories. Let us now hope that we are going to have a female reign illustrious in its deeds of peace – an Elizabeth without her tyranny, an Anne without her weakness.'[7]

If only because Victoria became monarch while a Whig ministry was in power, the new reign was also identified with the theme of political reform. Ever since 1830 (except for a few months in 1834–5) a government dominated by the Whig party had been in charge of the cabinet, and in the course of that decade, first under Earl Grey and then under Viscount Melbourne, it had reformed the major institutions of the kingdom. The Reform Act of 1832 significantly altered the distribution of parliamentary seats in favor of growing industrial cities at the same time that it expanded the electorate by one half and set up a far more uniform system of voting registration both in the boroughs and in the counties. In 1835 the government of most of the cities of England and Wales was revamped also, and virtually all house-owners became voters in local elections. The Church of England was deprived of its monopoly position, and the right to vote and to hold public office was extended to non-Anglican Protestants (such as Baptists and Methodists, Quakers and Unitarians) as well as to Roman Catholics. An Ecclesiastical Commission was set up to overhaul the finances of the Church of England, and the registration of births, marriages, and deaths was taken out of the hands of that institution and given over to a civil registrar's office. Non-Anglican clergymen were granted the legal right to conduct marriage services in their own religious houses. In the meantime, a statute of 1833 began a five-year apprenticeship period destined to abolish once and for all the institution of slavery within the entire British Empire.[8]

The queen's first direct encounter with Parliament took place on July 17, 1837, when she rode to Westminster Palace for the purpose of officially proroguing the last of the Parliaments of King William IV. The accession of a new monarch meant, within a few months, another general election and a new Parliament. According to one member of the cabinet,

> the day was fine, the crowd was great and the whole spectacle very beautiful. I thought the equipage more gay, the attendants and all the accompaniments of the process, horses, pages, and people more brilliant than I had ever seen them before. . . . [The queen] looked exceedingly well in her glass-coach, and she bowed repeatedly to the vast crowd . . . who, from every roof and window, were cheering and waving handkerchiefs as she passed slowly along. . . .[9]

Victoria thanked the assembled Houses of Parliament for the congratulations that they had extended to her on her accession, and she officially signed a bill to limit yet further the number of crimes punishable by death, a humanitarian goal with which she was pleased to associate herself. 'It will be my care,' she declared, 'to strengthen our institutions, civil and ecclesiastical, by discreet improvement, wherever improvement is required.'[10] A few months later, on her first official visit to the City of London and its Lord Mayor, she conferred a knighthood on one of the elected city sheriffs, Moses Montefiore, thereby becoming the first British monarch to grant such an honor to a professing Jew. He was an 'excellent man,' she noted in her journal 'and I was very glad that I was the first to do what I think quite right.' In the process, she strengthened her personal identification with the Whig tradition of religious toleration.[11]

But what were the powers of a British monarch in 1837? The answer is far from simple; for that reason most biographers of Queen Victoria fail to address it systematically. According to the Bill of Rights of 1689, the Act of Settlement of 1701, the Act of Union with Scotland of 1707, and other statutes that made up the late seventeenth-century 'Revolution Settlement,' a British monarch possessed approximately the same executive powers vis-à-vis the legislature (the two-chamber Parliament) and the independent judiciary that an American president was to be assigned by the Constitution of 1787. The monarch was commander-in-chief of the army and navy. The monarch appointed all the major officers of state at home and the diplomats who were sent abroad as well as the leading judges of the kingdom. The monarch had the power to transform commoners into hereditary peers of the realm – and thus into permanent legislators as members of the House of Lords. As governor of the Church of England, the monarch also chose the bishops and the two archbishops who presided over the Church of England and its sister body, the (Protestant) Church of Ireland. The monarch appointed the men who governed Britain's colonies in Canada, the British West Indies, and Australia, as well as (through the agency of the English East India Company) large parts of the Indian subcontinent. The monarch declared war and made peace and negotiated treaties with foreign countries. The monarch might propose legislation and ask Parliament to appropriate the funds and to levy the taxes necessary to administer and to defend the kingdom. At the same time, monarchs could neither tax their subjects nor enact laws without the approval of Parliament, nor could monarchs arbitrarily remove judges once they had been appointed.

Although the executive powers of the Crown in 1837 were as great as – and in some respects greater than – the relative powers of an American president, a tradition fifty to a hundred and fifty years old held that most of these powers would be exercised on behalf of the Crown by the monarch's advisers. They would be exercised by the prime minister of the day and by the other members of the cabinet, all of whom were expected at the same time to serve either as elected members of the House of Commons or as (hereditary or newly appointed) members of the House of Lords. There was general consensus, however, that a monarch needed to be consulted before ministers exercised any of the powers of the Crown in that monarch's name. There was consensus also that, although the monarch had the right to appoint a prime minister in the first place, that prime minister could successfully 'form a government' and manage the business of the Crown only if he could gain and retain the support of Parliament – most of all, if he could gain and retain the support of a majority of the elected members of the House of Commons.

The degree of influence that a monarch had in choosing his or her chief minister depended therefore on the balance of political power in the House of Commons. If one political party controlled a clear majority of seats and if it was led by a single, generally acknowledged leader, then the monarch presumably would have little option but to ask that individual to 'form a government'. But if no single party held an overall majority of seats in the House of Commons or if the party recognised no single leader, then the monarch might well have considerable choice as to whom to ask first – or second or third. The monarch might also express strong preferences as to the other ministers whom the prime minister wished to have join his cabinet and as to which precise posts they should hold. A monarch's wishes as to appointments to other executive positions, such as ambassadors abroad and bishops at home, might also have weight. A prime minister was expected to explain and to justify to the monarch any significant alterations in either foreign or domestic policy. He would be expected to justify also a recommendation to have the monarch dissolve Parliament and to call for new general elections. According to law, no Parliament could last for more than seven years, but they could be much shorter than that. Thus, during the 1830s, general elections had taken place in 1830, in 1831, in 1832, and in 1835, and Victoria's accession necessitated yet another in 1837. In part because they were closely related to the other royal families of Europe, British monarchs retained an especially strong personal interest in both the fashioning of foreign policy and in the administration of the kingdom's armed forces.

If only because they believed that Great Britain should continue to be governed by a monarch as head of state rather than transform itself into a republic, successive prime ministers might do their best to honor their monarch's special concerns when it came both to laws and to appointments. The monarch played not only a utilitarian role in government, after all, but also a symbolic role – as the head of state who represented Britain and its Empire before the world and who also served as a hereditary link with the kingdom's earlier rulers through the entire previous millennium. It was Victoria's picture that appeared on the kingdom's coins and on the postage stamps (after 1840, when the postage stamp was invented in Britain) and not that of the prime minister. On appropriate public occasions, people sang 'God Save the Queen' and not 'God Save the Prime Minister.' It was the goings-on in royal palaces that constituted the focus of public curiosity and not the events at Number 10 Downing Street. In matters of fashion and of etiquette, the behavior of a monarch and a monarch's family was far more likely to be emulated than was that of members of the cabinet. The degree of political influence exercised by King George IV or King William IV or Queen Victoria on a specific decision or appointment had not been defined in a single written document, and legal authorities often differed therefore as to whether a particular action was 'constitutional' or not. Royal influence would be affected by public opinion as reflected in Parliament and in the newspaper press, and it would also derive from the personal predilections and even the foibles of both monarchs and ministers.[12]

On her first day as monarch, Queen Victoria assured Lord Melbourne that it had long been her 'intention to retain him and the rest of the present Ministry at the head of affairs.'[13] In practice, she had no alternative, because Melbourne's coalition of Whigs and Radicals and Irish MPs decisively outnumbered the opposition Tory (or Conservative) party headed by Sir Robert Peel in the

House of Commons and by the Duke of Wellington in the House of Lords. Before long, indeed, the young queen's prime concern would become that of having Melbourne retain his majority in Parliament and of having her retain Melbourne as her chief minister. Within a very few weeks she had persuaded herself, indeed, that Melbourne was 'a thoroughly straightforward, disinterested, excellent and kindhearted man.'[14] Whatever the subject – a complex legal case, or a historical event such as the South Sea Bubble, or the peculiarities of Melbourne's cabinet colleagues – the prime minister was able to explain it to Victoria 'like a *kind* father would do to his child; he has something so . . . affectionate and kind in him, that one must love him'.[15] The partnership that began in June 1837 between the fifty-eight-year-old prime minister and the eighteen-year-old queen remains one of the most unusual and most engaging of political romances in recorded history – if only because their deliberations, their conversations, and the gossip that they exchanged were recorded in candid detail by Queen Victoria herself in the entries that she inscribed each night in her journal.

In the queen's eyes, Melbourne was himself a truly romantic figure. He had served ever since 1806 as a Member of Parliament, first as an elected member of the House of Commons, and since his father's death in 1829, as a peer. He had survived the Napoleonic Wars and the era of domestic unrest that followed. He not only knew personally most of the influential people in the Britain of the late 1830s but he had also met, and could vividly describe, their parents and their grandparents. It was through Lord Melbourne therefore that Queen Victoria developed an immediate sense of what it had been like to experience not only the Regency era but also the world of her paternal grandparents, King George III and Queen Charlotte. Melbourne, she was aware, had had a difficult family life: his eccentric wife, Caroline Lamb, had been guilty of numerous infidelities including a passionate and widely publicised affair with the poet Lord Byron. She had died mad, and yet he had never deserted her. Their only surviving child, a son, was an epileptic who had died aged twenty-nine. Because he was an aging and often lonely widower, Melbourne possessed both the time and the inclination to serve for several years not only as the Queen's prime minister but also as her private secretary, as her riding companion at mid-day, and often as her dinner and after-dinner companion in the evening. They might spend as many as six hours together on a single day, talking not only about politics past and present but also about clothing and hair styles, about marriages historical and contemporary, and about the presence and absence of personal beauty among members of the court circle and elsewhere.

By the standards of the 1830s, Melbourne at fifty-eight was an old man, but for a time he was stimulated by the enthusiasm and by the energy of the young queen, who was happy to ride as many as twenty-five miles on a single excursion – as far to the north-west as Harrow, as far to the south-west as Wimbledon. On one occasion, when the queen tumbled from her horse, Melbourne was horrified, but Victoria found the episode highly amusing; laughingly she picked herself up from the ground to remount her steed.[16]

As time passed, she necessarily came to be very much influenced by Melbourne's Whig political philosophy, which was tolerant but mildly cynical and far from ardent. Victoria became so partisan a Whig in her private comments, indeed, that the prime minister felt compelled to remind his monarch at regular intervals that the Tory party too possessed able members who made useful contributions to public debate and who might one day serve as her ministers. Melbourne headed a reform ministry, but by 1837 his chief desire had come to be that of calming the political waters. He championed an ideological position half way between despotism and democracy. On the one hand, he deplored absolute rulers whether they be kings such as Louis XIV or revolutionary emperors such as the great Napoleon. On the other hand, he feared the prospect of popular democracy: if the illiterate masses were abruptly granted the right to choose their rulers – as the advocates of the People's Charter were contending[17] – then they would in all likelihood fall victim to demagogues prepared to set up an alternate despotism in their name. Melbourne much preferred the rule of law and of reason, even as he was fully prepared to concede, with a shrug of the shoulder, that most people failed to behave reasonably much of the time. 'You had better try to do no good,' he told Victoria on one occasion, 'and then you'll get into no scrapes.' Even as some of his cabinet colleagues sought to expand the role of the national government in subsidising elementary education, Melbourne preferred a regime that focused on two purposes: 'to prevent and punish crime, and to preserve contracts.'[18] Melbourne's caution was given new emphasis by the results of the general election of November 1837, which left his party and its political allies with an overall majority of fewer than forty seats in the House of Commons.[19]

Although most historians have credited Melbourne with the best of intentions in educating his new sovereign, many have been sharply critical about his failure to develop Victoria's social conscience.[20] Admittedly, he had no desire to abolish England's reformed Poor Law of 1834, which, though rigorous in detail, continued, by means of parish Poor Law unions and workhouses, to provide food, clothing, and shelter for the very poor, the very sick, and the very old. Somewhat grudgingly, he also went along with the Factory Act of 1833, which prohibited children under nine from working in cotton mills. Children aged nine to thirteen were to be limited to an eight-hour working day and to be given compulsory schooling. Melbourne's ministry also began to implement in Ireland a Poor Law comparable to that of England. Yet neither he nor any other notable political leader of his day expected to transform Britain into a society resembling the post-1945 welfare state. He took it for granted that although his ministry might pass regulations involving child welfare and public health, it lacked the authority, the personnel, and the financial resources to provide all of Victoria's subjects with cradle-to-the-grave security.

On such matters, Queen Victoria found it easy to concur with the conventional wisdom of the day. At the same time, her sympathies could readily be aroused by personal tales of distress that were called to her attention – whether they be real or fictional. Thus she became fascinated and disturbed by Charles Dickens's most recent novel, *Oliver Twist*, a tale of workhouses, pauper schools, pickpockets, and 'squalid vice' in the slums of London. Lord Melbourne, in contrast, preferred books that dealt with more elevated subjects; he wished to steer clear of 'that low debasing view of mankind.'[21]

If the youthful Victoria had no great social program in mind for her kingdom, she certainly had a systematic one for her immediate family's financial stability. At first the new monarch possessed no money at all, and at once she had to borrow a large sum from a private London banker while she waited for Parliament to vote her an annual income of £385,000 (worth more than £35 million in the year 2003). Four-fifths of that amount was designated to pay the salaries and the expenses of the royal household – which included some 445 persons ranging from the Lord Chamberlain and the Yeomen of the Guard to a rat killer, a chimney sweep, a stove and fire lighter, and a poet laureate (as of 1843 William Wordsworth).

Her predecessors had surrendered to Parliament almost all the independent sources of income that monarchs had once possessed, and the accession of Victoria meant that the Kingdom of Hanover (tied to the British Crown since 1714) would go its separate way under her uncle the Duke of Cumberland, who became King Ernest Augustus II. (The 'Salic Law' that applied to Hanover, and to the other German states, did not permit a woman to reign.) Victoria therefore obtained no independent income from Hanover, but she did still obtain some from the Duchies of Lancaster and Cornwall – at least until she bore a son. Thereafter the income from the royal possessions in Cornwall would go directly to him. As soon as she did have a Privy Purse to call her own, the young queen used a significant amount to pay off the debts contracted by her father twenty years earlier. In the course of the next two years, she used another large portion to pay off her mother's equally sizable accumulated debts. Quietly she also allotted to her paternal cousins, the surviving illegitimate children of her uncle King William IV, the same level of support that he had provided while monarch. Only then could she begin to use her Privy Purse income to buy paintings, to make charitable gifts, and to build up a small nest egg. The size of the annual parliamentary grant was to remain unchanged until the year of Victoria's death, a tribute both to parliamentary conservatism and to the financial stability of the entire Victorian era. The purchasing power of the pound might fluctuate from year to year and even from decade to decade, but its approximate value changed little over the course of three-quarters of a century.[22]

For Queen Victoria, the great event of the year 1838 was her coronation, which took place on June 28, and it was the high point of the year for many of her people also. By means of horses, coaches, private carriages, ships, and – for the first time – railway trains, more than 400,000 people reached London in order that they might line the roundabout route by which the procession made its way from Buckingham Palace to Westminster Abbey. It involved trumpeters and cavalry men, foreign ambassadors and their staffs, scores of carriages transporting the queen's relations and the royal household, more bands and more troops, and as climax the queen's own ornate carriage drawn by eight cream-colored horses. Westminster Abbey was colorfully decorated and filled with elaborately costumed peers and with peeresses wearing the most dazzling diamonds.

A ceremony that was to last almost five hours began with the boys of Westminster School shouting 'Vivat Victoria Regina.'

'Will you solemnly promise and swear,' asked the Archbishop of Canterbury, 'to govern this United Kingdom of Great Britain and Ireland, and the dominions thereto belonging, according to the statutes in Parliament agreed on, and the respective laws and customs of the same?'

'I solemnly promise so to do,' the Queen responded.

'Will you, to your power, cause law and justice, in mercy, to be executed in all your judgments?'

'I will.'

'Will you, to the utmost of your power, maintain the Laws of God, the true profession of the Gospel and the Protestant Reformed religion as established by law. . . .?'

'All this I promise to do.'

Having been anointed and crowned in the coronation chair of King Edward I (1272–1307), Queen Victoria then received the feudal homage of bishops and peers. The ceremony also involved a communion service, and it culminated with George Frederick Handel's *Hallelujah Chorus*. Not everything went like clockwork: several of the bishops proved maladroit, and one jammed a ruby ring on a royal finger for which it proved too small. Yet almost all the spectators found the coronation a moving event. As the skeptical diarist

Charles Greville observed, 'She never ceases to be a Queen, but is always the most charming, cheerful, obliging, unaffected Queen in the world.'

The hour-and-a-half procession back to Buckingham Palace attracted an even larger crowd than had the procession to the Abbey. That night London's theatres and other places of amusement were thrown open to the public free of charge, and the evening ended with spectacular fireworks above Green Park and Hyde Park. For the next four days, Hyde Park itself was transformed into a vast funfair for the people of London and out-of-town visitors. Whereas George IV's more costly coronation of 1821 had catered to a small elite, the coronation of 1838 seemed designed to interest and amuse the masses. For the moment, young Victoria had established herself as 'the People's Queen.'[23]

As the events of the year that followed were to demonstrate, royal approval ratings could go down as well as up. In Queen Victoria's case, it was the Flora Hastings affair that brought the post-accession 'honeymoon' to an abrupt halt. Early in 1839, Victoria's ladies and the queen herself began to suspect that Lady Flora, the 32-year-old unmarried lady-in-waiting to the Duchess of Kent, was pregnant. She had an enlarged abdomen, and she had recently traveled from Scotland to London in the same post-chaise as Sir John Conroy, the man whom Victoria privately denounced as that 'Monster and demon Incarnate.' When the delicate Lady Flora for a time refused to let herself be examined by a physician, the rumor spread. Eventually Lady Flora was found to be a virgin, and the queen privately expressed her regrets about the rumors, but in the meantime Lady Flora's brother had launched a public attack on Victoria's Whig court and had challenged Lord Melbourne to a duel. The latter confrontation was averted, but the staunchly Tory Hastings family blamed Baroness Lehzen for launching the diabolical whispering campaign against Lady Flora and publicly called for the dismissal and expulsion of Victoria's closest confidante. Victoria's court, according to one critic, was becoming as 'depraved and licentious as that of Marie Antoinette.' When, in July 1839, Lady Flora died of a cancerous abdominal tumor, the outcry in the early-Victorian equivalent of the tabloid press grew yet louder. The young queen was accused of being

far too preoccupied with dresses and dances to rid herself of conspir-
ators whose slanders had hounded an innocent maiden to her death.
At several public events, Victoria was greeted with hisses rather than
cheers.[24]

Two months before Lady Flora's death, Queen Victoria had been
afflicted by news that caused her even greater distress: Lord
Melbourne and his entire cabinet resigned. The immediate occasion was not technically a parliamentary defeat but a vote that
demonstrated how weak the government had become. The Jamaica
Bill of 1839 was designed to suspend the self-governing legislative
assembly of the West Indies island and restore it to direct British
rule. Why would a reform ministry reverse the trend to colonial
self-government? Because the assembly of white plantation owners
was doing its best to slow down or halt altogether the emancipation of black slaves on the island, on which more of them lived than
in any other British colony. With its House of Commons majority
down to five votes, Melbourne's divided cabinet chose to give up
the battle, and Melbourne recommended to Queen Victoria that
she call on the Duke of Wellington – the great national military
hero and prime minister (1828–1830) – to form a government.
Wellington insisted that he had become too old and too deaf, and
he recommended instead Sir Robert Peel, the Tory leader in the
House of Commons who had served as prime minister for six
months in 1834–5.

Unlike Melbourne, Peel had no notion as to how to deal with a
youthful female monarch, and Victoria found him equally difficult
to understand. In demeanor he seemed 'such a cold odd man' in contrast to 'that frank, open, natural and most kind, warm manner of
Lord Melbourne.'[25] Peel embarked with reluctance on the task of
forming a government in a House of Commons in which his own
party could not yet claim an overall majority, and he asked Victoria
to show her confidence in his effort by replacing some of her Whig
ladies-in-waiting with Tories. He remained vague as to how many
he wished to replace, but Queen Victoria came to the quick conclusion that if she stood firm she might not only save her Whig ladies
from dismissal but also preserve Lord Melbourne as her prime minister. She greatly feared a Tory demand that she dismiss her closest

confidante, Baroness Lehzen. A wholesale change in her household might well be interpreted, indeed, as a public admission on her part that her courtiers were as morally corrupt as the Tory *Morning Post* had charged. As she firmly told Peel, whatever the party affiliation of the husbands of her ladies, 'I never talked Politics with them.'[26] She therefore turned down Peel's request; as she reported to Lord Melbourne, 'The Queen of England will not submit to such trickery.'[27]

Her stern defiance on the matter and Peel's subsequent decision not to form a government at all were to be described as 'unconstitutional' partisanship on the part of the young queen. Half a century later Victoria herself observed that, had she been older, she might have handled the matter differently. Yet constitutional precedent was far from clear, and Peel, surprised by Melbourne's resignation, was from the first reluctant to set up a 'minority government.' That Melbourne *did* return as prime minister and that his cabinet *was* able to maintain a narrow House of Commons majority for two years more – until the general election of June 1841 – strongly suggests that Queen Victoria had read the parliamentary tea leaves with greater acuity than had the more timorous members of her Whig cabinet.[28]

For the moment, the episode did little to enhance Victoria's reputation in Tory circles, but it provided one of numerous reminders that the queen possessed a strong personal will. That will had already been demonstrated a year before when Melbourne had proposed a long list of 'Coronation Honours': new peers and baronets were named and old peers were promoted. 'I of course consented,' wrote the queen, thereby implying that she might well have withheld her consent. Indeed she immediately added three such 'honours' of her own to the prime minister's list.[29]

Indirectly, the 'bedchamber crisis' also raised anew the question of when and how Victoria might appropriately find a husband. As she herself sometimes conceded, to live among people most of whom were much older than herself was unnatural. Tories hoped that a husband might cause the 'Whig Queen' to become less partisan. Whigs were aware that, without a husband, Victoria could not continue the royal succession. Until she had a child, the heir presumptive remained her uncle the Duke of Cumberland, a deeply reactionary figure who had celebrated his accession as King of Hanover by abrogating that kingdom's constitution. To marry would mean that Victoria could rid herself of her mother as palace chaperone; to marry might also mean the possibility of disagreement with a husband. As the queen admitted to Melbourne, she was 'so accustomed to have my own way.' Melbourne responded: 'Oh! but you would have it still.'[30]

About one matter Victoria felt certain: she would marry only for love. In the course of 1837, 1838, and 1839, a number of young men presented themselves for Victoria's inspection, the sons of the Kings of the Netherlands and of Württemberg among them. The most dazzling of the lot was Grand Duke Alexander of Russia. When she danced the mazurka with him, he literally swept her off her feet, and as she conceded in her journal, 'I really am quite in love with the Grand Duke; he is a dear, delightful young man.'[31] Yet the future Czar Alexander II was obviously an inappropriate choice; so was a mere English subject. So, she decided, was her paternal first cousin George, the son of the Duke of Cambridge. She was very much aware that ever since her childhood, her Uncle Leopold had hoped for a marriage with Albert, the younger son of the Duke of Saxe-Coburg-Gotha and her maternal first cousin. His initial visit to England in 1836 had been at best a partial success, and although they exchanged occasional letters, she reminded her uncle in 1838 that she had made no formal commitment to Albert and that she might not marry anyone for several years more. As late as April 1839, Victoria assured Lord Melbourne that of the several princes whom she had inspected 'not one . . . would do,' and that 'at present *my* feeling was quite against ever marrying.'[32]

Such sentiments changed dramatically in October 1839, when Albert and his elder brother came to Windsor for a second visit, and Victoria found Albert *'beautiful.'* His blue eyes, his exquisite nose, his broad shoulder, and his fine waist, his conversational talents, his love of music, and (although it was hardly his favorite pastime) his ability to dance, were all beyond compare. Within three days she confided to Lord Melbourne that she 'had a good deal changed' her opinion as to marrying. In marital matters, a reigning queen had to take the initiative. Two days later, with Melbourne's encouragement, she therefore plucked up her courage to reverse traditional gender roles and to propose marriage to Albert. He said 'Yes,' and they melted into each other's arms. A wedding date was set for February 10, 1840.[33] Yet another chapter in Queen Victoria's life was about to begin.

4 *The Royal Family at Home (1843)*

A lithograph of 1843 (*To the Queen's Private Apartments*, by Dean & Co. – RCIN
605909) shows us how that life was visualised at the time. (The Royal
Collection © 2002, courtesy of Her Majesty Queen Elizabeth II)

4 The Model of Domesticity

Queen Victoria's wedding on February 10, 1840, to her first cousin Prince Albert of Saxe-Coburg and Gotha, changed her life in a dramatic manner. Although the young queen initially appeared to cherish her freedom, many of her immediate and more distant advisers believed that a husband would add stability to both Victoria's personal and her political life. Not the least important of these counsellors was King Leopold of the Belgians, who from the time of Victoria's babyhood had begun to dream of an eventual match between his niece Victoria (the daughter of his sister Victoire) and his nephew Albert (the younger son of his brother Ernest, the ruler of the Duchy of Coburg). Few contemporaries challenged the propriety of a marriage of first cousins; after all, the future King George IV had married one of his first cousins back in 1795.[1]

Although they were closely related, Victoria was not to meet Albert in person until his seventeenth year. Albert was three months younger than Victoria, and he had been brought into the world in 1819 by the same Madame Charlotte Siebold, an exceptional university-trained German female obstetrician. As a child, Albert was the favorite of his doting mother, the beautiful Louise. When Albert was only five, however, his mother's infidelity led to the divorce of his parents, and his mother was compelled to leave Coburg. Although she lived for another seven years, she was not permitted to see her two sons again. From the age of five until he was eighteen, Albert and his elder brother were therefore brought up in a predominantly masculine environment in the home of Albert's ducal father – a man notorious both for his debts and for his own infidelities and dissipations – under the tutelage of the dedicated Herr Christoph Florschütz.

That tutor imposed on his charges an educational regime devoted less to the Latin and Greek Classics and to Mathematics than was the custom in English public schools of the day. Instead he emphasised Modern Languages, History, the Natural Sciences, Geography, Philosophy, Music, and Art (Albert did also study Latin). Although German always remained his first language, he was introduced at an early age to the novels of Sir Walter Scott in English. At the age of sixteen he wrote a lengthy essay tracing 'through the course of History the progress of German civilisation.' Albert became a product of the German Enlightenment as exemplified in the writings, especially *Faust*, of Johann Wolfgang von Goethe, and he was affected also by that Romantic reaction against the Enlightenment that had influenced cultural attitudes throughout Europe.

Albert's education continued with ten months of study in Brussels (1836–7) and a year-and-a-half (1837–8) at the new University of Bonn, unusual among German institutions in being open to both Protestant and Roman Catholic students. There Albert came under the influence, among others, of August Wilhelm von Schlegel, famed as the co-translator of Shakespeare's plays into German, and of a Professor Fichte who taught Albert that 'through work and effort shall come salvation.' Baron Friedrich Christian von Stockmar (the long-time physician confidant of King Leopold of the Belgians and Queen Victoria's adviser during her first years as queen) served as guide to Albert on a tour of Italy that familiarised the young prince with ancient and Renaissance art. When Edward Everett, the American minister to Britain, met Albert in 1841, he found him to be 'an exceedingly modest, intelligent, well-educated person, greatly above the average, I should think, of those of his rank in Europe.'[2]

Albert was only one of many possible suitors for Victoria's hand, and Albert's first visit to England and to Kensington Palace in May 1836 had indeed proved only a modest success. The princess found her cousin 'very amiable, very kind and good' as well as highly musical, but Albert was quickly exhausted by the day-to-day rigors of court life. He had a penchant for falling asleep by 9.30 p.m., and he found it impossible to make small talk, especially with women. In the aftermath of that visit, Victoria gave a vague undertaking to her Uncle Leopold that she found Albert acceptable as a prospective husband, but the two cousins were clearly not in love. Although they exchanged letters from time to time, they were not to see one another again until October 1839. In the interval, Victoria often spoke to Melbourne of putting off any thought of marriage for at least three or four years – or perhaps forever.

Immediately upon Albert's arrival at Windsor, however, Victoria's feelings began to change, for Albert was 'so handsome and pleasing . . . so excessively handsome, such beautiful blue eyes, an exquisite nose, and such a pretty mouth with such delicate moustachios and slight but very slight whiskers; a beautiful figure broad in the shoulders and a fine waist.'[3] Only five days later, Queen Victoria formally proposed to Albert, and the two embraced and exchanged mutual endearments. For Victoria, Albert had suddenly been transformed into a knight in shining armor and a man she could not live without. At the same time, Albert, who had heard disquieting tales of his cousin's incredible stubbornness and of her obsession with court formalities, was overwhelmed by her vitality, her kindness, and her affection. 'Your image fills my whole soul,' he was to write. 'Even in my dreams I never imagined that I should find so much love on earth.'[4] A month after the private engagement, Victoria formally notified her Privy Council of her decision, one 'which deeply concerns the welfare of My people and the happiness of my future life.' One of her aunts asked Victoria whether this speech 'was not a nervous thing to do?' 'Yes,' agreed the queen, 'but I did a much more nervous thing a little while ago.' 'What was that?' 'I proposed to Albert.'[5]

In the meantime, Albert had returned to Germany to say farewell to Coburg and to prepare for the challenging role of royal consort. As he soon learned, not all of Britain's people or members of its Parliament welcomed with the same enthusiasm as did Queen Victoria the arrival as royal consort of 'a pauper German' princeling from 'a Pumpernickel state.' When the Whig Ministry proposed to Parliament that Albert be granted an annual income of £50,000 (the same sum that Prince Leopold had been awarded back in 1816 as the husband of Princess Charlotte), the House of Commons rebelled. Radicals argued that, at a time of economic depression, the country could not afford so large a sum, and Tories were also quite willing to rebuff the 'Queen of the Whigs,' who had fobbed off their leader Sir Robert Peel only a few months before. The Tories were also annoyed that the ministry had not formally proclaimed that, as the Act of Settlement of 1701 required, Albert was 'a Protestant prince.' Although a number of Coburg relations had converted to Roman Catholicism in the course of the early nineteenth century, Albert had been brought up a dutiful Lutheran. When Baron Stockmar was asked whether Albert 'belonged to any special Protestant sect that will prevent him from taking the Sacrament with the Queen,' Stockmar's reply was mildly indignant: 'There is no essential difference between the communion service of the Protestant German and the English Churches, except that perhaps the German is the more reverent.'[6]

Parliament was in due course assured of Albert's religious orthodoxy, yet it remains a fact that neither Albert nor Victoria was in accord with the major religious movements that affected Great Britain during the 1830s. They were not sympathetic to those evangelicals (both in the Church of England and among Methodists and Baptists) who at all times opposed attendance at the theatre and the reading of novels and who on Sundays forbade all activities other than religious worship. They were equally unsympathetic to the members of the Oxford movement – such as John Keble, Edward Bouverie Pusey, and John Henry Newman – who rejected the Protestant Reformation of the sixteenth century and preferred to see the Church of England as a Roman Catholic institution in every respect except that of giving formal primacy to the Pope. The mildly cynical Lord Melbourne had urged Victoria to focus on 'the simple truths' rather than on theological conundrums, and the far more earnest Prince Albert was to show similar revulsion toward disputes over conflicting interpretations of the Bible. It was far more important for monarchs to lead moral lives, Albert insisted, than to be 'slavishly attending services in Church.' As one of Victoria's religious mentors was to note: 'the Prince Consort brought into her life a large religious element, but I should think it was, in his case, of a very nebulous sort so far as Christian dogma goes.'[7]

The next dispute pitted Victoria against Albert. Who was to be Albert's personal secretary and aide on his arrival in England? Albert thought he should bring along a fellow German or, if Englishmen were to be chosen for his household, that they should transcend the

Whig/Tory divisions of politics. Victoria insisted instead on the youthful George Anson who had been serving as Prime Minister Melbourne's private secretary. He was, Victoria informed her fiancé, 'very modest, very honest, very steady, very well-informed, and will be of *much use* to you.'[8] Victoria won that battle, and Anson in due course was to prove a firm friend to Albert. Albert also wished to exclude as royal bridesmaid the daughter of any woman who had a dubious past, but the young queen observed that 'one ought always to be indulgent toward other people.... If we had not been well brought up ... we might also have gone astray.'[9] Albert lost that particular battle also, but he turned out to be a stickler for sexual purity, and in due course his influence was to sharpen the dicta of 'Victorian morality.'

The wedding at London's St James's Palace on February 10, 1840, involved a procession from and later back to Buckingham Palace. Unlike royal weddings earlier in the century, it therefore invited public participation. Although the wedding was not a grand ceremonial event, neither the wind nor the rain deterred thousands of Londoners from cheering the royal couple. Albert, who had been formally naturalised as a British subject only the night before, wore the uniform of a British Field Marshal, while Victoria was attired in an elegant white satin dress decorated with orange blossoms and a veil of Honiton lace – all specially manufactured in England. At an afternoon Buckingham Palace 'wedding breakfast,' a relatively small assembly began the process of consuming a wedding cake nine feet in circumference and sixteen inches high. Then the wedded pair went off to Windsor Castle for a three-day honeymoon. Albert would have preferred at least a fortnight, but Victoria brought him up short: 'You forget, my dearest Love, that I am the Sovereign, and that business can stop and wait for nothing. Parliament is sitting ... and it is quite impossible for me to be absent from London.'[10]

In the aftermath of the wedding, the young queen felt deliriously happy. As she wrote to a Coburg cousin a few weeks later, 'You cannot imagine how delightful it is to be married. I could not have dreamed that anyone could be so happy in this world as I am.'[11] Albert for his part took delight in the numerous endearing qualities of his bride – her zest for life, her sense of fun, her ready displays of affection for him. What Victoria failed fully to appreciate, however, was how different Albert's personality was from her own. He was 'an early bird' and she 'a night owl.' She was an extrovert and he an introvert. She acted impetuously while he brooded silently. She was prepared to continue to play a central role in the sociable court life to which she had become accustomed during the previous three years; he was something of a pedant who preferred to devote himself to the drafting of memoranda on political and scientific topics and to associate with scholars rather than with aristocratic courtiers.

At first Victoria seemed oblivious to the fact that, for the moment, Albert lacked any formal post in which to exercise his acknowledged talents. At the same time, Victoria's surviving paternal uncles and their families objected to all attempts to grant Albert ceremonial precedence ahead of them. For several months after the wedding, therefore, the queen's daily routine was scarcely affected by Albert's presence. When it came to politics, Victoria continued to consult her prime minister, Lord Melbourne, and Albert did not participate in their meetings. Almost a year was to elapse, indeed, before the queen granted her husband a key to the government dispatch boxes that were ferried to and from the palace each day so that Victoria could review the policies that her ministers were implementing both at home and abroad. When it came to the day-to-day management of the royal household, of her personal correspondence, and of her Privy Purse, it was the queen's lady companion, the Baroness Lehzen, who continued to guide Victoria. As Albert explained to a childhood friend, 'In my home life I am very happy and contented; but the difficulty in filling my place with the proper dignity is, that I am only the husband and not the master in the house.'[12] Albert was conscious, at times unduly conscious, of the fact that, by the standards of the patriarchal nineteenth century, his was an all too obvious example of role reversal. He was to devote his first two years as royal consort to efforts to alter that state and to attain a meaningful societal and political role.

Two events began the process of altering Albert's status. The first was the queen's pregnancy; by May 1840 it had become clear that Albert was soon to be a father as well as a husband. The second, one month later, was an attempted assassination. While Victoria and

Albert were driving in an open carriage near Buckingham Palace, an eighteen-year-old lad armed with a pistol in each hand fired at them. A bullet missed them by inches. The horses shied, the carriage halted, and the gunman fired and missed a second time before a group of nearby pedestrians tackled and disarmed him. The pregnant queen showed remarkable courage and self-possession as she and her consort were triumphantly escorted back to the palace by Green Park riders amidst a crowd of cheering spectators. At the opera and at the Ascot race course, the queen was hailed once more as a popular heroine. Her brush with death motivated Parliament to pass a Regency Bill that named Prince Albert as sole regent in the event that the queen should die before her prospective heir attained the age of eighteen. In the meantime, the assassin, one Edward Oxford, was declared insane and he spent the next twenty-seven years in a lunatic asylum.[13]

On the afternoon of November 23, 1840, with Prince Albert at her side and with a group of government witnesses in the adjoining room, a baby was born. 'Oh Madam, it is a princess,' called out Dr Charles Locock. 'Never mind', replied the new mother, 'the next one will be a prince.'[14] During her weeks of recovery, Albert served as the most solicitous of caretakers. He sat by her side; he read to her; he wrote on her behalf. He lifted her from the bed to the sofa and back. There could not have been, Victoria was to recall, 'a kinder, wiser, or more judicious nurse.'[15]

No sooner had the queen recovered from the birth of her daughter than she discovered, to her chagrin, that she was pregnant again. Her second pregnancy proved more troublesome and painful than her first, but once again Albert served as prime comforter, and on November 9, 1841, the baby arrived, 'a fine large boy.' Albert Edward ('Bertie' to his parents) became the immediate heir to the throne, the first Prince of Wales to be born to a reigning monarch in eighty years. To the relief of many Britons, Bertie and Vicky (the first-born) had replaced the unpopular Duke of Cumberland (since 1837 also King of Hanover) as next in line for the succession. Albert had also established himself as paterfamilias, but he had not yet become the master of Victoria's household.

During the summer of 1842 the long-standing rivalry between Albert and the Baroness Lehzen reached a climax. For more than two years, Victoria had remained loyal to the governess who had served as her chief support as a princess and who now steadfastly resisted Albert's efforts to alter the royal routine. Albert in turn became deeply troubled by a lady whom he came to see as 'a crazy, stupid intriguer, obsessed with the lust for power, who regarded herself as a Demi-God.'[16] He also held Lehzen responsible for the long-time breach between Victoria and her mother and for the mismanagement of both the royal household and the new royal nursery. Every few weeks a heated argument would break out between husband and wife in which Victoria's passionate outbursts were countered by Albert's lengthy memoranda. Finally, with a push from Baron Stockmar, the queen let herself be persuaded that it was time for Baroness Lehzen's permanent retirement. She would move to a small town in the Kingdom of Hanover with a new carriage and a pension of £800 a year, and Albert would become the master of his household. Victoria wrote to her old governess at least once a month until Baroness Lehzen's death in 1870, but the baroness never visited England again, and the two women met in person on but a handful of occasions.[17]

Even before Lehzen's departure, the royal nursery had been placed under the care of a highly respected and competent aristocrat, Sarah Lady Lyttleton, a widow with five grown children of her own. In the course of the next five years, she added a spirit of calm and consistency to the supervision of Vicky and Bertie and of their younger siblings as they arrived: Princess Alice in April 1843; Prince Alfred in August 1844; Princess Helena in May 1846; Princess Louise in March 1848. Three more children were to appear later: Arthur in 1850; Leopold in 1853; and Beatrice in 1857. In the aftermath of Lehzen's departure, Albert secured a genuine reconciliation between Queen Victoria and her mother. The Duchess of Kent was provided with both a reliable financial adviser in place of the ambitious and dishonest Sir John Conroy, and a home of her own in London as well as one in the Windsor Castle grounds. There she could play the role of doting grandmother to a growing number of grandchildren.

By 1844 Queen Victoria could boast to her Uncle Leopold about the gratifying reviews that her private life was now receiving in the British press: 'they say *no* Sovereign *was more* loved than I am . . . and *that*, from our *happy domestic home* – which gives such a good example.'[18] She liked to sketch her children and, when they behaved, to show them off. She boasted of the fact that neither Germany nor France but 'England is the country of family life.'[19] When Alfred Tennyson, the new poet laureate, saluted Victoria in 1851, he celebrated her domestic role:

> Her court was pure; her life serene;
> God gave her peace; her land reposed
> A thousand claims to reverence closed
> In her as Mother, Wife, and Queen.[20]

As the century wore on, it became an axiom that, as Benjamin Disraeli was to tell the House of Commons in 1861, 'She who reigns over us has elected amid all the splendour of empire, to establish her life on the principle of domestic love.'[21] In the words of one early twentieth-century biographer, 'The Victorian court, with a husband and wife living in domestic contentment, singing Mozart in the evening and going to bed at half-past ten was the symbol of something new.'[22]

If only because Albert was an expert organist, an able pianist, and a facile composer, much domestic music-making did indeed go on in the royal household. Although the queen continued to adore Italian opera, Albert introduced her to the music of German composers such as Ludwig van Beethoven and Felix Mendelssohn. Frequently the two would play four-hand piano transcriptions of Beethoven's symphonies, and in 1842, the renowned Felix Mendelssohn came to Buckingham Palace in person so that he could admire the new pipe organ that had just been acquired by Albert. The visitor agreed to play for the royal couple, and he accompanied on the piano while the queen sang several of his songs; according to the composer, she did so 'without a single mistake and with truly felt expression.'[23] Queen Victoria, in turn, granted the composer the authority to dedicate his new symphony (No. 3, the 'Scottish') to her. During the years that followed, there were further meetings with Mendelssohn, and Victoria and Albert continued to attend scores of opera performances as well as to encourage the revival of the English theatre. The queen remained as fond as ever of the works of Bellini and Donizetti and she admired those of the French composer Giacomo Meyerbeer and of the young German composer Richard Wagner. Victoria and Albert were also pleased to encourage the development of opera in English, but only a few composers could boast of even short-term success. Oratorios in English proved more popular, as, in the theatre, did Victorian melodramas and revivals of Shakespeare's plays.[24]

As Queen Victoria's private letters confirm, her devotion to her husband was eminently genuine, and she increasingly came to resent the growing number of obligations, both public and private, that kept him from her side. In Victoria's case at least, the 'Royal *We*' dates from the time in 1843 when the queen ceased to speak of herself as *I* and began to include Albert in every pronouncement. She was often to look back on her own childhood as a lonely and unhappy one. As a result, she explained to her eldest daughter while Albert was yet alive, 'I owe everything to dearest Papa. He was my father, protector, my guide and adviser in all and everything, my mother (I might almost say) as well as my husband.'[25]

Victoria looked on her own marriage as a uniquely blessed one, but she took no joy whatever in what she called the shadow side of marriage, the state of pregnancy. 'What made me so miserable,' Victoria was to write two decades later, 'was – to have the two first years of my married life utterly spoilt by this occupation!' Nor did she remember with satisfaction the process of childbirth itself. 'What you say of the pride of giving life to an immortal soul is very fine, dear,' she told her daughter, 'but I own . . . [that] I think much more of our being like a cow or a dog at such moments.'[26] As a baby, Victoria had herself been breast-fed, but as queen she found the practice disgusting and she relied instead on the importation of wet-nurses from the countryside – even as the practice of wet-nursing was dying out among upper-class women in Victorian Britain.[27]   *contradictory of popular image.*

Most of the time Queen Victoria did not care for toddlers either, and she deplored the cult of 'baby worship.' She was, indeed, to caution her eldest daughter against developing 'rather too great a passion for very little babies,' and when in 1870 she became a grandmother yet again, she greeted the news in a remarkably matter-of-fact manner: 'The baby . . . the seventh grand-daughter and the fourteenth grand-child becomes a very uninteresting thing – for it seems to me to go on like the rabbits in Windsor Park!'[28]

The queen had certainly been more intrigued by her own children in their early years, and she spent a good deal of time with them.[29] Yet the evidence suggests that Prince Albert found child care far more palatable than did she – or, for that matter, than did most Victorian fathers. Lady Lyttleton took note of his patience and kindness toward children, and in her daily journal Victoria described him eagerly flying a new kite with his two elder sons, playing hide-and-seek with Vicky and Bertie with the gusto of a boy, and teaching Bertie how to turn somersaults. 'He is so kind to them and romps with them so delightfully,' the queen remarked.[30] He often read to the children at bed-time, and, as they grew older, he would accompany them to the waxworks and the circus and the zoo. Their mother found it far more difficult to enter into such activities; as she was to concede later, 'I often grudged you children being always there, when I longed to be alone with dearest Papa! Those are always my happiest moments!'[31]

The child with whom both parents felt most frustrated was their eldest son and heir, little Bertie. Vicky, his elder sister, may have been temperamental, but she was also astonishingly bright and clever. By the age of three, her father boasted, she could speak French, German, and English with 'great fluency and choice of phrase.' It was Victoria's earnest hope that Bertie, the future king, would prove equally bright and 'resemble his angelic dearest Father in every, every respect, both in body and mind.' The royal couple therefore devoted anxious days and nights to what one courtier described as 'the minutest details of the physical, intellectual, and moral training of . . . their eldest son.'[32] 'Be not over solicitous about education,' cautioned Lord Melbourne. 'It may be able to do much, but it does not do so much as is expected from it. It may mould and direct the character, but it rarely alters it.'[33]

Melbourne's advice was disregarded by the royal couple in their dealings with little Bertie, who proved to be an amiable child but an exceptionally slow and uncooperative learner. Twenty-first-century American child psychologists would probably have diagnosed dyslexia or attention deficit disorder – or both – but his mother simply called him 'a stupid boy' and his father was to describe him as 'the most thorough and cunning lazybones' he had ever met.[34] Conscientious parents as Victoria and Albert were, they failed to comprehend that the rigorous educational program that they imposed on Bertie (and on the tutors whom they hired to teach him) could prove both cruel and counter-productive. The royal couple continued to take pride in the fact that theirs had come to be seen as a model family. Albert proved an attentive father to his children in their earliest years, and he doted on his two eldest daughters as they grew up; for some years he became their personal tutor. Victoria privately conceded that she found it difficult to deal with her adolescent children and that she took no special pleasure in their company.[35] For Victoria and, to a lesser degree, for Albert the realities of day-to-day family life often failed to coincide with the ideals of domesticity that they continued to profess for the rest of their respective lives.

During the 1840s, the growing family spent most of its time at Windsor Castle, but Windsor Castle, Albert soon decided, was a less than ideal home. The grounds were beset with undrained cesspools and the kitchens were rat-infested; even a generation unacquainted with the germ theory of disease had come to equate filth and bad smells with sickness, and digestive upsets were all too frequent there. Secondly, no one seemed to be in charge – or rather too many individuals were: thus, the Lord Steward was responsible for laying fires, the Lord Chamberlain for lighting them. When the two officials failed to coordinate their activities, the fires were not lit and the castle rooms remained icy. In the same way, the Department of Woods and Forests cleaned castle windows on the outside while the Lord Chamberlain was responsible for having them cleaned on the inside. Hardly ever were both sides of a window clean at the same time so that the queen could enjoy the view. In the course of the years 1842–5 – under the guidance of Baron Stockmar – Albert found ways of centralising castle authority so that most such deficiencies were remedied and so that overnight visitors would be guided to their rooms by a servant rather than being left to wander idly through the halls. Such achievements made Albert intensely unpopular with certain members of the castle staff and with some of the inhabitants of the surrounding borough. Housemaids had their salaries cut; servants and visitors found their candle allotments sharply reduced; fewer of Windsor's poorer residents were able to cadge spare food at the castle kitchen door; the holder of many an ancient sinecure lost his income.[36]

Albert not only wanted to make more comfortable the life of his growing family, but he also wished to make it more secluded. When King George III and Queen Charlotte were surrounded by a similar young family in the 1760s and 1770s, spectators had often jostled members of the royal family as they strolled in the Windsor Castle grounds. Even in the 1830s and early 1840s, intruders such as 'the boy Jones' found it easy to wander into either Buckingham Palace or Windsor Castle and stay undetected for days. Albert sought far greater privacy for his family, and he persuaded Victoria that many of the paths and roads in the Windsor Palace grounds should be decreed off-limits to the public at large.[37]

The financial profit derived from making more efficient the administration of Windsor Castle as well as from the more systematic collection of income that the queen derived from the royal Duchy of Lancaster and the royal Duchy of Cornwall led in the course of the next few years to a situation in which for the first time in more than half a century royal finances were solidly in the black. It was also to lead to the acquisition of two additional homes for the royal family – Osborne House on the Isle of Wight off the south coast of England and Balmoral Castle in the Scottish Highlands. The romantic pavilion that the Prince Regent had built in the seaside resort of Brighton might also have served such a 'get away' purpose, but it was surrounded by other houses, and whenever the queen visited there in the early 1840s she was jostled by the crowds. The building itself, Victoria decided, was 'a strange Chinese thing, haunted by ghosts best forgotten.'[38] It therefore ceased to be a royal residence.[39]

Before additional homes could be acquired for the growing family, the royal couple set off during the years 1841–5 on a series of visits to the estates of the leading noble families of England and Scotland in a manner reminiscent of the 'royal progresses' of earlier centuries. Thus Victoria and Albert became acquainted with Woburn Abbey, the home of the dukes of Bedford, and with Hatfield House, the Elizabethan residence of the earls and marquesses of Salisbury. They spent three weeks at Walmer Castle, the ancient coastal fortress where the Duke of Wellington presided in his role as Lord Warden of the Cinque Ports. On another occasion they visited Drayton Manor, the home of their prime minister, Sir Robert Peel, and on yet another, they stayed at Chatsworth, the historic home of the dukes of Devonshire. The royal couple took delight in the Chatsworth gardens with their fountains and cascades, and in the gigantic display of fireworks that their host arranged in their honor. The Duke of Buckingham entertained the royal couple in so lavish a manner at Stowe – with the shooting of game by day and gigantic dinner parties at night – that the already debt-ridden aristocrat went bankrupt. Within two years, creditors had seized his residences and estates.[39]

The custom of prolonged royal visits to noble mansions was to die out in the course of Victoria's reign, but the desire of the royal couple to have a home away from London and Windsor was strengthened. Victoria had visited the Isle of Wight as a princess, and Osborne House there seemed a promising site, especially now that a railway connected London with Portsmouth and a steam ferry crossed the Solent. After renting the house and grounds for a year, Victoria and Albert decided to purchase the estate, to tear down the old house, and to build a brand new one. Unlike Windsor, the queen wrote, it would be 'a place of one's own, quiet and retired, and free from all Woods and Forests, and other charming Departments who really are the plague of one's life.'[40] To a large degree, Albert served as his own architect; to superintend the construction, he employed Thomas Cubitt, a noted 'master builder.' Because the view at Osborne reminded Albert of the Bay of Naples, he designed the building in the Italianate style with twin towers. One wing was reserved for the immediate family, another for guests, and a third for the royal household. The building proved innovative in several respects. In the principal reception rooms the shutters were lined with mirrors; in the evening, therefore, they not only reflected the light from the chandeliers but also created a sense of vast space. The structure was unusual in other ways: iron girders in place of wooden ones; a central warm-air heating system to supplement the open fires; and (for the first time in a royal residence) water closets and bathtubs with running hot and cold water. In the interior decoration of almost every room the letters V and A were ingeniously intertwined.

Albert was equally preoccupied with the two thousand acres of shore and parkland in which the new Osborne House was set. He enjoyed laying out gardens on a grand scale, and he planned the avenue of cedars that led to the main entrance.[41] It was at Osborne that Victoria bathed in the sea for the first time and that Albert taught his children how to swim. It was in the Osborne House grounds also that a few years later Prince Albert supervised the installation of a Swiss Cottage. The interior was child-size in every detail, and it included a fully equipped kitchen and range. Here the princes could learn carpentry and gardening, the princesses not only gardening but also cooking and housekeeping. The plates of the miniature tea, dinner, and dessert services were inscribed with the words, 'SPARE NOT, WASTE NOT, WANT NOT.' In one room there was a doll's house grocery shop, 'Spratt, Grocer to Her Majesty,' where the children could learn the price of everyday foodstuffs such as tea, coffee, cocoa, spices, dried fruits, and gelatine. The stones, fossils, and plants collected by the children under Albert's direction were displayed in a small 'natural history museum' upstairs. Separate garden plots for each child were laid out next to the cottage, and spades, hoes, and wheelbarrows were provided. The children were paid by the hour for their garden work, and they were taught both to make bricks and to erect tents. Not far away, a mock earthwork fort was set up with genuine brass firing cannons, so that the young princes could practice military tactics. No wonder that the royal children came to welcome the time that the family spent at Osborne and to cherish the Swiss Cottage most of all.[42]

Osborne was located in one of the warmest regions of Great Britain; the vegetation was luxuriant, and flowers bloomed early. Yet Queen Victoria was a hot-blooded individual who welcomed cool breezes and mountainous scenery – as soon as she became familiar with them. As a princess she had never set foot in Scotland – indeed few members of the Hanoverian royal family ever had – but in 1842, she and Albert, sailing amidst a squadron of vessels, traveled through the North Sea from London to Edinburgh. Victoria received a warm welcome in the city, whose monuments she admired, and the royal couple went on to visit other parts of Scotland including the estates of several noble families. In the course of the next month, inspired by the novels and poems of Sir Walter Scott, Victoria also acquired her first taste of the Highlands, and on her return to London she reported to Lord Aberdeen (her Scottish foreign secretary) that the

Highlanders were 'such a chivalrous, fine, active people' and that the Highlands meant 'a quiet, a retirement, a wildness, a liberty, and a solitude that had such a charm for us.'[43]

Different portions of Scotland reminded Albert either of Switzerland or of his native Thuringia, and he too felt certain that the Scottish air was purer and lighter than that to be found in southern England and that people were more honest and congenial there. During the years that followed, the family made additional visits to Scotland, which had become accessible by rail, and in 1847 they leased Balmoral. It was, Queen Victoria wrote, 'a pretty little castle in the old Scottish style,'[44] located in the Deeside region of the eastern Highlands near the city of Aberdeen. Balmoral became the site for all manner of expeditions: hiking, fishing, deerstalking (on the part of Prince Albert), pony-riding, picnicking, and mountain-climbing. On one occasion, Victoria and Albert reached the top of nearby Mount Lochnagar, at almost four thousand feet the third tallest peak in Scotland. For the queen it also meant becoming acquainted with the local Presbyterian kirk, with the Highland games, and with the near-by villagers whose houses she visited. She even made an effort to learn Gaelic, the ancient Celtic language still spoken in parts of the Highlands and the Hebridean islands. Unfortunately it proved to be 'a very difficult language, for it is pronounced in a totally different way from that in which it is written.'[45]

In 1852 the royal couple purchased Balmoral and the surrounding 17,400 acres of land. Soon thereafter, the old castle having proved too small, they laid the foundations of its successor, 'a building clad in granite which was part Flemish gables, part French Renaissance windows, part Scottish baronial grandeur, and part Thuringian Schloss, complete with pepper-pot turrets.'[46] Hoping to give encouragement to the declining Scottish woolen industry, Albert decorated the rooms – walls, floors, chairs, and curtains – with an exuberance of tartans such as the Royal Stuart. Noting that the wearing of kilts had largely died out in the neighborhood, the royal couple deliberately revived the practice, and Albert and his sons often wore kilts at Balmoral. Both Victoria and Albert gloried in the Highland atmosphere, and occasional visitors found Prince Albert far more relaxed and easygoing there than in London. Only a single policeman guarded the entire premises against intruders.[47] Even in the age of the railway, however, cabinet ministers (of whom at least one had always to be in attendance) found long sojourns to chilly northern Scotland far less palatable than did most members of the royal family.

It was in the year that the foundation stone was laid for the new Balmoral Castle that Queen Victoria became a mother for the eighth time, and for the first time the process was aided by the use of chloroform. Some religious leaders attacked that novel practice as interfering with a Divinely-appointed order that decreed pain as a natural aspect of childbirth. At the same time the leading medical journal, *The Lancet*, contended that the provision of anesthetics in childbirth was still too experimental a practice to be applied to so august a patient. The queen defied both the theologians and the doctors, however, and her example was soon followed by mothers throughout the kingdom. Although the queen initially imported a Gaelic-speaking wet-nurse to supply her new child with the pure milk of the Scottish Highlands, it prospered intermittently at best. Her mother thought the baby 'ugly,' and Leopold later turned out to suffer from hereditary hemophilia, a medical condition that caused his mother to become so over-protective as to make the young prince's childhood an often difficult one.[48] It was in the year that the family first occupied the new Balmoral Castle that their last child was born, the eminently healthy Beatrice, who understandably came to be known as 'Baby.'

By the mid-1850s Victoria and Albert were spending close to half of each year at either Osborne or Balmoral with their children. The queen may have found some of those children difficult to deal with as they grew up, but nonetheless in the course of two decades the manner in which the people of the United Kingdom visualised their royal family – in paintings, in cartoons, and in still novel photographs – had markedly changed.[49] During the first third of the century royalty had meant curmudgeonly elderly gentlemen. By the 1850s it had come to imply both youth and a keenly moral and domestically inclined family. Britain's people now found it as easy to visualise their queen and prince strolling through the Scottish heather as ensconced on gilded thrones in the House of Lords, their place at least once a year when a new session of Parliament began.

5 *The Royal Visit to Ireland*

In August 1849, as Queen Victoria, Prince Albert, and their four oldest children disembark at Kingstown Harbour, a mythical Sir Patrick Raleigh declares: 'May it please your Majesty to tread on the tail of my coat.' (*Punch*, July 28, 1849)

5 The Reigning Partner

A few months before Albert became her husband, Queen Victoria remarked to her Uncle Leopold that 'the English are very jealous at the idea of Albert's having any political power, or meddling with affairs here – which I know from himself he will *not* do.'[1] Albert may not have moved to England to *meddle*, but he was increasingly absorbed by the affairs of his adopted country, and his intention was to enhance the role of his new wife, the queen. As he was to explain to the Duke of Wellington a decade later, his purposes were

> to sink his own individual existence in that of his wife – to aim at no power by himself or for himself – to shun all ostentation – to assume no separate responsibility before the public – to make his position entirely a part of hers – to fill up every gap which, as a woman, she would naturally leave in the exercise of her regal functions – continually and anxiously to watch every part of the public business, in order to be able to advise and assist her at any moment in any of the multifarious and difficult questions brought before her, political, or social, or personal. To place all his time and powers at her command as the natural head of the family, superintendent of her household, manager of her private affairs, her sole confidential adviser in politics, and only assistant in her communications with the officers of the Government, her private secretary, and permanent Minister.[2]

highly influential position – could be good or bad concept

That's quite a bit

Albert preferred to see himself always as a servant, but he was obviously an intensely ambitious servant, one whose hope it was to strengthen the influence of the British monarchy not only as a symbol of morality and domesticity but also as an active player in day-to-day government. In the course of the 1840s, with Queen Victoria more often pregnant than regnant, Albert did indeed come to play an ever-more important political role. He examined the papers in the despatch boxes, and to an increasing degree he added comments to the despatches themselves. He participated in almost every personal meeting that Queen Victoria held with either her prime minister or with a member of the Cabinet. He accompanied Victoria to Parliament when she formally opened and closed each annual session and when she read her 'Speech from the Throne'. Indeed, he sat on a throne of his own next to hers. Occasionally he presided at royal receptions in her stead. Analogously, in every royal home – Buckingham Palace, Windsor Castle, and later Osborne and Balmoral – Albert and Victoria worked at adjoining desks for many hours each day. Theirs became therefore as much a political as a domestic partnership. It was Albert who wrote the lengthy memoranda and who increasingly came to draft her letters to her ministers. In fact, if not in name, theirs became a dual monarchy.

By 1845 a close observer of palace procedure took note of the fact that Albert and Victoria always met ministers together and began each sentence with 'We.' He went on:

> The Prince is become so identified with the Queen that they are one person, and as he likes business, it is obvious that while she has the title he is really discharging the functions of the Sovereign. He is King to all intents and purposes.[3]

Biographers who concur can cite her daily journal entry for June 8, 1846: 'Really when one is so happy & blessed in one's home life, as I am, Politics (provided my country is safe) must take only a 2nd place'.[4] Similarly, in a letter to her Uncle Leopold in 1852, she lamented that Albert was so preoccupied with political affairs as to have become 'really a terrible man of business... I am every day more convinced that we women, if we are to be good women, feminine and amiable and domestic, are not fitted to reign.'[5] The context of the latter comment is important: remarkably few early Victorian political leaders were as hard-working as Albert, and Victoria demonstrated time and again – both in her journal entries and in letters to her royal relations that had not been drafted by her husband – how assiduous remained her concern during the 1840s and 1850s with both domestic and foreign affairs.

But what precisely was the proper role of the monarch in Albert's and Victoria's eyes during these years? Inasmuch as most of the executive powers of the Crown were now exercised in the name of the monarch by the prime minister and his cabinet, what place remained for the monarch? Albert felt sure that Victoria had made a mistake by becoming identified in her early years as 'Queen of the Whigs'. In his judgment, the monarch should transcend political party differences and not campaign against the Whigs as King William IV had done in 1835 or for the Whigs as Queen Victoria was inclined to do as late as 1841. In Albert's eyes, to stand above the political battle was not, however, to become a cypher. Early in 1841, as it became increasingly clear that the Melbourne ministry would soon lose, once and for all, its overall majority in the House of Commons, Baron Stockmar set forth for Prince Albert, the following ideal:

> [The monarchy] supports frankly, honourably, and with all its might, the Ministry of the time, whatever it be, so long as it commands a majority, *and governs with integrity for the welfare and advancement of the country.*[6]

The first part of the statement would still hold true in our own century; the italicised portion implied that the monarch could strengthen or undermine a ministry independently of its success in retaining its support in Parliament. But how? As Albert was privately to complain a decade later:

> Why are Princes alone to be denied the credit of having political opinions based upon an anxiety for the national interest and honour of their country and the welfare of mankind? Are they not more independently placed than any other politician in the State? Are their interests not most intimately bound up with those of their country? Is the Sovereign not the natural guardian of the honour of his country . . . ? Has he no duties to perform towards his country?[7]

By then no one doubted that Prince Albert possessed an overwhelming sense of duty. It remains equally clear that his (and Victoria's) definition of the proper role of a constitutional monarch might from time to time clash with that of the ministers who were administering the country in Victoria's name.

By the time Prince Albert came to be involved in day-to-day policy-making, the prime minister was Sir Robert Peel. During the spring of 1841, the Melbourne ministry had lost a vote of confidence in the House of Commons. The Whig cabinet then asked Queen Victoria to call a new general election. The outcome was clear cut: the Whigs and their Radical and Irish allies won 290 seats; the Tories (or Conservatives), 368. Soon after the new Parliament met, Lord Melbourne resigned, and the almost daily meetings between the queen and her prime minister that had begun in 1837 came to an abrupt end. With Victoria's reluctant acquiescence, Prince Albert had already arranged for the retirement of several of the queen's most Whiggish female associates. As a result there took place no second 'bedchamber crisis'.

It took Queen Victoria several months to become accustomed to Sir Robert Peel, but Prince Albert took to him at once – if only because in temperament and personality Peel and Albert were far more alike than had been Albert and Melbourne. Melbourne remained the somewhat cynical, light-hearted, debonair, Regency-era ladies' man, whereas Peel, the son of a cotton manufacturer, was far more the earnest, hard-working, professional administrator, with a reserved personality very much like Albert's own. It was during the Peel ministry (1841–6) that Albert became ever more involved in politics and ever more sympathetic to Peel's reform program.

When Prince Albert first arrived in England, he possessed a curiously abstract and inaccurate notion of how the two-party parliamentary system operated there.

> Composed as Party is here of two extremes, both must be wrong. . . . The Whigs want change *before* change is required. The love of change is their great failing. The Tories on the other hand *resist change* long after the feeling & temper of the Times has loudly demanded it, & at least make a virtue of necessity by an ungracious concession.[8]

What Albert ignored, first of all, was the fact that many matters that Parliament discussed – such as 'social reform' – were not issues that divided the major parties from each other. During the later 1830s and 1840s a rapidly industrialising and urbanising Great Britain was beset by intermittent economic depression, but most political leaders concurred that the chief functions of the central government were to defend the country against foreign attack, to keep public order, to provide a legal system that ensured the fulfillment of contracts and the preservation of property, and to preserve a stable currency.

Many of the 'social reform' laws that were to create the early Victorian regulatory state were therefore not party measures. They were first introduced by private members of Parliament rather than by the prime minister and cabinet of the day, and they were supported, and sometimes opposed, by fluctuating combinations of Whigs and Tories. Such an individual initiative led to the Factory Act of 1833 that barred work in cotton mills by children under nine and that first set up a national system of factory inspectors. An evangelical Tory layman, Lord Ashley (after 1851 the 7th Earl of Shaftesbury), initiated what became the Mines Act of 1842, which barred women and boys from underground labour, and the Ten-Hour Act of 1847 which limited daily factory work for all women and children. In the course of the 1840s, such personal initiatives also led to the setting up of a national Board of Health to encourage British cities to build sewers and to secure clean water. Similar boards and inspectorates were set up to oversee savings banks, prisons, asylums for the mentally ill, conditions on merchant vessels, and private charities. Prince Albert demonstrated the monarchy's sympathy for such projects by praising Ashley for his efforts to protect exploited children and by becoming, in 1844, the president of the Labourers' Friends Society organised by Lord Ashley.[9]

These were all examples of intervention in the economy by central government, but – unlike many twentieth-century social reform measures – they did not involve the use of the tax system in order to redistribute income from the rich to the poor. The one institution that did so was the three-centuries-old Poor Law, which, in England at least, assured widows, orphans, the very old, and the very sick that they would not be left to starve. A degree of central government supervision was imposed on that ancient welfare system by the New Poor Law of 1834, but Poor Law guardians continued to operate at the smallest level of local government, the parish, or in unions of parishes. The poorer members of early Victorian society were discouraged by law and by custom from applying for Poor Law relief except when their situation was truly desperate. The wealthier members of society took comfort in the existence of numerous private philanthropic foundations – many of them religious – that supplemented the efforts of the Poor Law guardians, who relied on local property taxes. Each year private charities distributed twice as much money to schools, to model housing schemes, and to other projects as did all the Poor Law authorities together.

[If social reform was not the key issue that divided Whigs and Tories, then what was?] Back in 1832, the Whigs had favored the reform of the franchise laws and the Tories had opposed such change. In 1833 it had been a Whig ministry that had abolished slavery in the British Empire by compensating the slave-owners for the loss of their property; the inhabitants of Jamaica and other islands of the British West Indies were most immediately affected. The Tories had been reluctant to go along with these steps. Analogously, it was the Whigs and their allies who curbed the legal powers of the hitherto dominant Church of England and strengthened the role of both non-Anglican Protestants (such as Methodists, Baptists, and Congregationalists) and of Roman Catholics, who constituted a small minority in England and Scotland but a large majority in Ireland. The Tories, by contrast, sought to maintain the remaining privileges of the established Church of England.

By the time Peel became prime minister in 1841, he had assured the electorate that, if returned to power, his party would not seek to undo the Whig reforms of the 1830s. At the same time, it had no desire to change further the political structure of the state: the monarchy, the House of Lords, the House of Commons, the franchise rules, the Church of England. That did not stop Peel, however, from becoming a reformer in other matters: Ireland, the currency, and the regulation of foreign trade – and to an increasing degree, Albert and Victoria identified themselves with Peel's reform program.

One of the perennial concerns of nineteenth-century British government leaders was Ireland. Almost one-third of all the people who lived in the United Kingdom were Irish, but Ireland remained far more a land of poor tenant farmers and much less a land of factory workers and city-dwellers than were England and Scotland. It also contained many more people whose loyalty to the British Crown was suspect. During the later 1830s, it is true, Daniel O'Connell, the Irish Member of Parliament who had achieved 'Catholic Emancipation' back in 1829, was willing, together with his followers, to keep the Melbourne ministry in power. In 1841, O'Connell's party moved back to the Opposition benches, however, with the Whigs, and by 1843 O'Connell was leading an all-out campaign in Ireland to repeal altogether the Union of 1800. His goal was to enable the Irish to govern themselves domestically, by restoring to Dublin an Irish Parliament. Both the Whigs and the Tories opposed that proposal, but just as the Whigs during the 1830s had enacted reform measures in Ireland – such as non-denominational elementary schools and elective local government in Ireland's cities – so Peel, after 1841, sought to reform higher education in the land across the Irish Sea. His ministry established a new Irish University, with constituent colleges at Belfast, Cork, and Galway, open to all academically qualified applicants regardless of religious affiliation. Higher education in Ireland was no longer to be monopolised by the established Protestant Church of Ireland. Victoria and Albert strongly favoured Peel's design. They also supported Peel's plan to triple the amount of, and to make permanent, the annual government grant to Maynooth, the Roman Catholic seminary near Dublin that educated two-thirds of Ireland's priests.[10]

The youthful royal couple came deeply to admire the courageous manner in which Peel carried the Maynooth Bill through to ultimate triumph despite the opposition of many members of his own party. As the queen reported privately during the spring of 1845:

> Here we are in a great state of agitation about one of the greatest measures ever proposed; I am sure poor Peel ought to be *blessed by* all Catholics for the many and noble ways in which he stands forth to protect and do good to poor Ireland. But the bigotry, the wicked and blind passions it brings forth is quite dreadful, and I blush for Protestantism! . . . The Protestant Establishment in Ireland must remain untouched, but let the Roman Catholic Clergy be well and handsomely educated.[11]

Most of Peel's other reforms involved finance and foreign trade. Early in his ministry he moved in the direction of freer trade by reducing import tariffs on hundreds of items and by removing tariffs altogether from hundreds more – including raw cotton, the fiber imported from the United States that had become the basis of Britain's most important industry. By 1845 all remaining taxes on British exports were ended as well. Since four-fifths of the income collected by the British state came from excise taxes and customs duties, Peel had to find a new way of balancing the annual government budget. He found the solution in the income tax, a Napoleonic War expedient that had been abolished back in 1817 but which he now brought back to serve as a supplementary source of revenue. In the twentieth century, the income tax was to become the single most important financial tool by which the central government financed welfare state services, but during the nineteenth century it remained a secondary source. Poor people were exempt, but the heads of middle-class and upper-class Victorian households were expected to pay an annual tax that ranged between two and five percent of their income.

Intermittently during the later 1830s and 1840s two well-organised protest movements operating outside Parliament competed for public attention. The Chartists sought to turn Britain at once into a democratic state in which every adult male became a voter, in which all electoral districts were equal in population, and in which parliamentary elections took place every year by secret ballot. The Chartist movement involved mass petitions as well as gigantic demonstrations and parades all over England. Every now and then demonstrations turned violent, but although the movement struck fear into the hearts of some Members of Parliament, it did not gain their support. They would not vote for so abrupt a change in the constitution, one in which the average voter would be a dependent propertyless labourer or servant under the spell of a deluded demagogue.

A more successful extra-parliamentary organisation was the Anti-Corn Law League, first organised by a group of Manchester businessmen during the economic depression of 1837. Their long-range goal was a system of international free trade in which British industrialists would be free to import their raw materials and the food for their workers and export their manufactured goods without any interference by the government. They believed not only that such a system would secure economic prosperity and cheap food for the people of the British Isles but also that it would bring an end to what they called 'aristocratic misrule'. Because they were persuaded that most wars between nations had been caused by disputes over trade, they also felt certain that, if Britain adopted a policy of 'free trade' and if other nations followed Britain's example, the long-term result would be international peace. *idealistic*

A majority of British landlords and farmers and tenants felt equally sure that the still vital agricultural sector of the economy depended upon the Corn Laws (i.e. on protective tariffs) for its survival; they also argued that for Britain to become an industrial country primarily dependent on imported food would, in case of war, endanger its national security. Although both political parties might agree to amend the Corn Laws, as of 1841 neither was prepared to end them altogether, and Richard Cobden, the Anti-Corn Law League leader who was elected to Parliament that year, waged a war of words that he seemed unlikely to win for many years. Behind the scenes, however, Sir Robert Peel became ever less certain that the program of agricultural protection that his party had espoused at the general election of 1841 was any longer valid. Late in 1845, prompted by the potato blight that threatened famine in Ireland, Peel dramatically announced that he was prepared to recommend to the House of Commons that the Corn Laws be abolished altogether. By then Queen Victoria had became as staunch a supporter of Peel as six years earlier she had been his opponent. To her Uncle Leopold she confided her

> *extreme* admiration of our worthy Peel, who shows himself a man of unbounded *loyalty, courage,* patriotism, and *high-mindedness*. . . . I have never seen him so excited or so determined, and *such* a good cause must succeed.[12]

Albert was in the House of Commons gallery in January 1846 when Peel first introduced the resolution designed to end all Corn Laws within the next three years. To the surprise of both Albert and Victoria, one of the leading Conservative opponents of Peel's change of policy publicly criticised the prince for having been influenced by the prime minister

> to give semblance of the personal sanction of Her Majesty to a measure which, be it for good or evil, a great majority of the landed aristocracy of England, of Scotland, and of Ireland imagine fraught with deep injury if not of ruin to them.[13]

The royal couple was so caught up in Peel's 'great cause' that they celebrated his House of Commons triumph in May with delight. That victory came at a great cost, however. It depended on the support of the opposition Whigs and Radicals (by the late 1840s often known as Liberals). The members of Peel's own Conservative (Tory) Party had voted against him, by 231–112. That party was now divided between Peelites and Protectionists; and a month later the Protectionists allied themselves with the Whigs to vote Peel out of power. For the next five years the royal couple was compelled to deal with Lord John Russell as prime minister, a member of an ancient Whig family who had succeeded Lord Melbourne as head of the Liberal Party. Victoria and Albert never became as fond of Russell as Victoria had once been of Melbourne and as Albert had become of Peel, with whom he continued to correspond regularly until Peel's unexpected death in 1850 after a fall from a horse. In a public tribute to Peel, Albert described the statesman as 'a Liberal from feeling, but Conservative upon principle,' as a man whose 'impulses drove him to foster progress' in a gradual manner within established institutions.[14] The words could as readily have described the prince's own sentiments.

In the course of the later 1840s, Albert and Victoria reflected Peelite attitudes both in their political and in their ceremonial practices. The catalyst to Peel's conversion to the abolition of the Corn Laws had been the onset of the potato blight in Ireland, a land of over eight million people, half of whom had become dependent almost solely on the consumption of several pounds of salted, boiled potatoes per day. The potato was easy to grow and easy to store, but not for longer than a year. And when the blight struck, there was no easy remedy. Emergency shipments of grain, large-scale soup kitchens, and jobs created by local Poor Law authorities did not suffice. Rural western Ireland almost totally lacked the highly developed network of merchants, shops, and roads that British ministers took for granted in England, nor did the government possess the administrative machinery to handle such a crisis at a time when the prevailing political theory did not regard relief to be one of the proper functions of central government. According to *The Economist*, 'A government may remove all impediments which interfere to prevent the people from providing for themselves, but beyond that they can do little'.[15] Both the Peel and Russell ministries did a good deal more than that, but not enough to prevent almost a million Irish people from dying directly or indirectly of starvation. The young contracted dysentery, the old, typhus. During the ten years after 1845, at least a million and a half more Irish people sought refuge abroad: in England and in Scotland as well as in the United States, Canada, and Australia.

Some later Irish nationalists came to believe that many British political leaders actually welcomed the depopulation of Ireland and that Victoria and Albert were at best indifferent. The surviving evidence contradicts such a conclusion. Both in her private conversations and in her semi-annual speeches to Parliament, Queen Victoria showed herself deeply sympathetic to the plight of Ireland's peasants, whose sufferings 'were really too terrible to think of.'[16] Her private journal includes entry after entry reporting that 'the news from Ireland is appalling.' 'The people are starving & the landlords are ruined, & there does not seem to be a ray of hope, as to matters improving.'[17] At her side, Albert drafted memorandum after private memorandum assessing official and unofficial reports from Ireland and outlining possible ameliorative measures.

In 1848, the queen took comfort in the thought that the 'Distress in Ireland consequent upon successive Failures in the Production of Food has been mitigated by the Application of the Law for the Relief of the Poor, and by the Amount of charitable Contributions raised in other Parts of the United Kingdom.'[18] British and American Quakers had set up a Central Relief Committee in 1846, and early in 1847 Baron Lionel de Rothschild and other London bankers and merchants organised 'The British Association for the relief of the extreme distress in the remote parishes of Ireland and Scotland,' in order to distribute food, clothing, and fuel to 'the multitudes who are suffering under the present awful calamity.'

Queen Victoria headed the list of patrons with a pledge of £2,000 from her privy purse, and Prince Albert followed her with a pledge of £500. According to one estimate, at that time the sum of one pound could feed eight families of five for a week.[19] The royal couple's pledge was therefore the equivalent in 2003 of at least £250,000.[20] By the spring of 1849, destitution in Ireland was as severe as ever, however. The land was afflicted by cholera, fever, and dysentery; 250,000 people lived in workhouses and more than 750,000 subsisted on 'outdoor relief.' Russell's ministry was so shocked by such reports that each member of the cabinet contributed £100 to a new private subscription; Victoria once again headed the list with a donation of £500 (worth at least £50,000 today).

Victoria's concern was not limited to public speeches in Parliament or to private contributions to charity. Thus in February 1847, she attended an opera performance of which the proceeds were given to 'the Distressed Irish & Scotch.' Every few weeks thereafter she and Albert patronised yet another charity event designed to aid the deeply afflicted Irish. In the meantime, Victoria was happy to go along with Prime Minister Russell's request that she provide the 'authority of a Queen's Letter for collections in all the Churches for the destitute in remote districts of Ireland and Scotland.'[21]

Whereas during 1846 and 1847 Albert's and Victoria's correspondence with their chief ministers had focused on the best ways of relieving the famine, in the course of 1848 their attention was concentrated on the revolutions that had broken out first in France and then elsewhere in Europe, and on the scattered outbursts of revolt in the Emerald Isle led by Smith O'Brien and the other leaders of 'Young Ireland.' In April, Albert warned Russell that his ministry not only must suppress the rebels but also must 'express its readiness . . . to listen to any complaint & to take any proposition for the Amelioration of Ireland into the most serious consideration.' The famine years had brought in their train a quadrupling in the rate of murder, of cattle-stealing, highway robbery, and other 'outrages of every kind.' Ireland was also beset by the mismanagement of relief supplies and by inflammatory proclamations by the Roman Catholic Archbishop John MacHale, who alternately accused the British government of failing to feed the hungry and of seeking to convert them to Protestantism by handing out free soup.[22]

Albert's own long-range plans included a Roman Catholic clergy whose salaries were paid by the British government – at an expected cost of £350,000 per year to the British taxpayer – and the abolition of the post of lord-lieutenant in Dublin. Now that it had become possible to travel from London to Dublin in only fourteen hours – by a combination of steam railway and steamship – Ireland should no longer be governed as a separate province; rather it should be elevated to complete 'equality with England & Scotland.' Russell and Lord Clarendon, the astute new lord-lieutenant, were sympathetic to both plans, but considered them premature. Clarendon strongly supported the notion of regular royal visits to Ireland, however. As he wrote privately to Russell, 'whatever may be the political feelings or animosities of the Irish, their devotion to the Queen is unquestionable'.[23]

As late as October 1848 Queen Victoria wrote privately of 'Ireland quivering in our grasp, and ready to throw off her allegiance at any moment,'[24] but by then the Irish insurrection was largely over. Its leaders had been captured, tried, and exiled to Australia. In May of 1849, it is true, the queen became directly involved in Irish violence when a young man shot at her while she was driving in a carriage in London; he turned out to be an unemployed Irishman from County Limerick. By then, however, it was generally agreed, the time had come for the queen to make her oft-postponed first visit to Ireland. Even modest preparations for such a visit might stimulate the depressed Irish economy. In the words of one Dublin merchant, the visit would prove 'a great godsend to raise the country from its present deplorable condition.'[25] An army of Dublin workmen therefore repaired and decorated the Castle, the vice-regal Lodge, and St Patrick's Hall, while regular army troops rehearsed their parade drill in Phoenix Park. *Civic pride*

On August 1, the royal yacht, the *Victoria and Albert*, steamed into the harbor of Cove, which the monarch honored by renaming it Queenstown – in emulation of her uncle King George IV, who a generation earlier had renamed the town of Dun Loghaire as Kingstown. On board a smaller vessel, the *Fairy*, the queen swept into Cork, where she received a triumphant reception. Cannons saluted, flags flew, and thousands of onlookers cheered. Having knighted the city's mayor, the royal couple then toured Cork in an open carriage amidst a crowd that Victoria described as 'noisy, excitable, but very good-humoured . . . running and pushing about, and laughing, talking and shrieking.' Many of the banners were inscribed with the words: 'Hail Victoria, Ireland's Hope and England's Glory.'[26]

The next day the *Victoria and Albert* continued to steam along Ireland's south-east coast. The vessel anchored for the night near Waterford, but, unlike her husband and her two eldest sons, Victoria felt too sea-sick to go ashore. On Sunday, August 5, a flotilla escorted the royal vessel into Kingstown harbor. There thousands of enthusiastic spectators welcomed the royal couple and their four oldest children. As Victoria and her family disembarked the next morning, a stout old woman shouted, 'Ah, Queen dear, make one of them Prince Patrick and Ireland will die for you.' In Dublin the enthusiasm of the citizens seemed to grow by the day, and Victoria was deeply impressed by the beauty of the city and its surroundings – Sackville Street and Merrion Square, Trinity College and the old Parliament House. With its attractive parks and its riverside, the city resembled Paris, and the apparent joy of the people in seeing their Queen in person was 'a wonderful and striking spectacle.' On the one hand, she was shaken by the poverty of the masses. As she noted in her private journal, 'The raggedness of the people is beyond belief, man & boy having really hardly any covering, for they never mend anything.' On the other hand, she was struck by the attractive appearance of even the poorest women; they had 'such beautiful black eyes and hair and such fine colours and teeth.'[27]

In the course of the next several days, the queen drove about the city informally, and she visited the botanical gardens, the Bank of Ireland, a model school, a hospital for army veterans, and numerous other sites. At Trinity College the royal pair inspected the early medieval Book of Kells. 'I gladly share with you the hope,' she told assembled Dubliners,

> that the heavy visitation with which Providence has recently visited large numbers of people in this country is passing away. I have felt deeply for their sufferings, and it will be a source of heartfelt satisfaction to me if I am permitted to witness the future and lasting prosperity of this portion of the United Kingdom.[28]

On August 8, in the magnificent Throne Room of Dublin Castle, two thousand people were individually presented to the monarch in the course of a four-and-a-half-hour levée. At a formal state dinner that evening Victoria wore a dress of green Irish poplin lavishly embroidered with gold shamrocks and adorned by the blue ribbon and star of St Patrick. By then she could do no wrong in the eyes of Dubliners. 'The enthusiasm and loyalty were beyond everything', Victoria noted privately, and the O'Connellite *Freeman's Journal* readily acknowledged that 'the more the citizens of Dublin see Queen Victoria the more she wins their affections.'[29] In the meantime Prince Albert made visits to the Royal Irish Academy, the Royal College of Surgeons, and the Royal Dublin Society. He strongly urged his hosts to make their prize cattle and their agricultural implements 'the harbinger of a termination to those sufferings under which the people have so lamentably, yet with such exemplary patience, laboured.'[30]

While in Dublin, one of the queen's purposes was to meet the leaders of Ireland's three major churches, the (Protestant) Church of Ireland, the Presbyterian Church, and the Roman Catholic Church, and Prince Albert was able to take comfort in the thought that – contrary to his earlier fears – 'the Catholic clergy are quite as loyal as the Anglicans, the Presbyterians, and the Quakers.'[31] The final days of the royal visit included a gigantic military review and a visit to the Roman Catholic seminary at Maynooth, where the students loudly cheered the royal couple. A gigantic crowd surrounded Victoria when she returned to Dublin, and another highly enthusiastic one assembled at Kingstown, where she re-embarked on her yacht and waved to the crowd as the vessel drifted slowly into the Irish Sea. A brief but successful visit to Belfast followed before the yacht sailed on to Glasgow in Scotland; from there the queen went overland to Balmoral, her 'dear Highland home'. As a parting gift to the Irish, the queen divided £1,000 among the hospitals and charitable institutions of Cork, Dublin, and Belfast.[32]

All observers were in agreement that the visit to Ireland in 1849 constituted one of the great ceremonial success stories of the early Victorian monarchy. The oft-cynical viceroy, Lord Clarendon, reported to London that 'all classes and all parties' in Ireland had become 'enchanted' by a monarch who in her punctuality, her neatness, her apparent child-rearing ability, and in her kindliness served as a model for all womankind. Victoria, in turn, took comfort in the hope that the visit would 'promote among all Her Faithful Subjects

in Ireland that Union of Heart and Affection, which is essential to
the prosperity of their common country.'[33] In the immediate aftermath of the visit, the queen formally created her eldest son, then
seven, Earl of Dublin, and when her third son was born on May 1,
1850, he was christened Arthur William Patrick Albert – 'Arthur' for
the Duke of Wellington, 'William' for the Crown Prince of Prussia,
and 'Patrick', wrote Albert, 'for the Irish to show our gratitude for
their friendly reception of us last year.'[34] Although the royal couple
were to visit Ireland again in 1853 and 1861, later historians were to
criticise Queen Victoria for failing to build systematically on the
bond with the Irish that she had formed on her first visit to that
famine-afflicted land.

Prince Albert was a scholar at heart, and he and Victoria were
delighted by the warm welcome they received in 1843 on their first
visit to Cambridge University; the ancient institution conferred on
Albert an honorary degree. The post of Chancellor of Cambridge
University, an essentially honorific position, had often been filled
by an eminent political figure, and when the Duke of
Northumberland died in 1847 it fell vacant once more. The head of
Trinity College, the philosopher Dr William Whewell, who had
served as Albert's host four years earlier, strongly urged the prince
to stand for election. Albert was given the impression at first that
there would be no opposition, but St John's College was involved in
an internal academic quarrel with Trinity and put forward its own
candidate, the 2nd Earl of Powys, a Cambridge alumnus and erstwhile Tory MP. Albert was therefore inclined to withdraw, but former prime minister Peel urged Albert to persist. In the course of
three days of polling, graduates of the university traveled to
Cambridge from all over the country to cast their non-secret bal-
lots, while undergraduate students milled about the university's
Senate House. The results were: Albert, 953; Powys, 837. In the face
of so modest a victory, Albert was again tempted to withdraw, but
Sir Robert Peel and Queen Victoria jointly persuaded Albert to
accept. In March in Buckingham Palace the 27-year-old prince was
officially inaugurated, and in July the royal couple made a formal
visit to the ancient seat of learning.[35]

The heads of the Cambridge colleges may have sought a ceremonial royal patron. What they found instead was an eager academic reformer who was deeply disturbed by the fact that almost the only subjects taught well – or taught at all – were Classics and Mathematics and that the prime career for which the university prepared its students was the Anglican ministry. Albert was astonished to learn that, for practical purposes, the institution taught no history, economics, law, psychology, modern languages, geography, chemistry, art, astronomy, or natural history. With the assistance of the vice-chancellor, Dr Henry Philpott, Prince Albert set forth a significant set of reforms, adding to the university curriculum new subjects and lectures for undergraduates. It was adopted by a reluctant university senate late in 1848, and it proved to be only the first of many interventions by Albert in university affairs, making him, in the judgment of one of his biographers, not only 'the pioneer of the principles of enlightened scholarship' but also 'the greatest Chancellor Cambridge University has ever had.'[36]

Just as it was Sir Robert Peel who had encouraged Prince Albert's involvement with educational reform, so it had been Peel who even earlier had appointed Albert as president of the Fine Arts Commission. As head of that organisation, Albert had encouraged a revival of fresco painting in the remodeled Gothic Palace of Westminster, which was completed during the 1840s as the home of the House of Commons and the House of Lords; most of the earlier palace had burned down in 1834. It was Albert too who encouraged the creation of Schools of Design in London and a number of other cities. As president of the Royal Society of Artists, he also promoted the growth of the National Gallery and helped enlarge the royal couple's own collection of paintings.

The project that became peculiarly the prince's own was the Great Exhibition of the Works of All Nations, which opened in London's Hyde Park in May 1851. The underlying theme of this first true World's Fair was not only to celebrate Britain's own achievements in industry and the fine arts but also to include exhibitors from all over the world and to encourage the movement toward international free trade and international amity that Peel had done so much to advance. The Russell ministry had furthered that cause in 1849 when Parliament abolished the centuries-old Navigation Acts that had confined much trade with Britain to British ships and predominantly British crews.

Albert was the workaholic president of the Royal Commission that organized the exhibition and that decided that it should be set in the Crystal Palace, a gigantic iron-and-glass version of the greenhouse that the royal couple had encountered at the Duke of Devonshire's country manor some years earlier. It was 400 feet wide and 1,800 feet long, and high enough to enclose several of the tallest elm trees in Hyde Park; it was indeed, as of 1851, the largest enclosed space on the entire globe. Albert's professed purpose was to have the exhibition present 'a true test and a living picture of the point of development at which the whole of mankind has arrived.' The thousands of exhibits included a new sewing machine from the United States and a French medal-making machine that could produce fifty million medals in the course of a week. British exhibitors provided a gigantic 1,000-horsepower railway locomotive, a direct telegraphic link to Edinburgh, 'an alarm bedstead, causing a person to arise [quite literally] at any given hour', and 'a cricket catapulta, for propelling the ball in the absence of a first-rate bowler.'

Parliamentary spoilsports had warned that the Great Exhibition would attract to London not only vagrants, thieves, pickpockets, and prostitutes but also domestic and foreign revolutionaries. All those warnings proved unfounded. May 1, the day on which the royal couple and their two oldest children presided over the formal opening, turned out, in Queen Victoria's words, to be 'one of the greatest and most glorious days of our lives'. It resembled a second coronation. In Victoria's eyes, the enthusiastic but well-behaved crowds, the numerous dignitaries including the octogenarian Duke of Wellington, the trumpeters, and the six-hundred-person chorus were all saluting 'my beloved Husband, the creator of this great "Peace Festival", uniting the industry and arts of all nations of the earth'. As she wrote to her Uncle Leopold, it was 'the *greatest* day in our history, the *most beautiful* and *imposing* and *touching* spectacle ever seen, and the triumph of my beloved Albert.'[37] In the course of the spring and the summer, some six million visitors were to tour the Great Exhibition, and, according to the historian Thomas Babington

Macaulay, '1851 would long be remembered as a singularly happy year of peace, plenty, good feeling, innocent pleasure and national glory.' For once even his critics were willing to give Albert the praise that Victoria regarded as his due. The royal partnership had reached its heyday.

6 *England's War Vigil*

Punch (May 6, 1854) takes note of the Day of Fasting and Prayer that begins the Crimean War with a picture and with a poem that includes the following stanza:

> So kneels our England ere she goeth out
>   A knight – to battle in a godly cause
> Humbling herself – but not as one in doubt,
>   If God will bless the weapon that she draws.

6 Britain's Champion

Concerned as Victoria and Albert sometimes were with developments on the domestic scene during the 1840s and 1850s, they became yet more absorbed by events abroad. Albert felt persuaded, indeed, that a monarch had a special responsibility to oversee Britain's relations with the neighboring kingdoms and empires that lay across the English Channel. As Commander-in-Chief of the Army and the Navy, the monarch was also expected to use her influence to make sure that the kingdom maintained a military power sufficient to protect all of its possessions and to deter all possible attackers. During these years, therefore, Queen Victoria came more and more to see herself, in highly personal terms, as Britain's champion. That development was to reach a climax at the time of the Crimean War of 1854–6.

During the 1840s and 1850s, several of Victoria's ministers – such as the Duke of Wellington and Viscount Palmerston – retained immediate personal memories of the era of the French Revolutionary and Napoleonic Wars (1792–1815). Britain had been involved in no comparable Continental conflict since the signing of the Treaty of Vienna in 1815, but the peace among the 'Big Five' powers was at times an uneasy one. To Britain's east lay the great despotic empires, Russia, Austria, and Prussia – the latter two loosely bound together (along with dozens of smaller states) in the German Confederation. In those three eastern empires, parliaments and constitutional procedures had made little headway, and the Russian Empire had yet to abolish the practice of serfdom. The two great western powers were Britain and France; in both lands elected parliaments played an important role as did a belief in a high degree of freedom of speech and of the press. Since 1830, France had been ruled by its 'citizen-king,' Louis Philippe of the House of Orleans, one of whose daughters, Louise, was the wife of Victoria's favorite uncle, King Leopold of the Belgians; she had also become one of

Queen Victoria's dearest friends. Belgium, Spain, and Portugal were often also seen as part of 'the liberal West.' In the course of the 1810s and 1820s both Spain and Portugal had lost all or most of their once gigantic empires in the Americas, and both lands were afflicted by intermittent civil war, but – if only because a Coburg cousin of the royal couple was married to the Queen of Portugal – British foreign-policy makers were often deeply involved with events on the Iberian peninsula.

The Englishman who became most directly concerned with British foreign-policy making during the early Victorian years was Henry Temple, the 3rd Viscount Palmerston. As an Irish peer, it was possible for Lord Palmerston to sit in the House of Commons, and it was to an English constituency in that chamber that Palmerston had first been elected way back in 1807 at the age of twenty-three. During the Napoleonic and post-Napoleonic years he had served as Secretary of State at War, and in 1830 he became one of several erstwhile Tories who joined the Whig ministry headed first by Lord Grey and then by Lord Melbourne.

As foreign secretary, Palmerston saw it as one of his necessary tasks to cooperate with the other 'Big Five' powers to preserve the European peace. The French Revolution had made him fully aware of the horrors of mob rule, but he was in no way a friend to despotism. Indeed, he became an avowed champion of the abolition of slavery and of the slave trade wherever in the world it yet persisted. A staunch proponent of Britain's government as reformed in 1832, he also sympathised with Continental liberals and nationalists who sought to transform Europe's autocratic kingdoms and empires into constitutional monarchies with elective parliaments such as Britain's. At times Palmerston's roles as preserver of the peace and as advocate of liberal constitutionalism would therefore come into collision, but early in his tenure he had to his credit one great diplomatic success: the peaceful creation of a constitutional Belgium with Leopold as king. He persuaded all of the 'Big Five' powers to recognise the legitimacy of that new state, whose inhabitants had rebelled against the authority of the Dutch king set over them by the Treaty of Vienna.

By the time Victoria ascended to the throne in 1837, Palmerston had become an experienced and versatile statesman, and he provided the young queen with her first direct lessons in diplomatic protocol and international relations. He had a clear head and a trenchant mind, and his façade of leisured *savoir faire* hid an exceptionally energetic and hard-working administrator. Time and again the young Victoria marveled that, however difficult a subject might be, 'Lord Palmerston explained it in such a very clear, plain and agreeable manner.'¹ His marriage in 1839 to his long-time lady love, the widowed Countess Cowper (who was also the sister of Lord Melbourne and a one-time lady-in-waiting to the queen), tied him even more closely to the Whig ministry.

When that ministry fell two years later, so did Palmerston, and for the next five years the Foreign Office was directed by Lord Aberdeen, in many ways a rather less combative and independent-minded department head than Palmerston had become. During the years of the Peel ministry (1841–6), Aberdeen successfully brought to a close the so-called Opium War with China with a settlement that opened major Chinese ports to trade with British and other European merchants. The peace treaty also provided for the British annexation of the largely uninhabited island of Hong Kong off the China coast. Along with Singapore at the base of the Malay peninsula, acquired in 1824, Hong Kong became one of Britain's two chief outposts in East Asia. With the Webster–Ashburton Treaty of 1842, Aberdeen also brought to an end an undeclared war with the United States fought in the forests of Maine. A possible Anglo–American war over the north-west American–Canadian boundary line was averted four years later by means of a treaty with the James K. Polk administration. During those same years the royal couple paid a path-breaking visit to the French king and queen in Normandy and welcomed to London the Russian czar, Nicholas I.

The downfall of the Peel ministry in 1846 meant the return of Lord Palmerston to the Foreign Office, and it soon became clear to Victoria and Albert that Palmerston could sound far more bellicose and act in a manner far more independent of royal wishes than had the easy-going Aberdeen. Victoria and Albert agreed with Palmerston that it would be desirable for Continental monarchs to act in a more constitutional manner, but they became uncomfortable when British ministers abroad seemed deliberately to encourage revolutionary movements that threatened to undermine the stability of the thrones held by the queens of Spain and Portugal. Lord Palmerston patiently explained that

The Spanish Government seem to be pursuing the same course which proved fatal to the Stuarts in this country and to Charles X [in 1830] in France and it is to be apprehended that it will at last produce the same kind of resistance. The Spanish Government wishes to govern despotically a nation which thinks itself entitled to be governed constitutionally.[2]

[Palmerston's warnings seemed to be borne out by the events of 1848, when revolution broke out not only in Paris but also in Berlin and Vienna and in many of the capitals of the smaller states of Europe] The Prussian and Austrian thrones were only shaken, but the French monarchy was overthrown and replaced by a republic. King Louis Philippe and his family were given refuge in London by Victoria and Albert. London also became the home of numerous other Continental exiles ranging from Prince Metternich, Austria's influential foreign minister since the war against Napoleon, to Karl Marx, the co-author of the *Communist Manifesto*, whose efforts to stir up a working-class revolution in the German states had failed.

Palmerston did his best to make sure that Continental revolts did not lead to international warfare, but the events of 1848 – which England had escaped with no more than a large Chartist demonstration – confirmed his belief in the superiority of his native land above all others. He also remained persuaded that he, a veteran statesman in his sixties, understood international relations far better than could a presumptuous Prince Albert or Queen Victoria, both of them yet in their twenties. One of the rulers whom Palmerston seemed ever ready to lecture was King Otto of Greece, a land at whose birth in the 1820s, after a rebellion against the Ottoman Empire, Britain had served as midwife. Whether the problem was brigandage on Greek highways or the failure of the Greek government to pay in a timely fashion the interest due on its debts to foreign bondholders, that government seemed always to be in the wrong. As Palmerston noted privately to Queen Victoria, 'the defects of the King of Greece lie quite as much in his moral as in his intellectual qualities.'[3]

In 1847, the Athens home of Don Pacifico, a moneylender of Portuguese–Jewish ancestry, was pillaged by a Greek mob. The Greek government eventually provided partial compensation, but Don Pacifico was not satisfied and appealed directly to Palmerston with a detailed list of his claims. He had been born in Gibraltar, Don Pacifico pointed out, and he was therefore by law a British subject who held a British passport. Palmerston interpreted the entire episode as yet another example of Greek skullduggery, and he formally asked the Greek government for appropriate compensation. When, time and again, Athens hesitated, Palmerston ordered a British naval squadron of fourteen ships to enter Greek waters. In January 1850, the British envoy gave the Greek government a twenty-four-hour ultimatum. When he received no reply, a British admiral proclaimed a blockade of Greece and seized several ships. France and Russia, Britain's rivals for influence in the eastern Mediterranean area, protested loudly, but the Greek government capitulated.

Not the least of the monarchs who objected to Palmerston's gunboat diplomacy was Palmerston's own. Victoria and Albert once again protested vigorously to the prime minister, Lord John Russell, about Palmerston's reprehensible 'political doings and tricks.'[4] The House of Lords passed a motion of censure on the actions of the Russell ministry, and in a subsequent five-day debate in the House of Commons, numerous political leaders urged the foreign secretary 'to heed the general sentiments of the civilised world' rather than to challenge all comers like a medieval knight at a tournament.[5] In the course of that debate Palmerston defended his handling of foreign affairs in general and of the Don Pacifico case in particular in an eloquent five-hour oration. He firmly denied that the British Goliath had bullied the Greek David: 'Does the smallness of a country justify the magnitude of its evil acts?' It was said, Palmerston went on, that the claimants against the Greek government were unimportant people,

> as if because a man was poor he might be . . . tortured with impunity, as if a man who was born in Scotland might be robbed without redress, or, because a man is of the Jewish persuasion, he is fair game for any outrage.

In a final flurry, he summed up the moral foundations of what was to be called the *Pax Britannica*: ✱

> While we have seen . . . the political earthquake rocking Europe from side to side; while we have seen thrones shaken, shattered, levelled, institutions overthrown and destroyed . . . this country has presented a spectacle honourable to the people of England, and worthy of the admiration of mankind. We have shown that liberty is compatible with order; that individual freedom is

reconcilable with obedience to the law. . . . I contend that we have not in our foreign policy done anything to forfeit the confidence of the country. . . . I therefore fearlessly challenge the verdict which the House . . . is to give on the question now brought before it . . . whether, as the Roman, in days of old, held himself free from indignity, when he could say *Civis Romanus sum* [I am a Roman citizen]; so also a British subject, in whatever land he may be, shall feel confident that the watchful eye and the strong arm of England will protect him against injustice and wrong.

Palmerston carried the day in the House of Commons by a vote of 310 to 264, and he won yet wider popularity in the country at large.[6]

Once again the royal couple had been frustrated in their now increasingly insistent efforts to remove Palmerston from the Foreign Office. Although Prince Albert readily acknowledged that Palmerston was 'an able politician' and 'an indefatigable man of business,' he was equally persuaded that the foreign secretary possessed 'no very high standard of honour and not a grain of moral feeling.' Albert also reminded Russell of a twelve-year-old tale of Palmerston, then a bachelor, committing 'a brutal assault' on one of the queen's ladies-in-waiting in a Windsor Castle bedroom. (Apparently a switch of rooms had occurred, and the lady whom Palmerston expected to encounter there awaited him in another room of the castle.) Albert concluded, more to the immediate point, that Palmerston had antagonised numerous foreign governments and that his policies had fomented unrest abroad and lowered Britain's reputation for fair-dealing.[7] Prime Minister Russell demurred, but he felt compelled to agree that Palmerston should solemnly promise in the future to consult the queen fully before sending out despatches in her name and not to alter them after she had given her approval. Albert and Victoria had become almost obsessive in their antipathy toward a statesman with whom – as matters turned out a few years later – they often differed far more in style than in substance.

Like Lord Palmerston, Queen Victoria envisaged herself as the champion of Britain's honor, and in 1850, the very year of the Don Pacifico *imbroglio*, she was provided with an opportunity to demonstrate the fact. During the early nineteenth century, the Roman Catholic Church in England resembled a Protestant Nonconformist sect in that, unlike the established Church of England, it was one of numerous small religious groups whose members had been granted substantial political equality only three decades earlier. As of 1850 it claimed fewer than 250,000 adherents in an England and Wales of almost eighteen million people. Roman Catholic numbers were growing, however, because of conversion – on the part of eminent Anglican clerics such as John Henry Newman and Henry Edward Manning and of scores of other notables – and, to a far greater degree, because of the influx of hundreds of thousands of refugees from a famine-stricken Ireland.

Then in September 1850 the Pope promulgated a Papal Bull formally restoring the Roman Catholic hierarchy to England and dividing the land into twelve episcopal sees. Named to oversee the restored church, as the new Archbishop of Westminster, was Cardinal Nicholas Wiseman, who added oil to the flames by means of a triumphal letter: 'Catholic England,' he declared, 'has been restored to its orbit in the ecclesiastical firmament, from which its light had long vanished, and begins anew its course of regularly adjusted action round the centre of unity, the source of light and of vigour.'[8] John Henry Newman, the most eminent of recent converts to the Roman faith, warmly applauded the manner in which 'the people of England are about of their own free will to be added to the Holy Church.'

Queen Victoria's immediate reaction was one of deep anger at this

> extraordinary proceeding of the Pope, who has issued a Bull, savouring . . . of the time of Henry VIII's reign, or even earlier – restoring the Roman Catholic 'hierarchy' . . . saying that England was restored to the number of Catholic Powers, & that her religious disgrace had been wiped out. . . . All this is inconceivable, & it is in the highest degree wrong . . . of the Pope to act in such a manner, which is a *direct* infringement of my prerogative, without *one* word as to his instructions having been . . . communicated to this Gov[ernmen]t.

Ultra-Protestant organisations throughout Britain erupted in fury, and even such cosmopolitan Whigs as the lord-lieutenant of Ireland, the 4th Earl of Clarendon, felt indignant: 'It is high time to resist the encroachments of Rome and to let His Holiness know that we are still Protestants, and that the Reformation was not an error of our forefathers for which the present generation is desirous of atoning.' Lord John Russell, the prime minister, gloried in his reputation as a religious liberal, but even he decided that his government would have to provide a formal response in order to allay public discontent. Albert's hope that Uncle Leopold might persuade the Pope to revoke the Bull was soon dashed, and Victoria in turn discouraged Russell from sending a special envoy to Rome. The queen declared that it was 'entirely against her notions of what is *becoming* to *ask* the Pope for a *favour*', '[T]he best and wisest course,' according to Victoria, was a statute that outlawed the assumption, by Roman Catholic bishops, of English territorial titles – such as Westminster, the borough in which Parliament met and in which Westminster Abbey was situated. It was in collaboration with the royal couple at Windsor that the prime minister drew up the controversial Ecclesiastical Titles Bill of 1851. In June 1851 it was approved by the House of Commons by a vote of 433 to 95, and the House of Lords followed suit. The law proved to be at best a symbol of public outrage inasmuch as none of the fines that the measure called for were ever collected from the prelates who had illegally assumed English territorial titles. Nineteen years later the statute was to be quietly repealed.

In the meantime Queen Victoria praised 'the many good and innocent Roman Catholics',[10] members of her household such as the Duchess of Norfolk and Lord Edward Howard. At the same time she criticised the militant English converts who had given the Pope such poor advice, who had caused the Roman Catholic clergy to act in so 'injudicious' a manner,[11] and who had prompted Cardinal Wiseman to show himself as both 'ambitious & entirely wanting in judgment.' Although the Roman Catholic communion continued to grow during the mid-Victorian years, the controversy over 'Papal Aggression' died down for a time.

Victoria's and Albert's distrust of Lord Palmerston persisted, however. It was confirmed by the foreign secretary's open display of sympathy with British and foreign critics of the emperors of Austria and Russia, who had cooperated to suppress, in the harshest manner, rebellions against Austrian rule in Budapest and elsewhere. According to a delegation of radicals that called on Palmerston, the two emperors were 'odious and detestable assassins' and 'merciless tyrants and despots.'[12] The straw that broke the proverbial camel's back involved not Russia or Austria, however, but the France of the Second Republic, which since February 1848 had been convulsed by street battles and by rapid changes of policy and personnel. In early December 1851, Louis Napoleon (a nephew of the Emperor), who had been elected as

President of the Republic, staged a *coup d'état* that dissolved the French National Assembly and that, in effect, made him president for life and led to his proclamation as Emperor Napoleon III a year later. Without consulting his cabinet colleagues, his monarch, or even the British ambassador to Paris, Palmerston told the French minister to London that he approved of an action whereby Louis Napoleon had saved his country from anarchy. Prime Minister Russell thereupon demanded that Palmerston give up the seals to the Foreign Office, and Victoria and Albert were privately exultant at this 'great and unexpected mercy.' As Queen Victoria confided to her journal, 'our anxiety and worry during the last five years and a half, which was indescribable, was mainly, if not entirely, caused by him!'[13]

The royal couple could not escape Palmerston so readily, however. Scarcely a month later, the Russell ministry without Palmerston was defeated in the House of Commons, and for the next ten months a protectionist Conservative ministry headed by Lord Derby as prime minister and by Benjamin Disraeli as leader of the House of Commons and Chancellor of the Exchequer was in power. That minority government was defeated in turn before the year 1852 was out, and it was succeeded by a Peelite/Whig coalition government headed by the same Lord Aberdeen who had served as Peel's foreign secretary during the early 1840s. Victoria and Albert could not prevent Palmerston from becoming a leading member of that government, but they could prevent him from becoming foreign secretary again. Instead he took on the post of home secretary, and in the course of the next two years he carried through Parliament a number of pieces of significant social legislation such as a Factory Act forbidding children from working earlier than 6 a.m. or later than 6 p.m. on any given day. Other measures mandated compulsory vaccination against smallpox and sought to abate the smog that enveloped metropolitan London, where open coal fires served as the prime source of winter-time warmth.

The Aberdeen ministry (1852–5) came to be best known, however, not for its social legislation but for the manner in which it drifted into a war against the Russian empire. For more than a century successive Russian czars had sought to enlarge their influence in the Black Sea region and to diminish that of the Ottoman Empire. In the long run they hoped to take over Constantinople and establish a naval outpost on the Mediterranean Sea. In the short run they sought recognition of their right to serve as the protectors of the many Eastern Orthodox Christian subjects of the Moslem sultan. Britain and France were determined to halt such expansion and to maintain the neutral status of the Dardanelles, the straits that joined the Mediterranean and Black Seas. The Ottoman Turks soon learned that no matter how irresponsibly their leaders behaved, France and Britain might feel obliged to back them up. In May 1853, diplomatic relations between Turkey and Russia were broken and a British fleet was sent to the Aegean Sea. When the Turks refused to acknowledge Russia's special role as protector of Orthodox Christians, the czar's troops marched into the Balkan provinces of the Ottoman Empire that were later to become Romania. When the czar refused the Ottoman demand that the provinces be evacuated, Turkey declared war. Late in November an inept Russian fleet sailed across the Black Sea to the Turkish port of Sinope and sank an even more inefficient Turkish flotilla. Four thousand Turkish sailors drowned.

The 'massacre of Sinope' aroused British public opinion as no event of recent memory had done. In the words of the London *Chronicle*: 'We shall draw the sword, if draw we must, not only to preserve the independence of an ally, but to humble the ambitions and thwart the machinations of a despot whose intolerable pretensions have made him the enemy of all civilised nations!'[14] As the ministry of a reluctant Lord Aberdeen was drawn step by step into a war against Russia in collaboration with the France of Napoleon III, all manner of rumors swirled around Prince Albert. In several London newspapers his direct involvement in the queen's meetings with her ministers was revealed for the first time. He was accused of being a foreigner who had been meddling unconstitutionally in the making of British foreign policy. He was reproached (accurately enough) with being in large part responsible for Palmerston's dismissal as foreign secretary back in 1851. He was also stigmatised as pro-Russian, and it was certainly true that, until Britain formally declared war against Russia, Albert worked desperately to achieve a peaceful resolution of the Russo-Turkish conflict. He was more conscious than were many of the generals that Britain's small army was ill-prepared for war against a major European power. A few scandal sheets accused Albert of being an outright traitor to his adopted land, who had been – or ought to have been – imprisoned in the Tower of London.[15] When Parliament assembled early in 1854, Lord Aberdeen and other ministers stoutly defended Albert against his calumniators, and after a British force had set off for the Black Sea, press criticism of Albert died down. Victoria was deeply disappointed, however, to discover that her faithful helpmeet, who for more than a decade had been working overtime in the service of her kingdom, remained the subject of so much suspicion and distrust.

During the winter of 1853–4, Victoria felt as 'anxious' and 'alarmed' and gloomy as did her prime minister about the prospect of war with Russia. In February she reluctantly consented to have ten thousand troops sent to Malta, 'to be ready to proceed to Turkey, in case of war really taking place, which God forbid!' By then, however, a war fever held the nation in its grip, and on March 28, 1854, Britain – in alliance with France – formally declared war on Russia. Because of 'unprovoked' Russian aggression on Britain's ally, the Turkish empire, and because of the czar's rejection of honorable peace terms, Queen Victoria formally told Parliament, she had been compelled – 'by a sense of what is due to the honour of her crown, to the interests of her people, and to the independence of the states of Europe' – to declare war. Britain's purpose was 'to save Europe from the preponderance of a Power which violated the faith of treaties and defies the opinion of the civilised world.' By then she felt certain that the Crimean War 'was a glorious, honourable war.'[16]

Day after day, she stood proudly at the Buckingham Palace balcony, amidst tremendous crowds of cheering bystanders, as the troops bid a fond farewell to their kingdom's capital and to their queen. 'It was,' she wrote, 'a touching and beautiful sight.' When the royal couple watched thirty British warships with more than a thousand guns sail off from Portsmouth to the Baltic Sea, that too was, according to the queen, 'a most glorious, interesting, and never to be forgotten sight.' A few weeks later at Woolwich, before a hundred thousand cheering spectators, Victoria launched a brand new warship, the 5,000-ton *HMS Albert*.

By the summer of 1854, Queen Victoria described herself as 'very enthusiastic about my dear army and navy' and regretful only that none of her four sons was yet old enough to fight. She deplored the lukewarm attitude of her prime minister as she became totally absorbed with the naval campaign in the Baltic and the Anglo-French expeditionary force that had landed in the Crimea. Happily, by autumn, there were victories to celebrate both in the Baltic and on the Crimean peninsula at Alma and at Inkerman. As Victoria privately conceded,

> My whole soul and heart are in the Crimea. . . . I regret exceedingly not to be a man & to be able to fight in the war. My heart bleeds for the many fallen, but I consider that there is no finer death for a man than on the battlefield![17]

The late autumn and winter of 1854–5 were filled with numerous setbacks, however. Russian forces successfully defended their great naval base at Sevastopol, whose surrender had become the primary Anglo-French goal. A devastating Black Sea storm destroyed allied supply ships, tents, stores, and horses. More than eight thousand Britons died, and cholera drove more than ten thousand British troops from the battlefield to the hospital. The army transport system broke down. Discontented officers and pioneer war correspondents were happy to use the new electric telegraph to speed the bleak tidings back home to London, and – as Prince Albert was to complain – also to St Petersburg and Moscow. In December 1854, *The Times* protested that 'the noblest army ever sent from these shores has been sacrificed to the grossest mismanagement. Incompetency, lethargy, aristocratic hauteur, official indifference, favour, routine, perverseness, and stupidity reign, revel, and riot.'

In the course of the year 1855 Queen Victoria became a one-woman fighting machine. When in January the House of Commons voted 'no confidence' in the Aberdeen ministry, the queen – after unsuccessful consultations with alternate candidates – invited her old nemesis, Lord Palmerston, to become prime minister. He was a far more single-minded war leader than Aberdeen had proved, and he provided Prince Albert with an opportunity to become 'a decisive voice' on a government committee to promote recruiting and to reorganise the army. Palmerston and the royal couple were in full accord that the time to make a compromise peace with Russia had not yet come. When the Emperor Napoleon III made a state visit to London, the allied heads of state not only participated together in a military review – 'a most beautiful and exciting affair' according to the queen – but they also joined forces in a bi-national Crimean War planning council. 'It was,' wrote Victoria in her daily journal, 'one of the most interesting scenes I was ever present at. I would not have missed it for the world.' In August 1855, Victoria and Albert paid a return visit to Paris where they were received with banners, bands, arches of flowers, illuminations, and enormous enthusiasm. It was, Victoria observed, 'like a fairytale, *so* beautiful and enchanting,' and for her punctilious host, the Emperor Napoleon III, she 'conceived a *real* affection and friendship.'[18] The ceremonial highpoint was the occasion on which the queen and her eldest son knelt at the tomb of the Emperor Napoleon I while aged French generals wept and a Parisian band struck up 'God Save the Queen!'[19]

As the siege of Sevastopol dragged on, Queen Victoria insisted that she be shown every message from General Raglan in the Crimea to Lord Panmure, the new Secretary of State for War, and all instructions of importance despatched by Panmure 'if possible *before* they are sent.' According to Panmure, 'You never saw anybody so entirely taken up with military affairs as she is.' Indeed, he compared his monarch's desire for the latest war news to 'that of the parched traveller in the desert.' Yet still the siege in the Crimea dragged on, and when Lord Cardigan visited Windsor, one of the royal children told him: 'You must hurry back to Sebastopol, and take it, else it will kill Mama!!!'[20]

In the meantime, the queen wrote eloquent letters of condolence to the widows of generals who had died in the war and letters of consolation to veteran officers who had been passed over for command. Queen Victoria spoke so persuasively to 'the brave and chivalrous Old Highlander' Sir Colin Campbell, that Campbell agreed to return to the battlefield: 'If the Queen wished it,' he declared, 'he was ready to serve under a corporal.' In a precedent-breaking personal ceremony at London's Horse Guards parade ground on May 18, 1855, in the presence of tens of thousands of spectators, she pinned 450 medals individually on the heroes of Alma, Balaclava, and Inkerman. Some of them limped by on crutches; others were carried in bath-chairs. 'From the highest Prince of the Blood to the lowest Private,' the queen reported, 'all received the same distinction for the bravest conduct in the severest actions. . . . Noble fellows! I own I feel as if they were *my own children; –* my heart beats for *them* as for my nearest and dearest.'[21]

The queen and other members of the royal family visited military hospitals where she spoke to and became familiar with the detailed personal history of hundreds of wounded soldiers, and she inspired the opening early in 1856 of a giant new Victoria Hospital for wounded soldiers at Netley near Southampton. In the meantime, the monarch had also taken a keen interest in the activities in the East of Florence Nightingale and her nurses, and she soon expressed the wish that 'we had her at the War Office.'[22] After the war, she and Florence Nightingale held lengthy discussions at Balmoral. According to the queen, Florence Nightingale had 'a rare presence, very simple, gentle, and ladylike and modest to the last degree. At the same time she has a man's intelligence.'[23] In the meantime the queen launched – under the presidency of Prince Albert – a Patriotic Fund to relieve the widows and orphans of soldiers and sailors who died on active service during the war. More than £750,000 (worth about £75 million in 2003) was collected for the fund, in part by the sale of specially designed ceramic 'Royal Patriotic Jugs'.

The capture of Sevastopol in September 1855 was celebrated by the royal family with a tremendous bonfire and stentorian singing at Balmoral. Yet the queen was far from convinced that Russia had been taught the required military lesson. While the diplomats were gathering in Paris in January 1856, Victoria was still busily planning a new Black Sea campaign and 'dreading' a peace that 'would not leave *us* in a good position.' 'Much as the Queen disliked the idea of *Peace' –* her words – she did reluctantly acquiesce in its reality after the signing of the Treaty of Paris in March 1856. Albert had persuaded her that once the French army withdrew from the Crimea – and it outnumbered the British force there by a ratio of over three to one – then '*no*' further 'glory could have been hoped for by us.'[24]

The Crimean War had cost Britain the lives of more than 22,700 soldiers and £76 million (about £7,600 million in 2003). It had not been a total triumph, but Russian naval power in the Black Sea and Russian influence in the Balkans had encountered a major set-back. For the next half year Queen Victoria was engrossed by the process of personally greeting her soldiers as they came back from the East, regiment by

[handwritten margin note: Bolitho, Further Letters, 185.]

regiment, and of welcoming the return of a fleet of 240 ships-of-war from the Baltic and Black Seas in a giant naval review near Portsmouth. In July there were giant parades and reviews at London, Woolwich, and Aldershot, where the queen thanked her troops personally for their heroic deeds in a distant land. She spoke, according to *The Times*, 'with that propriety of emphasis, and that silvery sweetness of intonation for which she is so remarkable.' Charles Greville, the veteran diarist, complained privately that the queen remained in the grip of a 'military mania.' That mania had not abated a year later, when for the first time the queen awarded in person the bronze Victoria Cross, the medal for exceptional valor that she had personally helped to design and to establish by royal warrant. A hundred thousand spectators in London's Hyde Park watched the queen as, seated on horseback, she pinned the cross with her own hand on the uniforms of sixty-two Crimean War veterans. It was, Prince Albert thought, 'a magnificent spectacle.'

Military reviews had played an important role in Victoria's life from the time of her accession, and in 1853 Prince Albert helped inspire the custom of a huge military summer camp, which from 1854 on was held at Aldershot in Hampshire. It was Albert, also, who was instrumental in setting up Wellington College at Crowthorne, not far from the Royal Military Academy at Sandhurst, which had been established back in 1799. Wellington College was designed to educate the sons of army officers and encourage them to follow the paternal example. Prince Albert endowed Aldershot with the Prince Consort's Library, the largest collection in Britain of works in military science. At Wellington College, in the meantime, Queen Victoria established an annual good conduct medal for the cadet who best demonstrated 'fearless devotion to duty, and unflinching truthfulness.'[25]

During the next several years the royal couple also reminded first Lord Palmerston and then Lord Derby about 'the helpless state of the Navy'[26] and of how foolish it would be, now that peace had returned, 'to let our poor little army be wasted away' again in the interests of financial retrenchment. Lord Palmerston thanked Victoria for one such detailed cautionary warning with the following words:

> Viscount Palmerston . . . has had the honour to receive your Majesty's communication . . . stating what your Majesty would have said if your Majesty had been in the House of Commons. Viscount Palmerston may

perhaps be permitted to take the liberty of saying that it is fortunate for those from whose opinions your Majesty differs that your Majesty is not in the House of Commons for they would have had to encounter a formidable antagonist in argument.[27]

At the same time, Victoria warmly commended her prime minister for 'the manner in which both the War has been brought to a conclusion, and the honour and interests of this country have been maintained by the Treaty of Peace, under the zealous and able guidance of Lord Palmerston.'[28] She named him Knight of the Garter – the highest such distinction she could bestow – and the prodigal statesman proudly accepted the honor. He added profuse thanks for 'the firm and steady support which in all these important transactions your Majesty's servants have received from the Crown.'[29]

Hardly had echoes of the Crimean War begun to fade than a major revolt broke out in Britain's largest and most populous colony, India. The British Empire of the early and mid-Victorian era consisted of at least two gigantic regions – Canada and Australia – with a small population, and that made up primarily of immigrants from Britain and Ireland. India differed in that it was a subcontinent populated even then by more than 200 million people speaking scores of distinct languages and practicing numerous religions, of which Hinduism and Islam were the most prominent. Britain's interest in India had begun early in the seventeenth century as a commercial venture by the English East India Company. In the course of the eighteenth and early nineteenth centuries, by a combination of war and of treaties with Indian princes, the company became the administrator and tax-collector for an increasing number of provinces, and European rivals such as the French, the Dutch, and the Portuguese were deprived of all or most of their influence there. In the 1770s and 1780s, the British Crown became formally involved in the government of British India, but it continued to use the East India Company as its agent. Under company auspices, western reform was introduced to many parts of India – in the form of schools teaching English as well as in the form of irrigation canals, harbors, railways, telegraphs, and the abolition of ancient Indian customs (such as widows burning themselves on their husbands' funeral pyres).

In 1857 the army directed by the East India Company was made up of 40,000 British officers and 230,000 Sepoys (natives), and it was the well-attested rumor that the cartridges in the new Enfield rifle were greased by both cow and pig fat (thereby offending the religious scruples of both Hindus and Moslems) that led to a revolt in the army. In the course of the spring and summer, native members of several regiments shot their British officers and marched on Delhi where they killed all the English men, women, and children they could find. Several other major cities in the Ganges Valley were taken over as well.

Queen Victoria took an intense interest both in the revolt and in its suppression, and she was rightly skeptical of the more extravagant tales of cruelty by the native rebels. She suspected from the start that 'a fear of their religion being tampered with' lay at the root of the struggle. 'I think that the greatest care ought to be taken not to interfere with their religion,' the queen insisted. Faithful Christian as the monarch may have been, she remained doubtful throughout her life about the desirability of a large-scale Christian missionary campaign in India. She also urged sharp limits to the measures of retribution inflicted by British soldiers (and by Sepoys who had remained loyal) as they recaptured Cawnpore and Delhi and lifted the siege of Lucknow. She urged on the wife of the British governor-general, Viscount Canning, the principle that all old men, women, and children should be spared. The governor-general concurred, and revenge-minded Britons were to criticise him as 'Clemency Canning.' The Government of India Act of 1858 abolished both the East India Company and the shadowy claims of the old Mogul emperor at Delhi, and transformed two-thirds of the subcontinent into the Crown Colony of India. The remainder was governed by Indian princes, who, in matters of domestic policy, remained independent. Victoria and Albert insisted that the Royal Proclamation announcing this transformation should breathe a spirit of 'generosity and benevolence'[30] and include the following words: 'we disclaim alike the right and desire to impose our [religious] convictions on any of our subjects.'[31] As she wrote to Viscount Canning, now her direct representative in India as Viceroy,

It is a source of great satisfaction and pride to her to feel herself in direct communication with that enormous Empire which is so bright a jewel in her Crown, and which she would wish to see happy, contented, and peaceful.[32]

As the 1850s drew to a close, other challenges to British foreign-policy makers arose in Germany, in France, in Italy, and in the United States. In Britain, Albert may sometimes have been seen as far too German and far too eager to enhance monarchical power, but by Continental standards he was a liberal constitutionalist. His long-term goal was a German nation, federated under the leadership of the Kingdom of Prussia, that would serve as an example of liberal constitutional government in Europe. Such a possibility was briefly promised by the Revolution of 1848–9, but it failed to materialise. The prospect revived in Albert's mind in 1855 when – with parental encouragement – his eldest daughter Vicky fell in love with Prince Frederick William, the heir to the Prussian throne. She was only fifteen at the time, and the engagement had to be kept secret until shortly before the wedding at Windsor Castle in February 1858. The prospect of an Anglo-German alliance was not popular in Britain, where the Kingdom of Prussia was blamed for failing to ally itself with Britain in the Crimean War. Neither was it particularly popular in Prussia, where it was widely felt that the prospective heir to the throne should be married in Berlin. Queen Victoria found such a notion absurd: 'Whatever may be the usual practice of Prussian Princes, it is not *every* day that one marries the eldest daughter of the Queen of England. The question therefore must be considered as settled and closed.'[33]

The engagement and wedding enabled Victoria and Albert to relive the days of their own romance and nuptials eighteen years earlier. The ceremony was both beautiful and sad, sad because it meant the separation of Albert and his adored daughter, the child who resembled him most closely and who worshipped him as a model father. The wedding might take place at Windsor, but the life had to be lived in Berlin, and – for a complex of reasons – the German nation that did materialise under Prussian leadership was to be guided far more by the 'blood and iron' dicta of Chancellor Otto von Bismarck than by the constitutional handbook entrusted by Prince Albert to his favored daughter as she set off for her new home.[34]

Two years later it was her Crimean War ally, the Emperor Napoleon III, who had become – Victoria privately complained – the ruler who 'must needs disturb every quarter of the Globe and try to make mischief.'[35] In order to discourage the French from any fleeting temptation to invade Britain, Victoria and Albert welcomed the rapid creation of a 130,000-man Volunteer Force. In the summer of 1860, the queen took enormous pleasure in reviewing some 20,000 of these volunteer soldiers who had come to London's Hyde Park at their own expense.[36] Soon thereafter she attended a meeting on Wimbledon Common of the new National Rifle Association. Queen Victoria was the very first person asked to fire a shot at a target, and the association organisers so fixed the apparatus that, when she pulled the trigger, she scored a bulls-eye.[37]

As matters turned out, Napoleon was far more interested in intervening in Italy than in Britain. He assisted King Victor Emmanuel of Piedmont-Sardinia, and his chief minister, Count Camillo Cavour, in the process of uniting the entire Italian peninsula under their leadership. For Lord Palmerston and his foreign secretary Lord John Russell, this was a cause dear to all liberal hearts because Cavour promised to fashion an Italian kingdom with a parliamentary system and a policy of international free trade modeled on that of Great Britain. Queen Victoria was rather more disturbed by the manner in which, by a combination of war and popular plebiscite, the Austrian emperor was being deprived of his legitimate influence in the Italian peninsula. She was admittedly less troubled by the manner in which Pope Pius IX was being deprived of his authority as a territorial ruler over the tradition-bound Papal States that straddled the center of the peninsula. As she wrote privately to Lord John, 'How Italy is to prosper under the Pope's presidency the queen is at a loss to conceive.'[38]

By 1861, British diplomatic influence had done much to assist in the creation (except for Venetia and for Rome itself) of a single kingdom of Italy. Rather than censure that process, Russell announced that 'Her Majesty's Government will turn their eyes rather to the gratifying prospects of a people building up the edifice of their liberties, and consolidating the work of their independence.'[39] Queen Victoria acquiesced in that sentiment, even if she did not approve of all aspects of the Italian policy of her Liberal ministry. As she had reminded Lord Palmerston earlier in the year, she deeply resented any insinuation that she 'is no well-wisher of mankind and indifferent to its freedom and happiness.'[40]

During the 1840s and 1850s relations between the expansion-minded

United States and Great Britain were sometimes strained, but the queen herself was on cordial terms with successive American emissaries. She had known President James Buchanan (President 1857–61) well during his previous four years as American minister to London, and it was with President Buchanan that in 1858 she exchanged the first messages across the initial (and abortive) trans-Atlantic cable.[41] It was President Buchanan also who – learning in 1860 that the eighteen-year-old Prince of Wales was to visit Canada – invited him to cross the border as well. The prince became the first member of Britain's royal family to tour the independent United States as a guest. Prince Albert had long been fascinated by the New World, and he skillfully drafted the speeches that his son would deliver.[42]

That son proved to be a charming and engaging young visitor who adored the crowds that came to cheer him. In Canada he opened a new railway bridge across the St Lawrence River at Montreal. At Ottawa he laid the foundation stone for what became the Federal Parliament building. He crossed the American border at Detroit, and in the course of the next four weeks he was enthusiastically received in Chicago, St Louis, Cincinnati, Pittsburgh, Boston, and elsewhere.[43] In New York City he received his most tumultuous reception. Was that not remarkable, asked Albert, 'for the most republican city in republican America?'[44] So many young women sought to dance with the prince that the ballroom floor collapsed. In Washington, he was the guest of honor at a great state dinner in the White House. After the entire royal party had been accommodated for the night, President Buchanan discovered that all the White House beds were full and that the Lincoln bedroom was not yet available. The President therefore had to sleep on a sofa.[45]

Victoria reproved her eldest daughter for writing about 'those horrid Yankees' just after they had given her brother so 'marvellous' and so 'unexpected' a reception, a reception that the queen modestly attributed to 'the (to me incredible) liking they have for my unworthy self'.[46] President Buchanan judged the visit 'a triumph from beginning to end,' and Queen Victoria in turn described it as an 'important link to cement two nations of kindred origin and character.'[47]

That cement seemed likely to crack within the year, as the outbreak of the American Civil War soon threatened to involve Great

Britain. After a Union vessel had kidnapped two Confederate envoys from a neutral British steamer, the *Trent*, Lord Palmerston was prepared to demand immediate redress in peremptory terms. It was Prince Albert who redrafted the despatch so as to give President Abraham Lincoln and Secretary of State William Seward the opportunity to save diplomatic face. Queen Victoria became persuaded (as have many historians) that Albert thereby prevented an Anglo-American War. For that reason, Victoria felt more sympathetic to the cause of the Union than did most members of Palmerston's ministry. For the rest of her life, indeed, she remained an advocate of friendly relations between Britain and the United States.[48]

The redrafting of the *Trent* Affair despatch proved to be Prince Albert's last public act. Almost from the time that in 1857 he had been formally proclaimed Prince Consort by Letters Patent issued by Victoria's Privy Council, the Prince's health had been deteriorating. He was far less robust than was his wife, and during his later years reports of severe stomach disorders, sleeplessness, and rheumatism became ever more frequent. Albert was as insistent as ever on going on with his work, however, and he coped as well as he could with the departure of his eldest daughter and with the death of his mother-in-law in March 1861, an event that devastated the queen. In November came word that his eldest son, while temporarily stationed at an army camp in Ireland, had been involved in an affair with an attractive if highly indiscreet young actress. The news provided yet another blow to Prince Albert, who upheld scrupulously high moral standards for his entire family and for the heir to the throne most of all. As Albert admitted to Victoria, 'I do not cling to life. You do, but I set no store by it. . . . I am sure that if I had a severe illness I should give up at once. I should not struggle for life.'[49] That illness overtook Albert in early December 1861, and on the evening of December 14 he died. Victoria's world lay shattered. It was as widow rather than as wife that she would henceforth feel compelled to serve as exemplar of domesticity at home and as Britain's champion abroad.

7 *The Queen in Mourning*

A photograph of Queen Victoria, the Prince and Princess of Wales, and the bust of the Prince Consort (1863). (Courtesy of The Royal Archives, Her Majesty Queen Elizabeth II, and the photographer)

7 The Reclusive Widow

December 14, 1861 was a date that would be forever engraved on Queen Victoria's memory, and, she felt sure, on that of her children and her subjects. If her first years as Queen had sparkled with the vitality of youth, then the decade that opened with 'that dreadful day when she lost that bright Angel who was her idol, the life of her life'[1] would be enclosed symbolically by the inch-thick black borders that henceforth were literally to frame almost every piece of stationery on which Victoria wrote. In similar fashion, she would habitually dress in black except for a white cap and veil. For more than a decade also, death would increasingly intrude as a barrier between the queen and her people, many of whom came to assume that she had lost all interest in the world of the living. Such lack of concern was not the case for long, because even as the queen made a minimal number of public appearances, she remained very much involved in the private and public lives of her children, four of whom contracted marriages during the decade after 1861. Behind the scenes, she remained very much involved also with the work of her cabinet ministers and with the often dramatic changes in world history that were precipitated by the unification of Germany, the unification of Italy, and the American Civil War.

For a time, however, the queen's 'moments of calm resolution alternated with paroxysms of despair.'[2] Although the rooms and corridors of Windsor Castle were draped in so much black crepe as to exhaust the national stock, Queen Victoria found the funeral itself so shattering an ordeal that she fled to Osborne instead. She decreed official mourning 'for the longest term in modern times.'[3] What outlet remained, she asked rhetorically, for 'my warm passionate nature so full of that passionate adoration for that Angel whom I dared call mine. And at 42, all, all those earthly feelings must be crushed &

smothered.'[4] At times she wondered, indeed, whether she would ever truly awaken from the evil dream that afflicted her. As she wrote in January 1862:

> Oh! weary, weary is the poor head which has no longer the blessed precious shoulder to rest on in this wretched life! My misery – my despair increase daily, hourly. I have no rest, no real rest or peace by day or by night; I sleep – but in such a way as to be more tired of a morning than at night and waken constantly with a dreamy, dreadful confusion of something having happened and crushed me! Oh! it is too awful, too dreadful! And a sickness and an icy coldness bordering on the wildest despair comes over me – which is more than a human being can bear![5]

Ultimately she *did* learn to bear the burden without losing her powers of reason, but she often expressed the hope that before long she would literally be reunited in heaven with her beloved husband. She therefore envied Earl Canning, the Viceroy of India, who died unexpectedly only seven months after his wife had been felled by jungle fever.[6] In the meantime, she preserved and she cherished the innumerable reminders of Albert that could be found in the royal homes at Osborne, at Balmoral, and at Windsor.

The Blue Room at Windsor was photographed with care so that it could be preserved – except for cleaning and dusting – exactly as it had been at the moment of Albert's death. On his writing table lay the Prince's pen and blotting-book and his watch, wound daily. The Prince's rooms at Osborne and Balmoral were kept up in the same fashion. Each evening his clothes were laid out, and a jug of hot water and clean towels were brought in. Both the rooms and the routine were in this way preserved for the next four decades – not because Victoria believed in ghosts but because she took comfort in continuity of custom. She would privately recall how secure she had felt 'when in those blessed Arms clasped & held tight in the sacred Hours at night – when the world seemed only to be ourselves that nothing could part us!' Now she slept alone, comforted only by Albert's nightshirt, by a plaster cast of his arm, and by his portrait pinned above the empty pillow.[7]

For the next several years, the queen devoted much of her attention to the material ways in which Prince Albert was to be remembered.

She compiled an *Album Inconsolatium* in which she placed letters of condolence, extracts from books concerning life after death, and numerous German and English poems – including long portions of *In Memoriam* by the poet laureate Alfred Tennyson, which she copied out in her own hand. Tennyson also composed a special eulogy to Albert as a preface to a new edition of his *Idylls of the King*. With the assistance of one Arthur Helps, she compiled for publication in 1862 a collection of Albert's speeches prefaced with a sketch of the Prince's character that was largely drafted by the queen herself. In similar fashion she collaborated with her husband's long-time secretary, General Sir Charles Grey, on the preparation of *The Early Life of the Prince Consort* (1867). A younger son of Earl Grey, the Whig prime minister (1830–4), General Grey soon came to be recognised as Victoria's own private secretary, although only in 1867 was he formally so designated.

After December 1861, Queen Victoria sometimes saw her chief remaining purpose in life as that of bringing to fruition the plans of her deceased husband. Her 'sole future object' would be 'to *follow* in *everything all* HIS *wishes, great & small,* for then she will be doing *her duty!*'[8] In one important respect, she failed altogether to adhere to Albert's counsel: 'If I should die before you,' he had told her back in 1851, 'do not, I beg, raise even a single marble image to my name.'[9] To the contrary, Queen Victoria preferred to remember her husband as a secular saint, and during the decade that followed she was to unveil numerous statues and memorials dedicated to Albert, erected in Britain and elsewhere. Was the queen's absorption with death typical of her age or was it extreme? Public displays of grief that people of a later age might deem excessive were common in middle-class and upper-class Victorian society,[10] yet the degree to which the queen 'bedecked her person and crammed her residences with memorial images of her husband far exceeded normal nineteenth-century practice.' She could afford to act upon her inclinations, and as *The Times* noted two years after the Prince's death, mourning became 'a sort of religion' for her.[11]

Unlike most British monarchs and spouses, Albert was not to be buried in a public edifice, such as Westminster Abbey, but in a private building especially designed for him and Victoria on the Windsor

Castle estate; it adjoined the mausoleum that was even then being completed for the coffin of Victoria's mother. Victoria and Albert were thus physically dissociating themselves from their Hanoverian forebears. The sculptor Baron Carlo Marochetti was chosen to prepare in marble the 'sleeping statues' of the Prince and the Queen that would be set within the mausoleum atop their joint sarcophagus, a monument carved of Scottish granite, the largest block of granite that had ever been quarried in the British Isles. The building, an octagon in the Romanesque style, was formally consecrated just a year after Albert's death by Samuel Wilberforce, the Bishop of Oxford, in the presence of the queen and most of her children, and Albert's remains were in due course permanently buried within its walls.[12] The recumbent effigy of the Queen was carefully hidden away for that perhaps distant day on which it too would be needed. In the meantime, when resident at Windsor, the queen would make regular visits to her mausoleum, and she was to hold there an annual memorial service. It was to take another decade and much expense to decorate the interior of the mausoleum in High Renaissance style.

When the Dean of Windsor objected to the manner in which the queen was ignoring St George's Chapel at Windsor, a traditional royal burial site, she agreed to a compromise suggestion made by her eldest daughter: the Wolsey Chapel of St George's was to be remodeled into an Albert Memorial Chapel, a site of pilgrimage for the public. That chapel, paid for by the queen out of her own funds, was not to be completed until 1875. It was refashioned in the Gothic style as a 'veritable treasure-house of gilding, marble, mosaics, precious stones, and coloured glass,'[13] and a French sculptor, Baron Henri de Triqueti, prepared the recumbent marble effigy of the Prince. Below the statue he inscribed a Biblical citation, 'I have fought the good fight, I have finished my course.'

The true national Albert Memorial, paid for by funds formally voted by Parliament, was to be located not at Windsor but in London's Hyde Park not far from the site of the Great Exhibition of 1851. It proved to be the single most prestigious artistic commission of the entire era. The design that won Victoria's approval was that of George Gilbert Scott: a statue in gilded bronze of a seated Albert, partially protected from the elements by a canopy, beneath a gigantic

Gothic spire. That spire was the centerpiece of a much larger monument that was the work of numerous architects and sculptors, who carved groups of allegorical statues designed to illustrate the sheer breadth of the Prince's interests. These sculptures portrayed the cardinal virtues, the Emblems of Progress (Agriculture, Manufactures, Commerce, and Engineering), and the Four Continents (Europe, Asia, Africa, and America). Around the four sides of the podium of the memorial an elaborate frieze was carved displaying the world's 169 most eminent painters, sculptors, architects, and poets. The dedication to this extraordinarily elaborate memorial was affixed in glass mosaic: 'QUEEN VICTORIA AND HER PEOPLE * TO THE MEMORY OF ALBERT PRINCE CONSORT * AS A TRIBUTE OF THEIR GRATITUDE * FOR A LIFE DEVOTED TO THE PUBLIC GOOD.' In the course of the early twentieth century, as Victorian Gothic ornamentation fell into disrepute, the Albert Memorial was often to be deprecated as the philistine nadir of nineteenth-century art as well as an anachronistic symbol for a prince who had seen himself as the prophet of modernity. Newly restored and refurbished in the 1990s, however, the structure has been hailed as 'England's Taj Mahal,' as a fascinating material evocation of (at times contradictory) mid-Victorian ideals and assumptions.[14]

In metropolitan London, the Albert Memorial and, immediately to the south, that great concert auditorium, the Royal Albert Hall, were to provide the most monumental reminders of the Prince Consort. Within a decade of his death, however, every other important British municipality would also sponsor an Albert memorial. City fathers were motivated by sympathy for the grieving queen, by a belated public awareness of the Prince's numerous virtues, and by civic pride. Therefore Birmingham and Liverpool, Glasgow and Aberdeen, and more than a score of other cities could soon boast their own statue of the prince – as could the cities of Coburg in Germany, Sydney in Australia, and Bombay in India. A Scottish National Memorial to Albert was erected in Edinburgh, a Welsh National Memorial in Tenby, and an Irish National Memorial in Dublin. Not even the kingdom's greatest military hero, the Duke of Wellington, had been memorialised so often.

In keeping with the moral of Thomas Carlyle's famous lecture, *On*

Heroes and Hero-Worship, and the Heroic in History (1841), such statues were intended to serve a clear didactic purpose. As Queen Victoria remarked, when unveiling the statue in Perth in 1864, it would encourage 'those of future generations to the practice of those virtues which have rendered the memory of her beloved and great husband so dear to the people of this country.' As the statue at Balmoral reminded viewers, 'His life sprang from a deep inner sympathy with God's Will, and therefore with all that is true, and beautiful and right.'[15] Future generations were also encouraged to remember the prince in a more immediately utilitarian fashion – in the names of roads and bridges, of schools and libraries, of galleries and alms-houses, of drinking fountains and clock towers (helpful civic amenities at a time when pocket-watches remained rare and wrist-watches unknown).

One of Albert's wishes that *was* realised was the marriage in July 1862 at Osborne of Queen Victoria's second daughter, Princess Alice, to Prince Louis of the German Grand Duchy of Hesse-Darmstadt. The wedding, which was conducted by the Archbishop of York and which had the Duke of Saxe-Coburg (Albert's elder brother) give the bride away, was a strictly private ceremony. As the queen admitted to her elder daughter, the proceedings were 'more like a funeral than a wedding'; she felt that 'a dagger is plunged in my bleeding, desolate heart' when her self-possessed daughter spoke of how 'proud and happy' she was to become Louis's wife. Memories of all that the queen had lost enveloped her once more.[16] Alice, who had served her mother as a personal secretary since Albert's death, went off to Germany and left that task to the third daughter, Helena.

Necessarily more important in the queen's eyes than the marriage of her second daughter was the marriage of her eldest son, the trou-blesome Bertie whose brief affair with an Irish actress had, the queen felt sure, contributed to her husband's death. Bertie's salvation seemed to lie in his marriage as quickly as possible to an eligible and attractive young woman who would absorb his interests. Victoria's eldest daughter had therefore scoured the continent for appropriate German princesses, only to come to the reluctant conclusion that the girl that her brother would find most appealing was Danish. Alexandra, the daughter of Prince Christian, the impoverished heir to the Danish throne, was only sixteen years old in 1861, but she impressed Vicky as being the most appealing prospect in all of Europe. She had a beautiful complexion and a lovely figure; she was relatively tall as well as elegant and ladylike, and at the same time she behaved in a down-to-earth and unaffected manner.[17] She also spoke English well, if with the strong Danish accent that she was never to lose. Because of a looming Prusso-Danish conflict over the provinces of Schleswig and Holstein and because of the notoriously loose morals of the Danish royal family,[18] the princess initially impressed Queen Victoria as a far from ideal candidate; yet before his death Albert had given the match his blessing. At that time, Bertie had not yet met Alix (as she was generally called), and when he first did he was not bowled over. '[A]s for being in love I don't think he can be,' the queen observed privately, 'or that he is capable of enthusiasm about anything in the world.'[19] In September 1862, the Prince of Wales did formally propose to Alix, however, and she happily accepted.

A few weeks later, with Bertie away, Alix was summoned to Osborne to undergo for two weeks a personal inspection by her formidable prospective mother-in-law. The queen was rapidly won over:

[W]e all love her! She is so good, so simple, unaffected, frank, bright and cheerful, yet so quiet and gentle, that her presence soothes me. Then how lovely! . . . . She seems so religious – has such a deep and serious character, and is truly and laudably anxious to improve herself . . . . Oh! may Bertie be worthy of such a sweet wife! Does he quite deserve it?[20]

Queen Victoria fixed the date of the wedding for March 10, 1863, thereby overruling the Archbishop of Canterbury, who pointed out that Lent was an inappropriate time. 'Marriage is a solemn holy act,' the queen retorted, and 'not to be classed with amusements.'[21] Although the queen insisted that the wedding interrupt only briefly the prevailing mood of mourning and that it take place not in London but in the relative privacy of St George's Chapel on the Windsor Castle estate, her people were not to be denied. As the royal yacht bearing the princess sailed up the Thames estuary, it was surrounded by hundreds of rowing-boats and paddle-steamers. At Gravesend, the prince publicly welcomed his bride, and the railway line from Gravesend to London was festooned with flags and decorations. In central London itself the crowds were so great and so enthusiastic that the procession was repeatedly brought to a halt. Mile after mile, the princess bowed gracefully as the crowds cheered – an anticipation of the 'Diana-mania' of the royal wedding of 1981. On the wedding day itself, St George's Chapel overflowed with dignitaries. The queen, in deep mourning dress, watched from a private balcony as the Archbishop of Canterbury conducted the service, and the singing of a chorale composed by the Prince Consort caused the entire wedding party to burst into tears. Victoria stayed away from the meal that followed the ceremony, but she took 'melancholy satisfaction' in the family reunion that had been occasioned by 'this fearful ordeal.'[22]

During the years that followed, the queen often got on better with her new daughter-in-law than with her eldest son, but she did become aware that Alix's range of interests was remarkably narrow. She rarely read a book or a newspaper, and her growing deafness increasingly served as a barrier during social occasions. Yet in the course of 1864, 1865 and 1866, the Prince and Princess of Wales became the social arbiters of fashionable London. They dined; they danced; they attended race meetings; and – while Victoria scarcely set foot in the imperial capital – they made Marlborough House, their London home, the mecca for London high society. This was a world of which the queen did not truly approve. As she expostulated to her eldest daughter in 1867,

[T]he higher classes – especially the aristocracy (with of course exceptions and honourable ones) – are so frivolous, pleasure-seeking, heartless, selfish, immoral and gambling that it makes one think . . . of the days before the French revolution. The young men are so ignorant, luxurious, and self-indulgent – and the young women so fast, frivolous and imprudent that the danger really is very great.[23]

Her eldest son ought to serve as an example to the aristocracy, she believed, but she feared that he was far too weak and foolish to succeed in such a role. In 1870, he was even summoned to court as a witness in a dramatic divorce case.

During these years Alexandra remained immensely popular with the British public: she proved to be a devoted mother to five children, and she remained a striking (if perhaps somewhat chilly) beauty. Even as her husband often appeared fascinated with young women more lively than his wife had proved to be, she remained loyal to him. Whatever occurred, it was not she who would violate her wedding vows or disobey the queen or deliberately rock the royal boat. As her mother-in-law privately conceded, 'Alix is really a dear, excellent, right-minded soul. . . . I often think her lot is no easy one, but she is very fond of Bertie though not blind.'[24]

During these years Queen Victoria was prepared to travel as far as Coburg in Germany – as she did in August 1865 in order to unveil a new statue to Prince Albert – but she was unwilling to open Parliament, as she had done almost every year until 1862. Understandably, she failed to do so early that year, but she refused to do so again in 1863 and 1864. By the autumn of 1864, the London press was becoming restive about the queen's continuing seclusion, and an anonymous wag posted the following handbill on the gates of Buckingham Palace: 'These extensive premises to be let or sold, the late occupant having retired from business.'[25] In December 1864 Victoria wrote to Earl Russell, the foreign secretary, a plaintive letter explaining (in the third person) why she would not be opening Parliament in 1865 either:

> The Queen was always terribly nervous on all public occasions but especially at the opening of Parliament, which was what she dreaded for days before, and hardly ever went through without suffering from headache before or after the ceremony; but then she had the support of her dear husband, whose presence alone seemed a tower of strength, and by whose dear side she felt safe and supported under every trial. Now this is gone, and no child can feel more shrinking and nervous than the poor Queen does.[26]

For the time being, the queen similarly ignored the military reviews that had played so significant a role in her ceremonial life earlier in the reign.

What many ordinary Britons did not know was that at this time of apparent seclusion, Queen Victoria continued studiously to review cabinet papers and to follow with close attention the policies, especially in foreign affairs, pursued by her government – led since 1859 by Lord Palmerston. Thus, just a month after Albert's death, she reproved Earl Russell, the foreign secretary, for his failure to check the text with her before delivering a despatch to the American minister in London. At regular intervals, she asked him to rephrase despatches to British diplomats abroad – and he did. In April 1862 she reminded the prime minister that the Lords of the Admiralty had no business to add to the Queen's Regulations without first gaining her sanction. When she left for Belgium and Germany in the summer of 1863, she reminded Palmerston of 'her desire that *no step* is taken in foreign affairs *without* her *previous sanction* being obtained.' Should a true emergency arise, he could always use a cypher and communicate with her by telegraph.[27] Queen Victoria may have possessed neither the ability nor the inclination to draft as many memoranda[28] as her late husband had done, but by 1862 she possessed twenty-five years of experience in international affairs and she had personally met the chief monarchs and the leading statesmen and diplomats of Europe. Her continuing laments about the absence of Albert as her all-important adviser disguise both the breadth of her personal knowledge about matters of state and the strength of her will.

It had been Prince Albert's hope, when his eldest daughter wed Prince Frederick of Prussia, that Vicky could play a helpful role in strengthening the tendencies toward liberal constitutionalism in that state. Back in 1848, the Prussian monarch had reluctantly accepted a constitution that gave significant powers of legislation and taxation to the members of the Prussian Landtag (Parliament). It was Albert's hope that under the rule of Frederick's father, King William (who became Regent in 1859 and King of Prussia in his own right in 1861), the Prussian Crown would not only emulate the constitutional monarchy of Britain but would also peacefully unite with the other German states (hitherto only loosely allied as members of the German Confederation) to create a liberal constitutional German nation similar to the United Kingdom. Frederick and Vicky would in due course inherit that unified German Crown, which would then prosper in peace with its Continental neighbors and in fraternal friendship with its British counterpart.

During the years after Albert's death, his unduly optimistic hopes were repeatedly to be disappointed – as the Prussian monarch took far keener an interest in strengthening his army than his parliament and as he embarked on a series of wars rather than constitutional conventions. The man who taught King William I how to outwit his parliament and how to make Prussia the linchpin of a new German Empire was Otto von Bismarck. In 1862 he became, and for the next twenty-eight years he remained, the Prussian (and in due course also the German) chancellor; he refashioned the Europe of his day less by parliamentary debates than by 'blood and iron.' In the process Bismarck did his best to undermine both the liberal influence and the popularity of the Crown Princess Victoria. In the queen's judgment, her daughter was 'the best and wisest adviser' that her husband the Crown Prince could possibly have, but German critics condemned her as 'the Englishwoman' – a foreigner who had no right to meddle with the conservative autocratic structure of the kingdom of Prussia.[29] As she saw her late father's plans and her own desires for her adopted land repeatedly rebuffed, Vicky sometimes compared her lot – as a perennial object of suspicion – to that of the Austrian-born Queen Marie Antoinette in late eighteenth-century France. Her mother could do little more than convey her sympathy.[30]

Late in 1863, Bismarck had an opportunity to strengthen the Prussian state by challenging the Danish claims to Schleswig-Holstein asserted by Princess Alexandra's father when he took over the Danish throne as King Christian IX. Almost all inhabitants of Holstein were German-speakers and so were at least half of the inhabitants of Schleswig, and whatever their personal ties to the Danish Crown, the two provinces were also members of the German Confederation. As the two leading states in that confederation, Prussia and Austria insisted on German supremacy there. Princess Alexandra fervently sympathised with her Danish relations and so did the Prince of Wales – who at that time developed a detestation for German bullying that he retained for the rest of his life. In this instance, however, both the Crown Princess of Prussia and Queen Victoria agreed that the pro-German sentiments of the great majority of the inhabitants of the disputed provinces had to be respected. When Lords Palmerston and Russell threatened to aid the Danes if a

Prussian army were to occupy Schleswig, the queen reminded her
prime minister that she

> has never given her sanction to any such threat. . . . England cannot be
> committed to assist Denmark in such a collision . . . . The Queen has
> declared that she will not sanction the infliction upon her subjects of all
> the horrors of war, for the purpose of becoming partisan in a quarrel in
> which both parties are much in the wrong.[31]

A Prussian invasion of Denmark therefore did not result in British
military aid to Denmark, and the Danish king was compelled to sue
for peace and to surrender his claims to both provinces. Queen
Victoria expected that, in accordance with an earlier treaty (and with
Prince Albert's express desire), Schleswig-Holstein would henceforth
be ruled by the German Duke of Augustenburg, who happened to be
married to a daughter of Feodora, Queen Victoria's half-sister. It soon
became clear, however, that Bismarck's long-term intention was to
annex both provinces to Prussia outright. The queen's private verdict: 'Odious people the Prussians are, that I must say.'[32]

Austria and Prussia had collaborated against the Danes, but it was
Bismarck's purpose to make Prussia and not Austria the fulcrum of a
powerful new German nation-state, and in the Seven-Weeks War of
1866, a Prussian army defeated the Austrians. Both Prince Frederick's
wife and his mother-in-law took enormous pride in Frederick's success on the battlefield, but the war cost many thousands of Prussian
lives and even more Austrian ones. As Vicky wrote to her husband,

> The brilliant and glorious victories of our 'nation under arms' can never
> change my opinion of Bismarck. For me war will ever be a crime brought
> on by the irresponsibility and temerity of this one man, not by force of
> circumstances. . . . The work that is now (perhaps) being done by blood
> and iron should have been done by intellectual forces.[33]

Her mother concurred: 'I only wish it was all in a better cause and
against real enemies and not against brother Germans.'[34]

In the aftermath of the war against Austria, Bismarck created the
North German Federation and incorporated into Prussia one of
Austria's allies, the Kingdom of Hanover; he deposed its ruler,
George V, Queen Victoria's first cousin. In 1870, in order to achieve

Prussia's political union with the south German states – Baden, Württemberg, and Bavaria – Bismarck induced the Emperor Napoleon to declare war on Prussia. Because both sides respected the neutrality of Belgium, Britain stayed neutral. At that time, many Europeans still considered the French army the strongest in Europe; within a few months, however, the German army demonstrated its overwhelming superiority. Napoleon III was taken prisoner-of-war and abdicated his throne, Paris was surrounded by German troops, and in the Paris suburb of Versailles, King William I of Prussia was proclaimed Emperor William I of a revived German Empire incorporating the German states other than Austria. Once again, the Crown Princess of Prussia and her mother Queen Victoria found themselves cheering Prince Frederick's successes on the battlefield and hailing the creation of a German nation while lamenting the methods used by Bismarck and the militaristic and autocratic nature of the new state.

A majority of Britain's people had initially sympathised with Germany because the declaration of war by Napoleon III seemed unjustified. They ended up feeling sorry for the exiled emperor and empress and appalled by German war demands: a large reparations bill and the annexation of Alsace-Lorraine. Queen Victoria's own fluctuating private mood resembled that of her people in that she had considered Napoleon's declaration of war an 'act of mad folly' while her 'whole heart and . . . fervent prayers are with beloved Germany!' Even Albert, she thought, would have gone to fight on the German side. By January 1871, however, Napoleon, Eugénie, and their only son had been granted refuge in England by Queen Victoria. As she admitted to her daughter, 'the feeling in England is becoming sadly hostile to Germany' with the forcible annexation of Alsace and Lorraine making a future war all but certain.[35] That future war was to be deferred until after Queen Victoria's death, but in the meantime the European balance of power had been permanently altered, and on the European continent the new German Empire had become militarily, and was soon to become industrially, the most powerful state by far.

In the course of the 1860s, the queen took a keen interest in numerous other developments such as the transformation of the Italian peninsula into the constitutional kingdom of Italy. She vetoed the idea that her second son Alfred, her sailor prince, should became King of Greece; she similarly persuaded Albert's elder brother Ernest, the Duke of Saxe-Coburg-Gotha, not to assume that throne inasmuch as Alfred had been named heir to the childless duke.[36] The fact that Prince Albert's final public act had been to prevent war between Britain and Abraham Lincoln's government had caused the widowed Victoria to feel greater sympathy for the cause of the Union than for the Confederacy.[37] The American minister to Britain, Edwards Pierrepont, was to observe a few years later that there was 'a universal belief that the Queen, in our late Civil War, was on the side of freedom . . . and that she prevented a recognition of the rebel states . . . and thereby saved the lives of many thousands of our countrymen.'[38]

Only in 1866, in her Speech from the Throne (drafted by Lord Russell but approved by the queen), was Victoria able to observe

> with Satisfaction that the United States, after terminating successfully the severe Struggle in which they were so long engaged, are wisely repairing the Ravages of Civil War. The abolition of Slavery is an event calling forth the cordial Sympathies and Congratulations of this Country, which has always been foremost in showing its Abhorrence of an Institution repugnant to every feeling of Justice and Humanity.[39]

In the meantime, the queen had been deeply shocked by the 'dreadful and awful' news of the assassination of Abraham Lincoln. As she wrote to her Uncle Leopold, 'one never heard of *such* a thing! I only hope it will not be *catching elsewhere*.'[40] Two days later she had personally drafted the following lines to Mary Todd Lincoln:

> Dear Madam, Though a stranger to you, I cannot remain silent when so terrible a calamity has fallen upon you and your country, and must express personally my deep and heartfelt sympathy with you under the shocking circumstances of your present dreadful misfortune. No one can better appreciate than I can, who am myself utterly broken-hearted by the loss of my own beloved husband, who was the light of my life, my stay, my all, what your sufferings must be; and I earnestly pray that you may be supported by Him to Whom alone the sorely stricken can look for comfort, in this hour of heavy affliction! With the renewed expression of true sympathy, I remain, dear Madam, your sincere friend, VICTORIA R.[41]

'They say', wrote Walter Bagehot, the widely read mid-Victorian journalist, 'that the Americans were more pleased at the Queen's letter to
Mrs Lincoln, than at any act of the English Government. It was a
spontaneous act of intelligible feeling in the midst of confused and
tiresome business.'[42]

Behind the scenes, the reclusive widow may have been preoccupied with great affairs of state, but, in the eyes of many ordinary
Britons, the once eminently public monarch had become essentially
private. It was partly in the hope of bringing the queen out of her
shell and making court life less funereal that in late 1864, two leading
members of the royal household recommended that Victoria bring
south from Balmoral one John Brown, the Scottish gillie (personal
attendant) who had served the royal couple on their Highland picnics
and excursions in the years immediately preceding Albert's death.
His initial role at Windsor was simply to escort the queen when out
riding, but the experiment proved so great a success that Brown soon
took on many additional responsibilities, indoor as well as outdoor.
The son of a one-time schoolmaster turned tenant farmer, John
Brown was a tall, handsome, and rugged Highlander with both a
gruff demeanor and a fierce sense of loyalty to the queen. In her eyes,
he became the personal embodiment of a Scotland that was 'the
brightest jewel in my crown – energy, courage, worth, inimitable per-
severance, determination and self-respect.'[43]

Within a remarkably short time, John Brown came to play a central role in the daily life of a royal mistress who was at last beginning
to come to terms with life after Albert. 'It is a real comfort,' she told
her uncle, 'for [Brown] is so devoted to me – so simple, so intelligent,
so *unlike* an *ordinary* servant.'[44] A man as handsome and 'devoted &
attached & clever' as Brown, became, indeed, ever less an ordinary
servant. Instead, he served as the queen's one and only Highland
Servant with the salary of a professional doctor or lawyer. Persuaded
that his family was of gentry origin, in 1872 she formally named him
'Esquire' and he became *de facto* master of her personal household. As
she explained to her eldest daughter,

> He comes to my room after breakfast and luncheon to get his orders –
> and everything is always right; he is so quiet, has such an excellent head

and memory, and is besides so devoted and attached and clever and so
wonderfully able to interpret one's wishes. He is a real treasure to me
now, and I only wish higher people had his sense and discretion, and that
I had as good a maid. . . . It is an excellent arrangement . . . and God
knows how I want so much to be taken care of.[45]

That 'excellent arrangement' improved the queen's mood and
enhanced her sense of self-confidence, because at regular intervals
Brown would pledge his loyalty. Thus, after his first visit to the
mausoleum – in the company of the queen and her newly married
daughter, Princess Helena – he told his mistress:

> I felt sorry for ye; I know so well what your feeling must be – ye who had
> been so happy. There is no more pleasure for you poor Queen, and I feel
> for ye but what can I do so for ye? I could die for ye.[46]

At the same time, the new arrangement was often resented by the
queen's children, especially by her eldest son, because Brown soon
came to possess the full confidence of his mother and the immediate
access to her that Bertie was denied. Her children were also fearful
that Brown would use his office to exert an inappropriate political
influence. That he did not do, other than finding palace posts for
numerous relations. Instead, he assumed the liberties of a medieval
court jester. Thus, on one occasion when he was pinning a cape
about the queen's neck and accidentally scratched her chin, he was
heard to comment: 'Hoots, then wumman. Can ye no hold yerr head
up?' Victoria was un-Victorian in not being particularly fond of tea;
when she once congratulated Brown on the excellence of the tea that
he had brewed for her, he replied: 'Well, it should be, Ma'am. I put a
grand nip o 'whisky in it!'[47] Analogously, when more than once he
was found in his bed dead drunk, the queen made no remonstrance.
At times he even puffed on a Highland pipe in her presence, although
all other forms of smoking were banned on the royal premises. While
avoiding the formal dances of the London season, Victoria would
happily participate in the gillies' balls at Balmoral.

In London upper-class society during the later 1860s, rumors
spread that Brown had become far more than a servant but rather the
queen's lover or her secret husband and the father of a secret child, a
child that had been smuggled off to Switzerland to be raised by a

Protestant clergyman. Although such 'ill-natured gossip in the higher classes' (as Victoria called it) cannot be absolutely disproved, no persuasive confirmatory evidence has yet been found. There was, after all, little royal privacy in palaces filled with maidservants and dressers. It may be more appropriate to contend – as one biographer has done – that the queen's relationship with Brown became a 'closer and more intimate [one] than she had with any other man after her husband's death' and that it resembled far more 'that to be found in an affectionate marriage relationship than between mistress and servant.'[48] Queen Victoria might not have agreed publicly with such an appraisal, but she did candidly declare: 'He became my best & truest friend, as I was his.'[49]

In 1867 and 1868 the queen not only successfully resisted those high-born members of her household who sought to persuade her to get rid of Brown, but she also happily included a great many references to him in A Journal of Our Life in the Highlands, a book made up primarily of excerpts from Queen Victoria's journal up to the year 1861. With the assistance of Arthur Helps, it was first published privately in 1864 and then publicly in 1868: 18,000 copies were sold during the very first week, and additional printings and translations appeared every few months. Although her children and some of her courtiers privately deplored the publication of a book that seemed more preoccupied with footmen than with statesmen, Queen Victoria was certain that the work would prove beneficial. To the upper classes it would set a good example in proper behavior, and it would – in Helps's words – form 'a new bond of union' between the still reclusive queen and her people.[50] Perhaps it did.

Although reluctant as ever to appear in public, Victoria did agree to open Parliament in person in February 1866, in part, critics suggested, because she was about to ask the legislature to vote a £30,000 dowry for her third daughter, the Princess Helena – about £3,000,000 in the monetary values of 2003. The queen opened Parliament, but she refused to appear in state: there were no trumpet fanfares; there was no pageantry; there were no gingerbread coaches and no royal dress. Instead she wore a widow's cap. Her crimson robes were draped across the throne like a discarded skin. Nor did she read the speech herself – as she had always done before Albert's death. She merely nodded to the Lord Chancellor, and he read it on her behalf while she sat expressionless – as if she did not hear a sound. Privately, she likened the entire experience to a public execution. She failed to understand, she told Earl Russell, the prime minister, why the public should be so

> unreasonable and unfeeling . . . as to long to witness the spectacle of a poor, broken-hearted widow, nervous and shrinking, dragged in deep mourning, ALONE in STATE as a Show, where she used to go supported by her husband, to be gazed at, without delicacy of feeling, is a thing she cannot understand, and she never could wish her bitterest foe exposed to![51]

Queen Victoria had obviously forgotten that time long ago when she limited to three days her honeymoon with Prince Albert: 'You forget, my dearest Love,' she had then insisted, 'that I am the Sovereign, and that business can stop and wait for nothing. Parliament is sitting . . . and it is quite impossible for me to be absent from London.'[52]

At the special urging of Lord Derby, whose minority Conservative government shepherded through Parliament the Reform Bill of 1867, Victoria opened Parliament again that year. Her presence, Derby suggested, would signal the monarch's 'moral support' for a compromise political reform measure that in England and Scotland doubled the size of the electorate. Afterwards the queen regretted her decision. 'That stupid Reform agitation has excited and irritated people,' she concluded; it had caused a number of spectators to hiss, to groan, and to make nasty faces. Fortunately she had already made it clear to Derby that she had no intention of opening Parliament 'as a *matter* of *course*, year after year.'[53] During the remainder of her reign she was to open Parliament in person only five times more.

Initially Victoria was equally reluctant to resume her public role at military reviews. It was not the prime minister, however, but the queen who took the initiative in restoring such occasions, by writing to her first cousin, the Duke of Cambridge. He had participated in the Crimean War with greater discretion than valor, but that had not stopped his being named in 1856 as Commander-in-Chief of the British Army. He was to hold that position for the next four decades, thereby reconfirming the close traditional links between the army and the throne. In 1866 Queen Victoria offered to visit Aldershot again in order to review the troops there. Although she found it 'a painful trial' to revisit the Royal Pavilion for the first time since Albert's death, she felt certain that the prince would have wanted her to resume such visits. Her private secretary had 'seldom seen her more pleased.'[54] She returned to Aldershot a month later to present new colors to the 89th Regiment. Each year brought further visits to Aldershot, and in 1868 she fixed June 20 for a grand review of Volunteers in Windsor Park. Indeed she offered to increase the attendance by promising a holiday to Volunteers who ordinarily had to go to work that day. There were further reviews in 1869 and in 1870. She noted that when she arrived at an Aldershot review in the summer of 1870, the soldiers 'cheered me very much.' They, in turn, 'looked magnificent' when they gave the Royal Salute. In 1873, while at Osborne, she was

> much occupied with tomorrow's ceremony of presenting colours to the 79th Cameron Highlanders and preparing my little speech, which I had some difficulty at first in learning by heart. Repeated it several times & the last thing before going to bed.

After the ceremony was over, she recorded in her journal how fine the troops were, how well they marched, and how splendid they looked in their kilts. At the regiment's special request, she accepted their 'terribly tattered' old colors and promised them an honored home at Balmoral Castle.

Year after year the refurbished routine continued no matter what the weather. Thus in the autumn of 1881, Victoria held a review in Edinburgh's Queen's Park for more than 40,000 Scottish Volunteers. This is how one witness described the scene:

> The march past occupied more than three hours, during which the rain descended in torrents. The Queen was in an open carriage . . . [b]ut, true soldier's daughter as she was, she paid no heed to the weather, thinking only of her duty to let herself be seen by those who had come from all parts of the country. . . . She did not leave the Park until the last man had passed. By this time the carriage was full of water, and pools of it . . . dropped from the dresses of herself and [her] ladies when they returned to Holyrood.[55]

Eight years later one of Victoria's granddaughters was to report on 'the excitement and bustle' at Windsor when the queen prepared to present new colors to yet another regiment. '[I]t's such a touching moment when the old 'colours' are taken away and the band plays "for auld lang syne" – then Grandmama gives the new ones after her speech, which she said so well and without hesitation!'[56]

The later 1860s brought about a significant change in the political world: a new generation took power. In October 1865 came the death of the octogenarian prime minister Lord Palmerston, and within the next two and a half years followed the retirement of both Earl Russell, the other veteran Whig (Liberal) leader, and Lord Derby, since 1846 the leader of the Conservative Party. Palmerston had done his best to keep the domestic political atmosphere a placid as well as a prosperous one, but after his death, Earl Russell, the new prime minister, recalled that back in 1831 he had introduced into the House of Commons the measure that became the historic Reform Act of 1832. It was his intention to conclude his career with another major measure expanding the franchise; in this project, he gained the eager cooperation of the party's new leader in the House of Commons, the ex-Peelite William Ewart Gladstone. During the summer of 1866, the right wing of the Liberal Party rebelled against such political democratisation, however, and in collaboration with the Conservative opposition, defeated the ministry.

For the third time in fourteen years, it became possible, therefore, for the Conservative Party to form a minority government – with the 14th Earl of Derby (in the House of Lords) serving as prime minister and with Benjamin Disraeli serving as Chancellor of the Exchequer and as party leader in the House of Commons. It soon became clear to the Conservative Party chieftains that a major measure of political reform was in the air and that the Conservatives might just as well gain the political credit. In a masterful manner Benjamin Disraeli therefore guided through the House of Commons what became the historic Reform Act of 1867. When Derby retired from the prime ministership early in 1868, Queen Victoria had an opportunity to name a successor. Yet Conservatives who had grown accustomed to Benjamin Disraeli as the Number Two man in their party still shrank from the notion that he should become prime minister, that an upstart adventurer of Jewish origin should hold the most prestigious political position in the kingdom and the Empire and preside over a cabinet made up largely of hereditary landed aristocrats.

The queen too had long shared their doubts; when back in 1846 Disraeli's polemics had led to the downfall of Sir Robert Peel, Prince Albert felt certain that Disraeli had 'not one particle of the gentleman in him.'[57] When he first became a cabinet member in 1852, Victoria found him 'most singular, – thoroughly Jewish looking. . . . The expression is disagreeable.'[58] Even then she thought his official letters intriguing, however, and during the years since Albert's death (and Disraeli's eloquent eulogy) she had gradually warmed to the man. On Derby's resignation, she therefore named him prime minister without hesitation or further consultation. It was, she told her daughter, a 'proud thing for a man "risen from the people" to have obtained!' His father had been, after all, a 'mere man of letters.' Disraeli, she concluded, had not only proved himself a master parliamentarian, but he was also clever and sensible, and so 'loyal and anxious to please me in every way.' His words were indeed 'full of poetry, romance and chivalry. When he knelt down to kiss my hand which he took in both of his he said "in loving loyalty and faith".'[59]

Disraeli's tenure as prime minister was destined to be a brief one, because his party could hold on to office only so long as the Liberal majority (made up of Whigs and Radicals and erstwhile Peelites) was temporarily splintered. As soon as political reform measures had been passed for Scotland and Ireland and as soon as a new register had been prepared for the vastly expanded electorate, it would become necessary to hold a general election. That election took place in November 1868; it was hard fought, and its outcome was clearcut: Liberals, 382; Conservatives, 276. The Conservatives won almost as many seats as the Liberals in England alone, but the Liberals won the vast majority of Welsh, Scottish, and Irish seats. Disraeli decided not to wait for the newly elected House of Commons to assemble and vote him out, but to resign at once. As he once again embarked on long years of political opposition, he took delight in the fact that Queen Victoria agreed to honor his own services by ennobling his aging wife – she was 76, he 64 – as Viscountess Beaconsfield.

The personal victor in the general election of 1868 was William

Ewart Gladstone, who succeeded in reuniting his temporarily divided party on the issue of Irish Church Disestablishment. The sister church of the Protestant Church of England, to which at most one Irish man or woman in eight adhered, was no longer to be treated as the official religion of an island in which Roman Catholicism was the religion of three out of four people and in which Presbyterians were dominant in many towns of Ulster (north-eastern Ireland). The issue of Irish Church Disestablishment tied the Liberal Party once more to the historic cause of religious liberty, and it held great symbolic importance for the large numbers of Protestant Nonconformists (Methodists, Baptists, and Congregationalists) in England who voted Liberal. So did Gladstone's decision to appoint to his cabinet John Bright, a political Radical and a Quaker; he was the first Protestant Nonconformist since the middle of the seventeenth century to hold high political office.

Queen Victoria had known Gladstone since he had first entered the cabinet under Sir Robert Peel, and Prince Albert had developed a keen respect for Gladstone's abilities as Chancellor of the Exchequer. Gladstone sought to use his influence over the annual budget to reduce or eliminate the excise taxes paid by ordinary people for such necessities as soap and candles and to encourage individual thrift and industry. He shared Prince Albert's sense of moral duty and public service – as exemplified by strict financial accounts and by government civil service examinations based on merit rather than on patronage. He had spoken warmly of Albert after his death. For such reasons Queen Victoria might have welcomed Gladstone as prime minister. She was indeed cordial to him, but she felt certain that he had done 'immense mischief' by raising the Irish Church issue: it would promote religious discord rather than allay it. She therefore refused to open Parliament in person in February 1869; she had no desire to give the 'sanction of my presence' to a policy that she found mistaken if by then inevitable.[60]

After months of debate, Gladstone did carry his Irish Church Bill through both Houses of Parliament, and in the course of the next several years, the Gladstone ministry of 1868–74 also enacted numerous other reforms: a Bill to curtail the legal powers of Irish landlords; the setting up in England of a state system of tax-supported elementary schools (to supplement the church schools); an expanded civil service system; the enactment of the secret ballot; a restructuring of both the judiciary and the army; and the resolution by arbitration of long-standing American claims against Britain for having failed to stop the Confederacy from using British shipyards to build vessels afterwards used as commerce raiders. Queen Victoria ultimately supported or acquiesced in all of these reforms, but she protested strongly against Gladstone's reform plans for the monarchy itself.

The trouble was, as the prime minister privately observed: 'The Queen is invisible, and the Prince of Wales is not respected.' As the French empire gave way to a republic, there were republican murmurs in Britain also. In his *Impeachment of the House of Brunswick*, Charles Bradlaugh, a powerful Radical lecturer and an avowed atheist, condemned the Hanoverian dynasty as 'a race of small German breast-bestarred wanderers . . . here we pay them highly to marry and perpetuate a pauper-prince race. If they do nothing they are "good". If they do ill loyalty gilds the vice till it looks like virtue.'[61] Not only outdoor agitators but also influential Liberal MPs such as Sir Charles Dilke welcomed the prospect of a republic, and Joseph Chamberlain, soon to become the Radical mayor of Birmingham, predicted that it would come in his lifetime. The monarch and her children were paid large sums but appeared to do little in return, and her private secretary privately informed the prime minister that Victoria was in better health than she let on: 'It is simply the long, unchecked habit of self-indulgence that now makes it impossible for her . . . to give up . . . the gratification of a single inclination, or even whim.'[62] Some of her children privately concurred with this appraisal.

Gladstone wanted the queen both to spend more time in London and to set up a permanent royal residence in Ireland; he wanted the Prince of Wales to spend several months there each year as ceremonial viceroy. He wanted, he told her, 'to make the monarchy of this country, in Your Majesty's person, visible and palpable to the people.'[63] Although she would have been pleased to have her son forgo part of the lively London social season, ultimately Victoria resisted all of Gladstone's well-intentioned plans for the monarchy. 'What killed her beloved Husband?,' she asked rhetorically that same year. The answer was 'Overwork and worry! . . . and the Queen, a woman no longer young is . . . to be driven and abused till her nerves and health give way with this worry and agitation and interference in her private life.'[64] As for William Ewart Gladstone, he was 'a very dangerous Minister – and so wonderfully unsympathetic.'[65] Indeed, as the queen ultimately confided to her private secretary, 'Mr Gladstone would have liked to *govern* HER as Bismarck governs the Emperor. . . . [S]he always felt in his manner an overbearing obstinacy and imperiousness (without being actually wanting in respect as to form) which she never experienced from *anyone* else.'[66]

What caused the republican movement of the early 1870s to subside[67] was neither Gladstone's stratagems nor the queen's conversion to a program of royal splendor, but first, Queen Victoria's own very real illnesses – an abscess on her arm and rheumatic gout – in the autumn of 1871. Then in late November the Prince of Wales, at his home in Norfolk, fell gravely ill of typhoid. Newspaper reporters clustered at the gate of Sandringham House and kept the telegraph wires hot with whatever scraps of information they could elicit. The queen rushed to her son's bedside, and a sense of superstitious dread overtook the household as Bertie's condition worsened and the 14th of December approached, the tenth anniversary of the death of Prince Albert. That very day the fever broke. A genuine mood of relief swept the country, and, at Gladstone's behest, Victoria was reluctantly persuaded to join her son on February 27, 1872, in an open carriage in a procession of thanksgiving to St Paul's Cathedral. She long resisted the 'pomp or show' involved, but her prime minister insisted on the 'extreme solemnity of the occasion not only for the Prince . . . not only for the Queen and Royal Family, but for the future of the Monarchy.'[68] As even the queen conceded, the event became one of the triumphant ceremonial events of the Victorian era. She marveled at the gigantic crowds and the 'deafening cheers [that] never ceased the whole way' and 'the wonderful demonstration of loyalty and affection, from the very highest to the lowest.'[69] When the very next day an Irish lad pointed a pistol straight at the queen, and John Brown courageously jumped off the carriage and wrestled him to the ground, public rejoicing confirmed the revival of the queen's popularity.

She may never have truly appreciated how much the survival of the monarchy owed to Gladstone. Had the most popular and magnetic Liberal of the day chosen to join the republican movement, it might well have succeeded. Instead he repeatedly swallowed his frustrations with the person of the queen as he continued to exalt an institution that he revered as a symbol of national unity and continuity.

8 *New Crowns for Old Ones!*

A cartoon from *Punch* (April 15, 1876) shows Prime Minister Benjamin Disraeli (dressed as Aladdin) offering Queen Victoria the title 'Empress of India.'

8 The Guardian of the Constitution

Although she never truly ceased to grieve for Albert, in the course of the 1870s and early 1880s Queen Victoria came to play a more public role than she had done during the first ten years after the Prince's death. She was confirmed in the belief, especially by Benjamin Disraeli, that her role was not merely ceremonial but also consultative, that both foreign-policy decisions and particular legislative measures demonstrated 'how great is the power of the Sovereign in this country, if firm and faithfully served.'[1] On occasion she pondered the possibility that she might abdicate and 'retire quietly to a cottage in the hills and rest and see almost no one. . . . If only our dear Bertie was fit to replace me!'[2] Unfortunately, the queen felt certain, he was not. She had no alternative, therefore, but to carry on, and, as she reminded William Ewart Gladstone in 1881, '[h]er constant object, which only increases with years, is the welfare, prosperity, honour & glory of her dear Country.'[3] She had never opposed constructive reform, she insisted, 'but she also thinks, that the great *principles* of the *Constitution* of this *great country* ought to be maintained and preserved.'[4] Politicians might come and politicians might go, but in her eyes it was she alone who remained the permanent guardian of her country's constitution.

One aspect of that constitution that troubled her repeatedly during the later 1860s and the 1870s was the Church of England, its leaders, and its doctrines. For one thing, the institution that she served as governor seemed ill-equipped to participate effectively in the manifest renewal of Protestant/Roman Catholic rivalry throughout western Europe and to a lesser degree within Britain itself. During the papacy of Pius IX (1846–78), Roman Catholic theological claims had

135

become increasingly 'triumphalist.' In 1854 had come the promulga-
tion as church dogma of the immaculate conception of the Virgin
Mary, and in 1855 a concordat with the Austrian Empire gave the
papacy 'greater rights and privileges than had ever before been
extracted from any German sovereign.'[5] Less than a decade later, in
the Syllabus of Errors, the pontiff had condemned as heretical the
doctrine that Catholic lands might legally tolerate other religions or
that any form of Protestantism constituted a legitimate form of
Christianity. The papacy declared that it had no intention of recon-
ciling itself with 'progress, liberalism, and modern civilisation.' Then
in 1869 at Rome there assembled the first conclave in three centuries
of representatives of all Catholic Christendom. In 1870 that Vatican
Council formally proclaimed the dogma that, when speaking *ex cathe-
dra* on matters of faith and morals, the Pope was infallible. 'This
would seem rather disgraceful in the 19th century!' – so noted Queen
Victoria in her journal. Like her foreign secretary, Lord Clarendon,
the queen was astonished by the manner in which even clever
Roman Catholics first protested against the doctrine of papal infalli-
bility and then submitted to it.

During those same years, the states of central Italy that the Pope had
governed as political ruler first shrank in size and then in 1870 were
absorbed by a unified Italian kingdom while Pius IX became a self-
confessed 'Prisoner of the Vatican.' Despite such curtailment of the
pontiff's temporal authority, Queen Victoria's eldest daughter feared
that the political influence of the Pope remained 'far greater abroad
than it is at home – and to the German Roman Catholics he is still
enveloped with the awe and mystery to which Italians have long
become indifferent.' She was suspicious of the power exercised by
German Catholics as schoolmasters, as meddlers in politics, and as
instigators of 'a feeling of intolerance and hostility between
Protestants and Roman Catholics.' Queen Victoria fully concurred. In
the Britain of 1869 also, 'people will not see the danger of encouraging
the R[oman] Catholics which is too foolish. You can never conciliate
without their encroaching.' Suspicious of Bismarck as the two women
were on other matters, they therefore found themselves sympathetic
with the purposes, if not the tactics, of the German Chancellor as during the 1870s he sought to enhance German nationalism by waging a

Kulturkampf (a 'struggle for civilisation') against the international Roman Catholic Church. The queen agreed with her daughter that the outright persecution of Germany's Roman Catholic bishops was 'very wrong and a great mistake.'[6]

When Gladstone pushed through Parliament the disestablishment of the Irish Church, Queen Victoria protested, however, that his ministry appeared 'totally blind to the alarming encroachments & increase of the R[oman] Catholics in England and indeed all over the world.'[7] During the mid-Victorian years, Irish immigration and the conversion of scores of prominent Englishmen had caused the Roman Catholic population of England to quadruple. The queen privately deplored the conversion in 1868 of the 3rd Marquess of Bute and in 1874 of the Marquess of Ripon, the latter a member of Gladstone's cabinet. 'How dreadful this perversion of Lord Ripon's,' Victoria commented. 'I knew him so well and thought him so sensible.' As the queen had declared on an analogous occasion, 'I do blame those who go from light to darkness!'

It was during these years also that the queen brought up most often a favorite theme: that in the Church of England – unlike the Presbyterian Church of Scotland – the Reformation 'was *never* fully completed.' Back in 1866, Victoria had insisted on

> the duty which is imposed upon her and her family, to maintain the *true* and *real* principles and *spirit* of our Protestant religion; for her family was brought over and placed on the throne of these realms *solely* to maintain it; and the Queen will *not* stand the attempts made to . . . bring the Church of England as near the Church of Rome as they possibly can.[8]

What was desperately required, the queen felt sure, was not disestablishment but 'a *very sweeping* Reformation of the English Church.' In that spirit, Victoria insisted in 1868 on the appointment of Archibald Tait, a bishop who shared her views, as the new Archbishop of Canterbury. And it was in collaboration with the archbishop that she initiated what in 1874 became the Public Worship Regulation Act, a measure designed to enforce greater discipline on Anglican clerics and to rid the Anglican churches of the rituals and ceremonies, 'flowers, crosses, vestments,' that in England 'all mean something most dangerous!'[9]

Victoria felt certain that only a truly Protestantised Church of England could appropriately 'stretch out its arm to other Protestant Churches' rather than showing its contempt for them. Only a reformed Church of England could be expected to join with the Presbyterian Church of Scotland, the Lutheran Church of Germany, and the other reformed churches of the continent in 'a strong phalanx' to lead the 'universal struggle' against Roman Catholicism, 'a religion which is so aggressive, so full of every sort of falseness and uncharitableness and bigotry (unlike any other) that it must be resisted and opposed.'[10]

By the time the Public Worship Regulation Act had become law, Gladstone's ministry had been defeated in a general election. It had passed a sizable program of reform legislation, but as Disraeli observed, by 1873 the Liberal front bench had come to resemble a 'range of exhausted volcanoes.' Although Gladstone had pushed through Parliament both the disestablishment of the Church of Ireland and a measure to strengthen the legal rights of Irish tenant farmers, his effort to set up a new Irish university that would admit and satisfy the expectations of both Protestants and Roman Catholics was defeated. Queen Victoria had always been dubious about the prime minister's self-proclaimed ' "mission" to redeem Ireland,' and she was privately pleased when Gladstone resigned office. Disraeli refused to form a ministry, however, at a time when the Liberals retained a large majority of seats in the House of Commons, and the 'very tiresome and obstinate' Gladstone struggled on for another ten months.[11] Then came a new general election, and the greatest Conservative electoral triumph since 1841. A unified Conservative Party emerged with 352 seats, a temporarily divided Liberal Party was reduced to 242, and a new Irish Home Rule Party won 58.

Queen Victoria secretly rejoiced. Although she offered Gladstone an earldom and bade him a polite farewell, the election outcome confirmed her growing doubts about the Liberal prime minister. He had 'contrived to alienate and frighten the country,' whereas the new ministry was made up of 'distinguished and able men.'[12] The most distinguished of them all was the man who was destined to remain her prime minister for the next six years, Benjamin Disraeli. Throughout his life Disraeli had found both solace and delight in the company of women. 'I owe everything to women,' he once declared, and he took immense satisfaction in the very notion of serving a female sovereign. He was now himself a widower, and his relationship with the queen immediately began to resemble a political romance. 'He repeatedly said *whatever I wished* SHOULD *be done*,' the queen reported, and when, in accordance with custom, he fell to his knees to kiss her hand as her prime minister, he declared, 'I plight my troth to the kindest of *Mistresses*.'[13] There were all manner of personnel decisions to be made, and on more than one occasion her new prime minister both sought and abided by her advice. As he wrote in April 1874,

> It may be unconstitutional for a Minister to seek advice from his Sovereign, instead of proffering it; but your Majesty has, sometimes, deigned to assist Mr Disraeli with your counsel, and he believes he may presume to say, with respectful candour, that your Majesty cannot but be aware how highly Mr Disraeli appreciates your Majesty's judgment and almost unrivalled experience of public life.[14]

Never had William Ewart Gladstone written to her in such a manner.

The queen took a benevolent if not intense interest in a series of social-reform Acts sponsored by the Disraeli ministry. They included a strengthened Public Health Act, a measure allowing local authorities to demolish and to reconstruct city slums, and a Sale of Food and Drugs Act that banned all ingredients 'injurious to health.' A new Trade Union Act gave full legal sanction to such activities as peaceful picketing. As Disraeli happily reported to the queen, 'the working classes of the kingdom now felt persuaded that 'the object of all the measures of the present Ministry is really to elevate their condition and mitigate their lot.'[15] Other acts of social legislation were to follow between 1874 and 1880, but from 1875 on, the prime minister, his cabinet, and the queen were to become primarily absorbed with foreign affairs: the Suez Canal; the government of India; the Russo-Turkish War of 1877–8 and the revived 'Eastern Question.'

One of the engineering wonders of the century, the Suez Canal had been completed in 1869 by a French company. Palmerston had initially opposed the project because he feared that Britain would find it difficult to defend militarily what immediately became its 'lifeline to

India,' far shorter than the traditional route around the Cape of Good Hope. From the start, at least three of every four ships that traversed the canal flew the Union Jack. Yet it did not seem to worry Gladstone that this vital link was entirely under foreign control – that of the French and of the Khedive of Egypt, the largely independent ruler of a state that was in name still part of the Ottoman Empire. In November 1875 Disraeli learned that the bankrupt Khedive was prepared to sell his share – 44 percent – of the canal company to a syndicate of French investors. Taking into his confidence only the queen, who strongly encouraged him, and a few cabinet members, who were highly doubtful, Disraeli acted swiftly. Before any other country or company could take action, he bought the vital shares for £4 million on behalf of Britain. With Parliament not in session, he secretly borrowed the money from the London banking house of Rothschild until Parliament agreed several months later to appropriate the sum.

Queen Victoria was ecstatic. Thus to safeguard the route to India impressed her as an enormous advantage for her country, and she felt certain that the *coup*

> must be a source of great satisfaction and pride to every British heart! It is *entirely* the doing of Mr Disraeli, who has *very large ideas*, and *very lofty views* of the position this country should hold. His mind is so much greater, larger, and his apprehension of things great and small so much quicker than that of Mr Gladstone.[16]

Queen Victoria was somewhat less happy with the manner in which Disraeli managed to gain her grudging agreement to a proposed journey through the Suez Canal to India that her son and heir, the Prince of Wales, sought to undertake. Reluctant as the young man may have been to become ceremonial Viceroy of Ireland, he was deeply attracted by the prospect of exploring Asia's exotic subcontinent with its 250 million people. Disraeli persuaded the British Parliament and the British government of India to secure the necessary funds to enable the prince's party to travel in style on the luxurious *Serapis*. The formal purpose of the visit, the prince insisted, was to become better acquainted with the customs and beliefs of these distant subjects of his mother. 'If the result of my visit,' declared the prince, 'should conduce to unite the various races of Hindostan in a feeling of loyalty to the Queen, attachment to our country, and of goodwill to each other, one great object at least will be gained.'[17] The queen found suspect a number of the proposed companions of her son, who intended to leave his wife behind in England. Victoria could only concur in the hope voiced by Dean Arthur Stanley, that in the course of the journey, 'the standard of national morality shall not be lowered but raised aloft.'[18] The princely party traveled by train, first to Paris and then through southern France and the Italian peninsula to the port of Brindisi. From there the ship took them on ceremonial visits to Greece, where his wife's younger brother ruled as King George of the Hellenes, and then to Egypt, where he visited the pyramids and conferred the Order of the Star of India on the son of the Khedive. Then came the journey through the Suez Canal and the Indian Ocean and a triumphant reception by the Viceroy of India in Bombay to mark the prince's thirty-fourth birthday. As he toured the city in an open carriage amidst tens of thousands of cheering Indians, he spotted a sign in large square letters, 'TELL MAMA WE'RE HAPPY.' The next several weeks were filled not only with tiger shoots but also with a succession of ceremonial events, innumerable exchanges of gifts with maharajas, and the conferral of an honorary degree on the prince by the University of Madras. By February, his mother had come to find 'very wearing' the reports of her son's sojourn: 'there is such a constant repetition of elephants – trappings – jewels – illuminations and fireworks.'[19]

And yet, on balance, the journey proved a success. The Prince of Wales resembled his mother in that he did not look down on people of a different race or faith. As he wrote to Lord Granville from India, 'Because a man has a black face and a different religion from our own, there is no reason why he should be treated as a brute.'[20] The Prince of Wales performed his often tiring ceremonial duties with great aplomb; in India alone he survived a journey of almost 10,000 miles by land and sea, and for hundreds of thousands of Indians he brought a distant monarchy to life. When her son received an enthusiastic welcome on his return to London in May 1876, even the queen was compelled to concede that her misgivings about his Asian journey had been misplaced.[21]

While her son was putting India on the map anew for Britain's newspaper-reading public, Queen Victoria was also involved with India back home. Ever since 1858, when, in the aftermath of the Great Mutiny, India became a crown colony ruled by a British viceroy (rather than a governor-general), the question had arisen: who was truly the formal ruler of the subcontinent and the unequivocal head of the hierarchic order there? Now that the impotent Mogul emperor at Delhi had been formally deposed, had Queen Victoria become the Empress of India? Some people did apply that title to her, and she found it appealing, but British law did not formally authorise such usage. Early in 1876 Disraeli introduced into the House of Commons the Royal Titles Bill in order to make such usage official. Critics in the Liberal Party objected strongly: in their eyes the names 'King' and 'Queen' were grand and historic English titles whereas the name 'Emperor' connoted force, violence, and debauchery. William Ewart Gladstone, who had formally resigned the Liberal Party leadership a year earlier, urged the defeat of the Bill. According to Disraeli, during one debate 'he was in one of his white rages.' His 'glancing looks at me . . . w[oul]d have annihilated any man who had not a good majority and a determination to use it.' The queen very much regretted all the distress that the 'ill-advised and mistaken conduct of the Opposition' was causing her devoted prime minister, and she urged him to explain to the House of Commons that the new title would not supersede that of 'Queen' at home: it would 'apply *only* to India.'[22] In due course, the measure did pass both Houses, and at the end of the parliamentary session of 1876 the queen elevated Disraeli to the House of Lords as Earl of Beaconsfield. That way the aging and often sickly statesman could remain prime minister without being fatigued by having to lead his government in person night after night in the House of Commons.[23]

On January 1, 1877, Lord Lytton, the new Viceroy of India, presided over a gigantic 'Victorian Feudal' gathering of 84,000 people in Delhi, a *durbar* of Indians comprising maharajas, princes, landlords and gentlemen, with their attendants. There Lytton proclaimed the queen's new title and provided coats of arms, banners, and medallions to many of the assembled Indians. As Lytton had earlier explained to the queen,

Your Majesty's Indian Government has not hitherto, in my opinion, sufficiently appealed to the Asiatic sentiment and traditions of the native Indian aristocracy. That aristocracy exercises a powerful influence over the rest of the native population. To rally it openly round the throne of your Majesty, and identify its sympathies and interests with British rule, will be to strengthen very materially the power, and increase the *éclat*, of your Majesty's Empire.[24]

Lytton closed several days of elaborate ceremony in Delhi with a personal telegraphic message from the new Empress: 'Our rule,' it affirmed, was based on the great principles of liberty, equity, and justice, 'which would promote their happiness,' add to their 'prosperity and advance their welfare.'[25]

Back home at Windsor on the day of the formal proclamation, the queen sponsored a celebratory banquet at which she was dressed in an imposing array of Indian jewels. When her son Prince Arthur toasted the 'Queen Empress,' he was rewarded with a dazzling smile. She employed Lockwood Kipling (the father of Rudyard Kipling) to design, and Ram Singh, an Indian artist, to decorate, the exotic Durbar Room as an addition to Osborne House; it served as a site to display her ever-growing collection of Asian curios. She would dearly have loved to visit India in person, but although she relished the icy gales that sometimes swept the Scottish Highlands, she feared that she would be overcome by the heat of the tropics. Henceforth, the monarch signed her formal letters not 'Victoria R' but 'Victoria R & I,' *Regina* and *Imperatrix*. The queen always denied that a hidden purpose of the law that she had directly inspired had been to enable her to hold up her head and those of her children among the status-conscious emperors of Germany, Austria, and Russia. In practice, however, the exaltation of her formal status in India was accompanied by an enhancement of her place in the hierarchical ruling order of the continent of Europe.

It was in Europe also and not in distant India that war clouds were gathering once again. In 1876 and 1877 British policy-makers found themselves impaled on the horns of a painful dilemma: should they support their fellow Christians, such as the Bulgarians, rebelling against Ottoman rule in the Balkans or should they resist the power of the Russian Empire, the 'big brother' of those same Balkan rebels, as it sought to conquer Constantinople and dominate the eastern portion of the Mediterranean world? Queen Victoria deplored the massacre of any people – including Bulgarians – but she strongly rejected Gladstone's belief that such sympathy should alone determine Britain's long-term policy toward Russian ambitions in the Balkans. The 'Bulgarian Massacres' carried out by Turkish troops in 1876 caused the former Liberal leader to return to public life with eloquent speeches and a lengthy polemical pamphlet. In the queen's judgment, Gladstone was displaying a 'mawkish sentimentality for people who hardly deserve the name of real Christians.'[26] 'The Turks could easily be managed by kindness,' she felt sure, 'but we have done nothing but lecture them & tell them [that] we would not help them' in their struggle to resist Russia's might.

For Queen Victoria the Eastern crisis of 1877 represented a direct replay of the Eastern crisis of 1854. That was no surprise, because she had been conscientiously assisting Sir Theodore Martin as he brought to completion the portion of his five-volume biography of Prince Albert that recounted the beginnings of the Crimean War. The lesson that both Martin and Victoria drew from the earlier conflict was not that it had been an error for Britain to declare war on Russia but that it had been an error for her kingdom to be so ill-prepared for that conflict and so slow to appreciate the depths of Russian cruelty and duplicity. The Liberal *Spectator* dismissed the third volume of Martin's biography as no more than 'a party pamphlet' in support of Disraeli and in opposition to Gladstone. The Ottoman sultan was more tolerant of his Jewish subjects than was the (Eastern Orthodox) Christian czar, and Disraeli was sometimes criticised for letting his Jewish birth determine the foreign policy of Great Britain. Yet Judaism had obviously determined neither Lord Palmerston's suspicion of the Russian Empire in the 1850s nor Queen Victoria's hostility in the 1870s. Nor was the queen deterred by the fact that, in 1874, Czar Alexander II had paid a friendly visit to Windsor after his only daughter had married her second son, Prince Alfred.

'The Crisis has begun and I shall need all of Y[ou]r Majesty's support.' Those were Prime Minister Disraeli's words to Queen Victoria at a garden party on July 13, 1877. The monarch needed no such prompting. She was already preoccupied with worries about the implications for her empire of the war that had broken out between Russia and Turkey. In her daily journal, the queen included detailed descriptions of the battles of Shipka Pass and Plevna among other such 'most interesting and fearful things.' She also set forth full descriptions of the attitude of every major member of Disraeli's cabinet towards Britain's policy in the Near East. Time and again she admonished her 'peace at any price' foreign secretary, Lord Derby, and she criticised her colonial secretary, Lord Carnarvon, to his face for 'tamely submitting to Russia's ambition.' According to Victoria's own account, 'he looked like a naughty schoolboy who was being scolded.' The queen did everything in her power to strengthen Disraeli's hand against the cabinet pacifists and to insist on a pointed warning to Czar Alexander II that, if Russian troops seized Constantinople, then Britain would declare war. In the opinion of Queen Victoria's private secretary, 'she is more determined and energetic than her Ministers.' On one occasion, in order to emphasise her personal support, she and her youngest daughter Princess Beatrice made a much-publicised visit to Disraeli's country estate, Hughenden Manor.

At times the queen's militancy became too much even for her sympathetic prime minister. As he complained to one of his confidantes in July 1877, she 'writes every day, and telegraphs every hour' as she sought to mastermind a conflict that she had come to envisage as a personal struggle for supremacy between the czar and herself. The queen had no desire, she told Disraeli early in 1878, 'to remain the Sovereign of a country that is letting itself down to kiss the feet of the great barbarians, the retarders of all liberty and civilisation that exists. . . . Oh, if the Queen were a man she would like to go and give those Russians . . . such a beating!'[27] As things turned out, the queen did not abdicate nor did she lead her army into battle, but she did play a major role in persuading the Disraeli ministry to strengthen Britain's army, to send a British fleet to Constantinople, to encourage Lords Derby and Carnarvon to resign from the cabinet, to deter Russia from war with Britain, and in the course of the year 1878 to transform the one-sided Treaty of San Stefano into the far more acceptable Treaty of Berlin.

The latter treaty emerged from a month-long conference of representatives of the great powers in the German capital, over which

Bismarck presided. Disraeli broke with tradition by attending in person and by addressing the Congress of Berlin in English rather than in French – for the previous two hundred years *the* language of international diplomacy. He also kept a diary of the proceedings especially for the queen. During a private conversation with Bismarck in which the chancellor complained about the duplicitous manner in which the German emperor and members of his family had treated him, Disraeli responded that, in contrast, the sovereign whom he served was 'the soul of candour and justice . . . whom all Ministers loved.' So, at least, he reported to Queen Victoria. After long negotiations and the issuing of an ultimatum, Disraeli was able to report back to his monarch: 'Russia surrenders and accepts the English scheme for the European frontier of the [Ottoman] Empire.' The Russian quest for direct access to the Mediterranean Sea had been foiled once more at the same time that a defensive convention between Turkey and Britain ceded to Britain the island of Cyprus as Britain's chief future base in that part of the world. His monarch's appreciation was profound: 'It is all due to your energy and firmness.'[28]

Soon thereafter Disraeli and the new foreign secretary, Lord Salisbury, returned to London as heroes. At Number 10 Downing Street the prime minister assured a cheering crowd that, even as he and Salisbury had avoided war with Russia, they had returned from Berlin bearing 'Peace and Honour.' Queen Victoria was in raptures. She named both Disraeli and Salisbury Knights of the Garter, and she would gladly have raised Disraeli from an earldom to a dukedom – but he declined the honor. 'The Convention and the possession of Cyprus has given immense satisfaction to the country,' she assured her prime minister. 'High and low are delighted, excepting Mr Gladstone, who is frantic.'[29] According to *The Times* of London, Disraeli was now 'at the pinnacle of Ministerial Renown, the favourite of his Sovereign and the idol of Society.'[30]

Some historians have contended that the longer the queen conferred on an almost daily basis with Disraeli and the more frequent the exchanges of flowers, pleasantries, civilities, and courtesies between them, the more did she become a convert to Disraeli's form of Victorian conservatism. To the extent that such conservatism involved an elevation of the status of the monarchy and of other traditional British institutions, this assessment is accurate. It is true also to the extent that it involved looking upon Britain's heterogeneous overseas empire as a reason for pride rather than as a source of anxiety, difficulty, and expense – as Melbourne and sometimes Albert had done and as Gladstone still did. Yet as late as 1883 the queen would insist that 'I will yield to none in true liberalism,'[31] and she accepted the fact that her chief epistolary confidante, her eldest daughter, defined herself proudly as a 'liberal . . . a staunch and true one from deep conviction.'[32] The queen was equally aware that, like his predecessor General Grey, Sir Henry Ponsonby, her private secretary from 1870 to 1895, was politically a Liberal rather than a Conservative. Yet the thought of dismissing him never occurred to her. Admittedly, Ponsonby was a master diplomat, and time and again he served his mistress as a moderating force by persuading her to tone down her initial anger when men and events misbehaved. In his dealings with Disraeli, as the latter readily conceded, Ponsonby was 'scrupulously on his guard to be always absolutely fair.'[33]

Whatever her misgivings about some of the Gladstonian reforms of 1868–74, she reminded Disraeli soon after he gained office that it was 'essential to the well-being of the British Constitution' that his ministry not attempt 'a *retrograde* policy which would alarm the country'; that would be '*very* dangerous.'[34] The queen's Liberal tendencies remained notable with regard to Church appointments. She was prepared to acknowledge that Conservative ministries depended to a significant degree on the political support of Church of England clerics, but in 1875 she cautioned her prime minister that

> there are far *larger* questions at *stake* which the Queen, who has anxiously and carefully watched the subject for years . . . is bound to regard as all-important. . . . The Church is in *great danger* from its divisions within, and from the outward danger of Romanism and Popery, as well as from Atheism and Materialism, and the only way to counteract this is by promoting pious, intelligent, well-informed, moderate, but large-minded and liberal-minded men in the Church.[35]

In the queen's eyes, one example of clerical obtuseness was the opposition of the Anglican Church to a widower legally marrying a sister of his late wife, even though she was in every respect the appropriate choice and both parties were agreed. The theological objections impressed Victoria as spurious, and in 1879 the Prince of Wales personally presented a petition in favor of a Marriage with Deceased Wife's Sister Bill. The House of Commons approved the measure, but episcopal pressure caused the House of Lords to turn it down. 'Incredible!' was the queen's reaction. Although such a measure was debated almost every year, not until 1907 was that particular reform to become law. Analogously, just as back in the 1850s the queen had advocated that bands be allowed to play in Hyde Park on Sundays, so in the 1870s she strongly favored the opening of museums on that day. In her judgment, a rigid sabbatarianism did not make the lower classes more pious; it merely encouraged them to consume more alcohol. The queen also gave warm approval to a measure permitting non-Anglican Protestants to bury their dead in parish churchyards.[36]

Although the queen held no strong feelings about most social legislation, she pictured herself as a champion of the poor. Therefore, when Gladstone's ministry added to its proposed budget a new tax on matches, she protested strongly. Such a tax

> will be at once felt by all classes, to whom matches have become a necessity of life. Their greatly increased price will in all probability make no difference in the consumption by the rich; but the poorer *classes* will be *constantly* irritated by this increased expense. . . . Above all it seems *certain* that the tax will seriously affect the manufacturer and the sale of matches, which is said to be the sole means of support of a vast number of the very poorest and little children, especially in London, so that this tax, which it is intended should press on all equally, will in fact be only severely felt by the poor, which would be very wrong.[37]

The queen's objections were echoed by thousands of London matchmakers, and Prime Minister Gladstone's government ultimately decided to withdraw the proposal. When, a decade later, another Liberal government proposed to increase the tax on beer, the queen was similarly indignant. Whereas the 'richer classes who drink wine . . . can well afford to pay for wine,' she pointed out, 'the poor can ill afford any additional tax on what in many parts is about their only beverage.'[38] She even anticipated the 'welfare state' liberalism of the twentieth century in supporting government-sponsored slum clearance, and in 1884 she encouraged her son, the Prince of Wales, to become an active member of the Royal Commission on the Housing of the Working Classes.

During the Disraeli ministry of 1874–80, the queen was responsible for at least one other non-party measure that may readily be interpreted as 'liberal.' Throughout her life she was devoted to animals. 'How are all your dogs?' she asked her eldest daughter in 1875. 'I feel so much for animals – poor, confiding, faithful, kind things and do all I can to prevent cruelty to them which is one of the worst signs of wickedness in human nature!'[39] Did animals have souls? In defiance of the teachings of theologians, the queen felt persuaded they did – at least 'the very intelligent and highly developed ones.'[40] The anti-vivisection measure of 1876, which forbade cruelty when animals were used in scientific research, was passed at the queen's direct initiative.[41]

'What nerve! What muscle! What energy!'[42] That was Disraeli's private appraisal of the queen at the age of sixty. In the course of the previous decade, Victoria had demonstrated that energy not only in her involvement with matters of state, foreign and domestic, but also in her continued preoccupation with the lives, the marriages, and the concerns of her nine children and an increasing number of grandchildren. 'Believe me,' she told her eldest daughter in 1870, 'children are a terrible anxiety and . . . the sorrow they cause is far greater than the pleasure they give.' Sir Theodore Martin had remarked to her only the other day that he had ceased to regret his childless state because he had met so many 'parents whose hearts were broken, and lives rendered miserable by bad or thoughtless children. Believe me a large family is a misfortune.'[43] Six years later she reiterated that

> the very large family with their increasing families and interests is an immense difficulty & I must add – burden to me! Without a Husband and father, the labour of satisfying all (which is impossible), & of being just & fair & kind – and yet keeping often quiet which is what I require so much – is quite fearful![44]

Yet even Queen Victoria took quiet satisfaction in 1879 in the news that at the age of fifty-nine she had become a great-grandmother.

'Your Majesty has become "the mother of many nations",' Disraeli exulted, 'and your Majesty is still in the freshness and fullness of life.'[45]

During these same years, the queen kept her eldest daughter as her favorite epistolary confidante, and she remained in close touch with her other children also. Often she found it easier, indeed, to write to them than to talk to them, and, like her cabinet ministers, they sometimes used her private secretary, Sir Henry Ponsonby, as buffer and intermediary. Her daughter Alice had served as a comfort during the months immediately after Albert's death, and so for a time did her third daughter Princess Helena (Lenchen), who remained part of the court circle even after her marriage in 1866 to an obscure German prince. The somewhat dowdy Helena had been fearful of finding any husband at all, and she appeared happy with her dull, bald, and penniless spouse who was fifteen years older than she. In the queen's eyes Prince Christian possessed one significant redeeming feature: he was willing to live and to raise his family of four children at Windsor under his mother-in-law's eagle eye. A few years later, while Helena was in the South of France recuperating from an illness, the queen even agreed to serve as baby-sitter for the quartet, of whom the youngest, Louise, was not quite two. Victoria despatched to her daughter the following telegram of reassurance: 'Children very well, but poor little Louise very ugly.' Once she had grown up, Louise was to remonstrate: 'Grandmama, how could you send such an unkind telegram'? 'My dear child,' responded the queen, 'it was only the truth!'[46]

Sometimes her offspring were no comfort at all. When the queen was seriously ill during the autumn of 1871, the Master of the Queen's Household was asked why her children had not been summoned to her bedside. 'Good heavens!' he protested, 'that would have killed her at once.'[47] As the monarch's private secretary diplomatically explained on one occasion, Victoria loved her children 'generically not individually.'[48]

After Helena's marriage, it was Louise, the queen's fourth daughter, who often served as her mother's prime female companion – even though at times she proved 'dreadfully contradictory' and regrettably 'indiscreet.' She may not have been as clever as Vicky or Alice but she was by far the prettiest of the lot, and readily evident were her artistic talents not only as a painter but also as a sculptor. Her mother agreed to the employment of private tutors, and in 1868 she even permitted her daughter to study modeling at the National Art Training School in Kensington; Louise thus became the first princess to attend an educational institution open to the public. Louise's marble bust of her mother was exhibited by the Royal Academy in 1869 and won wide acclaim. At school she came to know a number of commoners and began to develop sympathy for such novel notions as higher education for women and the right to vote.

By 1870 her mother decided that the time had come for Louise to marry and that it might even be appropriate, in this instance, for a royal princess to marry not another German princeling but a British commoner. The man chosen was admittedly a most uncommon commoner. The Marquess of Lorne was the eldest son of the 8th Duke of Argyll, Scotland's most eminent nobleman, the chief of the Campbell clan, and a member of Gladstone's cabinet of 1868–74, while Lorne was himself an elected Liberal member of the House of Commons. The Prince of Wales privately objected to the marriage, and the Prussian royal family deplored the *mésalliance*, but at the wedding, in March 1871 Queen Victoria herself gave away the bride, the first daughter of a reigning monarch to marry a non-royal since Henry VIII's sister had wed the Duke of Suffolk back in 1515. A Radical minority in the House of Commons had objected to successive marriage settlements for Victoria's children, but in this instance the Commons approved the £30,000 marriage settlement and the £6,000 annuity with but three negative votes. As *The Times* observed, 'The daughter of the Queen, with her mother's full consent, descends from the charmed heights of Royalty and marries a subject. What can the most advanced Liberal object to in that?'[49]

Although Princess Louise was initially happy with her husband, with whom she shared many common interests, she felt frustrated as the sole child of the queen not to have children of her own – an after-effect, in all likelihood, of the serious case of tubercular meningitis that Louise had contracted in adolescence. Her time in Canada – after her husband had been named Governor-General at Disraeli's behest – was marred by a serious sleighing accident, and during the 1880s the couple drifted apart. Art and philanthropy preoccupied the princess's later years. Louise's full-length statue of the young Queen Victoria was unveiled in 1893; it continues to stand in the garden of Kensington Palace, the princess's own home for much of her long life, which did not end until 1939.

In Queen Victoria's eyes, the least satisfactory of her children was her second son Prince Alfred, who in 1866 was named Duke of Edinburgh. His long naval career should have pleased his mother, and on occasion she did find cause to praise him as 'a very dear, clever, charming companion.' More often than not, however, she found fault with his sexual escapades and with the manner in which he had been ruined by 'fine society.' He 'displeased high and low, and made mischief,' and he was intermittently a cause of 'bitter anguish' and of 'great, great grief.' After Alfred had loudly quarreled at Balmoral Castle with John Brown, the queen insisted that 'I won't have naval discipline introduced here.' For at least a decade she searched among Continental princesses to provide her son with a suitable wife, but he insisted on choosing his own, the Grand-Duchess Marie, the only daughter of Czar Alexander II of Russia. Such a match did not cheer either the czar or the queen, but both eventually gave way. The queen was not present at the wedding, at which her son wore the uniform of a Russian naval captain; it was celebrated in St Petersburg in January 1874 by an Eastern Orthodox priest. Not since the Revolution of 1688 had a member of Britain's royal family married a non-Protestant.[50] Whatever her reservations about the background of her new daughter-in-law, Victoria came to look on Marie as genial, even-tempered, and well-read. Marie may not have been particularly pretty, but she possessed a surprisingly good command of spoken English. The marriage, which produced five children, was reasonably happy for a decade. Thereafter the couple were often separated as Alfred pursued his naval career as Commander-in-Chief of Britain's Mediterranean fleet. His final years, during which he succeeded his Uncle Ernest (Albert's brother) as Duke of Coburg, were overshadowed both by alcoholism and by cancer of the tongue.[51]

Relations with her second daughter, Princess Alice, who had become the beloved Grand-Duchess of Hesse-Darmstadt, were also intermittently troubled. Victoria took a keen interest in her life, however, and in that of the Hesse grandchildren, and she was devastated late in 1878 when diphtheria struck the household. One of the children succumbed, and in the process of tending them, Alice contracted the disease herself. On the fatal December 14 – the date of Albert's death – Alice died also. As the queen lamented in her journal, 'Our darling precious Alice, one of my beloved five daughters, gone, after but six days' illness, gone for ever from this world, which is not, thank God, our permanent home!'[52] 'Look on me as a mother,' the queen urged upon her Hesse grandchildren, especially Victoria, the eldest, who would in due course become the grandmother of the current Duke of Edinburgh, the husband of Queen Elizabeth II.[53]

Leopold, Queen Victoria's youngest son, led a difficult life. He was afflicted by hemophilia, a genetic predisposition for which the queen served as carrier but that she was reluctant to acknowledge publicly. She was very much aware, however, that the slightest injury might threaten the boy's life; she therefore sought to wrap him in a protective cocoon and to make him, for a time, a veritable prisoner at Windsor and at Balmoral. The queen loved her Highland home, but Leopold came to see it as 'that *most vile* and *most abominable* of Places.' He also came to look on John Brown's younger brother, the valet whom she imposed on her son for nine years, as an insolent, impudent, and '*infernal blackguard*.'[54] 'Will the Queen never find out,' her private secretary wondered, 'that she will have ten times more influence on her children by treating them with kindness and not trying to rule them like a despot?'[55]

Leopold was by far the most studious of her four sons, and his protective mother reluctantly agreed to let him attend Oxford University. There he gloried in the company of the families of Henry Acland (the head of the Oxford Medical Faculty), Dean Henry George Liddell (the father of the Alice who inspired *Alice in Wonderland*), John Ruskin (the eminent art historian and critic), and Professor Max Müller (one of the leading linguists of the era). Leopold delighted in the cultural life of the university, and he subsequently became an eloquent advocate of the expansion of educational facilities, of the teaching of the deaf, of the curbing of air and water pollution by expanding public parks, and of better medical care for victims of epilepsy and tuberculosis. In 1882 he became one of the founders of the Royal College of Music. That was also the year during which Leopold, newly named Duke of Albany, was permitted to marry a German princess. One of his two children, Alice, the Duchess of Athlone, was to live long enough to participate in 1977 in Queen Elizabeth II's Silver Jubilee procession, but Leopold himself died in March 1884 – of a fall and a subsequent hemorrhage. For his mother, Leopold's death came as 'an awful blow' but not as a surprise; 'his young life was a succession of trials and sufferings though he was so happy in his marriage. And there was such a restless longing for what he could not have.'[56]

A year before Leopold's had come another death, one that affected the queen's daily routine in a far more immediate fashion. For two decades John Brown had been at her side almost every day, not only in Britain but also on her travels each spring to Germany or Switzerland or France, but then on March 27, 1883, he died. Only a few days earlier Victoria had suffered a bad fall at Windsor Castle, and so she was unable to visit his deathbed. As she lamented to her eldest daughter,

> I am crushed by the violence of this unexpected blow. . . . [T]he one who since '64 had helped to cheer me, to smooth, ease and facilitate everything for my daily comfort and who was my dearest best friend to whom I could speak quite openly is not here to help me . . . ! He protected me so, was so powerful and strong – that I felt so safe![57]

Nor did the queen keep her grief a secret from the wider public. Indeed, she compared the loss of Brown in 1883 quite candidly to the loss of Albert in 1861. Brown's body lay in state for six days prior to an elaborate funeral, and the queen compiled a scrapbook of tributes to him. She also commissioned one of the leading sculptors of the day, Sir Edgar Boehm, to memorialise the rugged Highlander in a life-size bronze statue that stood guard over the queen while she worked through her despatch boxes in the garden at Balmoral. The plinth bore lines proposed by Alfred Lord Tennyson, the poet laureate:

> Friend more than servant, Loyal, Truthful, Brave,
> Self less than Duty, even to the Grave[58]

In the case of Albert, the queen had commissioned a multi-volume biography. In the case of her faithful servant, she began to draft a *Life of John Brown* herself and sprinkled it with excerpts from the gillie's own diary. Members of her household were aghast – not because they expected the monarch to include such revelations as a secret marriage but because of doubts (that were tactfully expressed by Sir Henry Ponsonby) whether 'this record of Your Majesty's innermost and most sacred feelings' should be revealed to the world. Her courtiers' underlying premise was that monarchs did *not* write biographies of servants. It was Randall Davidson, as Dean of Windsor the queen's private chaplain (and a future Archbishop of Canterbury), who with enormous difficulty at length persuaded Victoria that the book should not be completed, and it was Ponsonby who ultimately consigned the manuscript pages to the flames.

The queen had to make do with the publication in 1884 of *More Leaves from the Journal of Our Life in the Highlands*, a compilation in which the name of John Brown appeared far more often than did that of Victoria's eldest son. The first volume of such excerpts had been dedicated to the memory of Prince Albert. This second volume (which dealt with the post-Albert years) was dedicated 'gratefully' to 'MY LOYAL HIGHLANDERS, and especially to the memory of my devoted personal attendant and faithful friend JOHN BROWN.'[59] The queen's children might remain privately dubious about such a publication, but the book received numerous friendly reviews – especially in provincial newspapers – and Victoria felt as certain as ever that she knew 'perfectly well what my people like and appreciate and that is "home life" and simplicity.'[60]

Such involvement with family and household affairs did not prevent the queen from maintaining a keen interest in the wider world. The Congress of Berlin in 1878 had marked the highpoint of Disraeli's prime ministership, but the next two years proved far more difficult for his ministry. Responsible in part was a war in South Africa; there, in the process of seeking to preserve peace between the Zulus and the Transvaal (the republic that had been fashioned by the descendants of Dutch settlers, the Boers), a British force met defeat at the hands of Zulu spear-throwers. The Boers, who had temporarily agreed to British annexation, now rebelled against British authority. In the meantime, the British Viceroy of India was seeking to turn Afghanistan into a friendly buffer state between the expanding Russian Empire to the north and British India to the south. He eventually succeeded, but not before a British minister to Kabul and his entire entourage had been massacred by a group of Afghan army mutineers.

Queen Victoria took greater satisfaction in such extensions of British influence than did her prime minister, even if there was a price to be paid, both in money and in lives – including in 1879 that of the Prince Imperial, the only son of the widowed Empress Eugénie of France. He had insisted on seeking military glory by accompanying a British force to South Africa. That same year the queen felt compelled to caution Disraeli not to cut the nation's defence budget:

> NEVER *let the Army and Navy* DOWN *so low as to be obliged* to go to *great expense* in a hurry. . . . *If we are to maintain* our position as a *first-rate* Power . . . we must, with our Indian Empire and large Colonies, be *prepared* for *attacks* and *wars somewhere* or *other* CONTINUALLY. And the *true economy* will be *to be always ready.*[61]

Events abroad combined with misfortunes at home to undermine the second Disraeli ministry. The mid-Victorian economic boom had given way by the later 1870s to a period of depression as international trade slowed and business profits fell. British agriculture was particularly hard hit; traditional wheat growers were beset not only with bad harvests but also with foreign competition. Grain was being transported ever more speedily and cheaply from the American midwest by a growing flotilla of steam-powered merchant vessels. Because it remained a predominantly rural country, Ireland suffered even more from the depression in agriculture than did Great Britain. Irish tenant farmers were far less likely to blame Americans for their plight, however, than Protestant landlords at home and the British government across the Irish Sea. By 1879, a militant Irish Land League headed by Michael Davitt and Charles Stewart Parnell was providing a mass popular base for an Irish Home Rule Party in the House of Commons that was acting in an ever more obstructive manner.

At the same time William Ewart Gladstone, still technically a mere back-bencher at Westminster, had become a parliamentary candidate for the Scottish county of Midlothian and was waging a whistle-stop campaign against 'Beaconsfieldism.' The one-time Tory was transforming himself into the most popular leader of Britain's first age of mass party politics. In domestic affairs, Gladstone upheld financial probity rather than unbalanced budgets. In foreign affairs, Gladstone insisted, Britain should neither act unilaterally nor attempt to dominate others. He therefore condemned Disraeli's concern with the advance of British *interests* and the upholding of Britain's *honour* – words that Gladstone found meaningless if they could not be reconciled with the cause of international justice, of humanity, of civilisation, and of religion. For Gladstone, the annexation of Cyprus had constituted an 'insane covenant' and 'an act of duplicity.' For Disraeli, Gladstone had become 'a sophistical rhetorician inebriated with the exuberance of his own verbosity' who was conducting a campaign of 'rhodomontade and rigmarole.'[62]

The results of the general election of 1880 came as an understandable disappointment to Disraeli and as a far deeper one to Queen Victoria herself: 347 Liberals, 240 Conservatives, 65 Irish Home Rulers. She confessed to Disraeli her 'intense astonishment, distress, and annoyance' at the outcome.[63] Only a year before, she had privately insisted that 'I could never take Mr Gladstone . . . as my Minister again, for I never COULD have the slightest *particle* of confidence in Mr. Gladstone *after* his violent, mischievous, and dangerous conduct for the last three years.'[64] Inasmuch as Lord Granville was the Liberal leader in the House of Lords, and the Marquess of Hartington[65] was the elected Liberal leader in the House of Commons, it was constitutionally proper for the queen – after Disraeli had resigned office – to invite Hartington to form a Liberal government. Hartington soon made it clear to her, however, that a Liberal ministry without Gladstone would be an absurdity and that, although he had formally resigned the Liberal Party leadership five years earlier, Gladstone would refuse subordinate office. Recognising with regret that she had no alternative, the queen did in due course invite Gladstone to form a ministry, one in which he intended to serve as both prime minister and as Chancellor of the Exchequer. With minor cavils, she also accepted his recommendations for the holders of cabinet and sub-cabinet office. Before she would agree to the naming of Sir Charles Dilke as under-secretary for foreign affairs, however, she insisted on a lengthy 'written explanation' of the anti-royalist sentiments that Dilke had voiced a decade earlier. She took what comfort she could in the thought that Gladstone 'looks very ill, very old and haggard and his voice [is] feeble.'[66] Gladstone's second ministry was to endure for the next five years.

Even as Gladstone sought to live up to the lofty principles enunciated in his 'Midlothian Campaign', he found the first two years of his second ministry mired in intermittent defeat and disorder both abroad and at home. As before, he saw himself as a friend to Ireland, and yet both Home Rule Party obstruction in the House of Commons, and land agitation, in the form of damage to property and refusals to pay rent, reached a fever pitch between the summer of 1880 and the spring of 1882. In the course of 1881, Gladstone piloted through Parliament a momentous Irish Land Act designed to provide Irish tenant farmers with the 'Three Fs' they had long sought (fair rent, free sale, and fixity of tenure). The queen corresponded with Gladstone repeatedly while the measure was being drafted and debated. She agreed that 'To do justice to the Tenants is right, but,' she went on to warn, 'if this is done at the expense of the innocent Landlord, the feeling of insecurity which exists in Ireland will be increased & capital, which is so much wanted there will fly *from* instead of *to* that Country.'[67] In the short run, such epic legislation failed to still the storm, and Gladstone reluctantly felt compelled to agree with the queen that sticks were required as much as carrots – in the form of Acts temporarily suspending the right of habeas corpus and restricting the importation of fire-arms. In October 1881 Gladstone at last agreed to use such laws to suppress the Land League and to arrest Charles Stewart Parnell on charges of criminal incitement. In the queen's eyes, such steps should have been taken much earlier and in a more comprehensive fashion. 'The queen hopes,' she wrote to Gladstone in December 1881,

> that *greater* efforts may be made to arrest the agitators who have created this state of affairs, to protect her loyal subjects and to punish those who are intimidating and alarming the well affected inhabitants. . . . If the *law* is powerless to punish wrong-doers, let increased powers be sought for and at *any rate* let no *effort* be spared for *putting an end to a state of affairs* which is a *disgrace to any civilised* country.[68]

The situation in Ireland did improve somewhat in the course of the next several years, and Parnell and his major lieutenants were released from gaol. In the meantime the House of Commons had changed its rules so as to make it far more difficult for a small minority to obstruct parliamentary business.

The queen was often as unhappy with Gladstone's foreign policy as with his Irish policy. Thus the insistence of the Liberal cabinet of including in the annual Queen's Speech of 1881 the decision to evacuate a British force from the Afghan city of Kandahar led to a constitutional contretemps. At the very time that a friendly amir had been installed on the Afghan throne, it impressed Victoria as absurd to show such military weakness. 'It may lead to another war,' she insisted, 'and so many more precious lives [may] be sacrificed.' The Liberal cabinet insisted and, after a four-hour argument, the queen gave way, protesting that she had 'never before been treated with such want of respect and consideration in the forty-three and a half years she has worn her thorny crown.' She had apparently lost the battle, but Gladstone felt compelled to hold a special cabinet meeting, to send a profuse apology, and to assure his monarch that, if circumstances arose making it desirable to continue to occupy Kandahar, then Britain would hang on.[69]

British forces did not hang on in the Transvaal and Orange Free State. With the Zulu threat overcome, the Boers were rebelling against their British overlords, and in 1881 a small British force was defeated at Majuba Hill. Gladstone, who had disapproved of the original annexation, decided to conciliate the Boers by restoring to them their independence except for a verbal fig-leaf, Britain's continuing theoretical 'suzerainty' over the two states. 'We must not give way to Boer demands,' Queen Victoria protested in vain. Appeasement at this time, she added, would only lead to a new military conflict with the Boers at a later date.[70] Although she sometimes privately complained that the prime minister talked too much, she was equally unhappy with the fact that, unlike Disraeli, he fobbed her off with generalities whenever she inquired into the details of intra-cabinet disagreements. Gladstone in turn complained privately to an associate in 1882, 'the Queen alone is enough to kill anyone.'[71]

Queen Victoria was happier with Gladstone's approach to Egypt, where the reigning khedive's financial extravagance had led in 1878 to the setting up of an Anglo-French control board to supervise Egyptian finances. Four years later, an outburst of Egyptian nationalism headed by one Colonel Arabi against the khedive and his European advisers led to a *coup d'état* that resulted in the killing in Alexandria of fifty Europeans. At Gladstone's orders, the British navy shelled the port city, and a few weeks later a British army of 14,000 men under General Sir Garnet Wolseley landed in Egypt. One of the brigades was commanded by the queen's third son, Prince Arthur the Duke of Connaught.

Of her four sons, only Arthur, the godson of the Duke of Wellington, had from the first shown promise as a soldier. Even as a child, he became for the queen, next to her husband, 'the *dearest & most precious* object to *me* on Earth.'[72] That sentiment seldom wavered during the decades that followed as Arthur was trained at the Royal Military Academy at Woolwich and then moved rapidly upwards in the ranks from captain in the Rifle Brigade to cavalry officer to Adjutant-General in Gibraltar to Lieutenant-Colonel in command of an army battalion in Dublin. At the Battle of Tel-el-Kebir in August 1882, the far smaller British force defeated 30,000 Egyptian rebels, and Arthur demonstrated his personal courage in battle. Queen Victoria's joy was unbounded. 'Perhaps not many Mothers may feel as proud as I do,' she explained, 'but I am so devoted to the Army.' It was an 'indescribable moment' for the queen to welcome the troops home to London and personally to award a victory medal to her cherished son. Arthur's military career continued both in India and in Ireland, where in 1895 he became Commander-in-Chief of the British army there. According to the queen, her soldier son was 'so like dear Papa – so dear & good & *wise* [and] such a help to me.' As she lamented to him on more than one occasion, 'Oh, if only *you* were the *eldest*.'

Having subdued Egypt and, in effect, turned that state into a British protectorate, Gladstone spent the remainder of his ministry in trying to extricate Britain from its new, but unintended, responsibilities. If the British could not withdraw from Egypt right away, they could at least relinquish all Egyptian claims to the territory to the south, the Sudan. General Charles 'Chinese' Gordon, a flamboyant soldier–adventurer, was unwisely entrusted with the task of supervising that evacuation.

He decided instead to make a stand to keep Khartoum and the Nile valley in Anglo-Egyptian hands in the face of attacks by the fanatical Sudanese Mahdi ('Messiah') and his followers. Gladstone's cabinet disagreed with Gordon's decision, but it delayed – against the advice of experts in Africa and of Queen Victoria at Windsor – in authorising a relief expedition up the Nile to bring back General Gordon. Eventually a relief force was sent, but it did not reach Khartoum until January 28, 1885, two days after the rebels had stormed the city and had killed General Gordon. No single event in his long career made Gladstone more unpopular; for many, the G.O.M. ('Grand Old Man') was transformed into the M.O.G. ('Murderer of Gordon'). The telegram from the queen to the prime minister was almost as scathing: 'These news from Khartoum are frightful and to think that all this might have been prevented and many precious lives saved by earlier action is too fearful.'[73] Ordinarily all telegrams exchanged between monarch and prime minister were sent in cypher. This telegram was sent by the queen *en clair.*

Privately the queen had been scathing about Gladstone from the onset of the second ministry. In 1880 he was the 'half-crazy enthusiast . . . ruining all the good of 6 years [of] peaceful, wise government.' In 1883 he was 'a very dangerous unaccountable man' and in 1885 he was 'the old sinner.'[74] The actual letters and telegrams exchanged between monarch and minister were, for the most part, eminently civil in tone, however, and from time to time, Queen Victoria even paid 'the People's William' a sincere compliment. Thus she was '*much gratified*' by Gladstone's speech proposing the raising of a monument to Disraeli after the latter's death in April 1881. She was similarly pleased by the joint congratulatory address from both Houses of Parliament that was moved a year later after she had escaped by inches an attempted assassination by a young man firing a revolver. It was the seventh such attempt of her reign and the last. 'It is very rare,' she admitted, 'that people are so kindly & lovingly spoken of & *appreciated* in their *life-time* as has fallen to *her* lot.'[75]

The queen had no overriding objection to the most important domestic legislative measure of the second Gladstone ministry, the Reform Bill of 1884. It enlarged the electorate from 3,160,000 to 5,700,000 by enfranchising rural laborers and indeed almost all men who either owned or rented the homes in which they lived. Gladstone was initially furious when the House of Lords, led by Lord Salisbury, refused its assent until both Houses had also agreed to a mutually acceptable Redistribution of Seats Bill. Gladstone was tempted for a time to use the obstinacy of the peers to introduce a measure permanently limiting the power of the House of Lords to block legislation: 'Peers versus People!'; 'Mend them or end them!'

When Gladstone pointed out to the monarch that the House of Lords had repeatedly opposed the will of the people, Queen Victoria disagreed. Was it not more likely, she responded, that on the subject of a Redistribution Bill, the upper chamber represented 'the true feeling of the country'? In any event, she went on,

> the existence of an independent body of men acting solely for the good of the country, and free from the terror which forces so many Commoners to vote against their consciences, is an element of strength in the State, and a guarantee for its welfare and freedom.[76]

The queen continued to urge conciliation on both major parties, however, and ultimately Gladstone had no desire to fight a new general election on the old electoral register. Eventually, indeed, even Gladstone felt compelled to acknowledge 'all the well-timed efforts your Majesty has graciously made . . . to avert a great public mischief and a fierce controversy.'[77] A conference in November 1884 involving the Liberal and Conservative leaders rapidly agreed on a surprisingly radical seat redistribution scheme. Henceforth a majority of parliamentary seats would be not double-member but single-member constituencies approximately equal in population. Henceforth it was to be the individual voter rather than a historic community that a Member of Parliament represented. Soon thereafter both the Reform Bill and the accompanying Redistribution Bill became law.

Like most Britons of the day, Queen Victoria was less conscious of the radical theoretical implications of these reform measures than of the inter-party cooperation that had brought them into being. She was increasingly aware also of the fact that in the aftermath, during the early months of 1885, Gladstone's divided Liberal ministry was falling apart. In June 1885 it suffered a vote of 'no confidence' on a budget measure and resigned. She decided that Lord Salisbury (the

Conservative leader in the House of Lords since Disraeli's death) would make a stronger prime minister than would Sir Stafford Northcote (the Conservative leader in the House of Commons since 1876), and she invited Salisbury to form a ministry. He agreed to head a minority government pending the general election due as soon as a revised electoral register had been prepared. The queen once again offered Gladstone an earldom as a farewell gift and as 'a signal mark of recognition of Mr Gladstone's long and eminent career.'[78] He respectfully declined that honor once more. Although an unusually tumultuous political year lay ahead for the queen, she was vastly relieved that Gladstone was no longer her prime minister and that her kingdom's constitution, though altered in detail, had been duly preserved.

9 *The Official Diamond Jubilee Portrait* (1897)
Signed and dated 'Victoria R 1837–1897'. Taken by W. & D. Downey.
(Courtesy of The Royal Archives; © Her Majesty Queen Elizabeth II and the
photographer)

9 The Imperial Matriarch

The final fifteen years of Queen Victoria's reign took on a flavor all their own. Several previously distinct strands of her long life became interwoven. First of all, there was her continuing absorption with the details of both foreign and domestic affairs. As she was to remind a fledgling foreign secretary in 1886, 'She has nearly fifty years' experience and has always watched particularly and personally over foreign affairs, and therefore knows them well.'[1] At home she became preoccupied with the task of preventing the advocates of Irish Home Rule from breaking up her kingdom. Historians who imply that, as Queen Victoria aged, her interest in public affairs flagged and her influence waned, have ignored her detailed correspondence with her leading ministers and her royal relations. As the editor of her letters reminds us, even as she approached and passed the age of eighty the monarch took 'a remarkably active part and interest in affairs'[2] and several cabinet ministers and at least one prime minister owed their appointment to her direct intervention.

Secondly, during these same years, the queen remained as concerned as before with her ever-growing family of grandchildren and great-grandchildren. It was during those years that she truly became 'the Grandmother of Europe.' It was during this era also that 'the scramble for Africa' and an expansion of British influence in East Asia caused the Victorian Empire to become greater in territorial extent and in population than ever before. When Walter Bagehot had set forth the queen's 'dignified' roles in The English Constitution (1867), it had not occurred to him to cite 'head of the heterogeneous British Empire' among them. Yet that had become her most significant role by the 1890s, and she took a keen personal interest in the Empire, especially in the Crown Colony of India. During the final years of the century that Empire was publicised and celebrated as never before as a cause for national pride – and so was the queen herself. The critics of monarchy did not disappear altogether, but never in the course of the century did their voices become more muted and never did the queen, as fountain of honor, as patron of philanthropy, and as symbol of the Victorian virtues, loom larger in the eyes of her subjects. For Queen Victoria, the decade between her Golden Jubilee (1887) and her Diamond Jubilee (1897) constituted an apotheosis.

The prelude to that apotheosis was a rocky one, however, because the apparent wishes of an electorate vastly enlarged by the Reform Act of 1884 did not initially accord with those of the queen. The results of the general election of 1885 decisively favored Gladstone over Salisbury: 335 Liberals; 249 Conservatives; 86 Irish Home Rulers. Some members of Salisbury's minority government – in office since June, 1885 – had drawn close to the Irish party in the course of 1884 and 1885 as fellow opponents of the Liberal government, and Parnell had even urged Irish voters in England to vote for Conservative candidates. The election results undermined, however, any possible long-term Conservative/Irish alliance; it had failed to secure an overall majority. As soon as the election was over, Gladstone began to hint that he was now prepared to introduce into Parliament a measure granting to the Irish both a Parliament and a prime minister of their own to deal with their domestic affairs. At the same time, in matters of foreign policy, defence, and currency, Ireland would remain part of a United Kingdom over which Victoria would continue to reign. Salisbury was still prime minister, but the Irish MPs now flocked to the Gladstone banner, and in late January 1886 they (along with most Liberals) voted 'no confidence' in the Salisbury government. Salisbury resigned, and with a heavy heart the queen felt compelled to call upon the 76-year-old William Ewart Gladstone to form his third ministry. At her insistence, he agreed to include in his cabinet two Scots, the Earl of Rosebery (rather than the aging Earl Granville) as foreign secretary and Sir Henry Campbell-Bannerman as Secretary of State for War.

In April 1886 the prime minister introduced an Irish Home Rule measure in the House of Commons. In Gladstone's judgment, rather than having London govern Ireland by means of repeated 'coercive' Acts, it was far preferable to grant domestic self-government to Ireland. Once the Irish identified the making and the enforcement of the criminal law with a government that they considered truly their own, he argued, then they would become more law-abiding and less radical in outlook. That the Irish wanted such self-government had been proved by the recent election: an electorate that now included a majority of Irish men had just chosen advocates of Home Rule for 85 out of 103 Irish seats in the United Kingdom Parliament.[3] Doubtless, unionists could also still be found throughout much of the Emerald Isle, but only in the eighteen constituencies of north-eastern Ireland, in and around the city of Belfast, did they still constitute the majority.

Queen Victoria did not see the question in such a light, however, and she took comfort in the fact that several leading Liberals (such as the Marquess of Hartington) refused to serve in Gladstone's cabinet and that others (such as Joseph Chamberlain) afterwards resigned. Gladstone's 'peculiar and very objectionable views' demonstrated to her that he had fallen under the spell of Charles Stewart Parnell, a man who had encouraged lawlessness in Ireland and who appeared totally unfit to become Ireland's prime minister. Rather than leading to peace in Ireland, the queen believed, Gladstone's plan was all too likely to break up both her kingdom and her empire. One Irish lady, the wife of the former mayor of Cork, pleaded with the queen to halt Gladstone's appeasement of 'the Irish desperados.' A separate Irish Parliament, she predicted, would plunge the island into 'a state of anarchy, and civil war.'[4] The queen fully concurred with that assessment. Privately she reminded undecided Liberals that 'true loyal patriotism must go before party.' She urged Gladstone himself to reflect on the fact that his proposal was 'condemned almost universally by the Press and by an immense number of the thinking and educated class!'[5]

The one anti-Home Rule argument that the queen did not put forward was that 'Home Rule means Rome Rule,' that a semi-independent Ireland would become an officially Roman Catholic state and would discriminate against its Protestant minority. By the mid-1880s, the queen's earlier anti-Catholic sentiments had faded. Her friendship with the widowed Empress Eugénie of France had played a role. So had her visits to continental Roman Catholic monasteries and convents. So did the supplanting in 1878 of the 'triumphalist' Pius IX by the far more diplomatic Pope Leo XIII. In 1887, indeed, she and Leo XIII exchanged personal letters in French, and she later sent the

pre-eminent English Catholic layman, the Duke of Norfolk, to Rome
to assure the Pope of the queen's 'sincere friendship and unfeigned
respect and esteem.' When a strong protest arrived at Windsor, the
queen commented that the Protestant objectors

> entirely forget how many 1000 Catholic subjects the Queen has who can-
> not be ignored – And it is grievous to think that what w[oul]d be good for
> the peace of Ireland will probably be prevented by these well-meaning but
> fanatical Protestants.[6]

During the spring of 1886 both the House of Commons and the
country at large were absorbed by the debate on the merits of Irish
Home Rule. It was an issue more politically divisive than any that had
preoccupied British politicians since the repeal of the Corn Laws in
1846 or even the Reform Bill of 1832, and a cause for which Gladstone
seemed willing to court political martyrdom. The decisive vote came
on June 8, when the measure was defeated by 343 votes to 313.
Gladstone had the support of all the Irish Nationalists, but 93 Liberals
(almost one-third of his party) voted against him. In the aftermath, the
prime minister asked the queen to dissolve Parliament, a request that
she gladly granted. In the electoral campaign that followed, Gladstone's
unprecedented nationwide speaking tour failed to persuade a majority
of the English electorate. Although he fared better in Welsh, Scottish,
and Irish constituencies, for him the overall results proved bleak: 316
Conservatives, 78 Liberal Unionists, 191 Liberals, 85 Irish Home Rulers.
'The Elections are going quite wonderfully,'[7] exulted the queen.
Gladstone's Liberal Party had split both at the constituency and at the
parliamentary level. Even though Liberal Unionists such as the whiggish Marquess of Hartington and the radical Joseph Chamberlain were
not yet prepared to join Lord Salisbury in a coalition government, they
were willing to heed the queen's plea that they 'support Lord Salisbury's
Government in all important questions . . . so that the country (not to
speak of herself) may not be perpetually exposed to changes of
Government, which . . . paralyse our actions and policy.'[8]

Queen Victoria was delighted with this turn of events. A year before,
she had formed a highly favorable impression of Salisbury as prime
minister. It had proved 'a pleasure and a comfort . . . to transact business with him.' He was a minister 'in whom she could thoroughly

confide, and whose opinion was always given in so kind and wise a manner.'[9] There was nothing flowery or exotic about Salisbury as there had been about Disraeli, but his very presence was reassuring. Only a few months later Lord Randolph Churchill, the self-professed 'Tory Democrat' and the most troublesome member of Salisbury's cabinet, resigned abruptly. The father of Sir Winston Churchill had streaked across the political sky like a meteor, and Queen Victoria conceded that he was immensely 'clever.' Unfortunately he was also 'mad and odd,' 'devoid of all principle,' 'impulsive and utterly unreliable' – and she succeeded in keeping him out of subsequent Conservative cabinets.[10] At the queen's strong urging, a reliable Liberal Unionist, George Joachim Goschen, replaced Churchill as Chancellor of the Exchequer, and soon thereafter Lord Salisbury took over the Foreign Office as well as the prime ministership. Queen Victoria's political world appeared truly in order both at home and abroad, and although the Irish and Liberal opposition repeatedly sought to obstruct the work of the House of Commons, several years of relative stability lay ahead.

The queen's domestic comfort was reconfirmed at about the same time. Like many a Victorian parent, the queen thought it altogether appropriate that her youngest daughter should remain single and at home in order to care for her aging mother. The subject of marriage was never even to be mentioned in the presence of Princess Beatrice. When, on the occasion of her seventeenth birthday, her eldest sister expressed the wish: 'may she be as good a daughter as I trust some day a wife and mother,' Queen Victoria was outraged. Beatrice was never to become a wife or a mother. According to her mother, 'a dearer, sweeter, more amiable and unselfish child I never found'; she was indeed 'My Beloved Baby – who is really the apple of my eye . . . and who I pray God may remain with me for as long as I live for she is the last I have and I could not live without her.' Besides, 'Thank God she is not touchy and offended like several of her brothers and sisters are.'[11]

In the course of two decades, Beatrice did not leave her mother's side for more than a week, and when, aged twenty-eight, she announced that she wished to marry Prince Henry of Battenberg, Queen Victoria was devastated. '[Y]ou . . . cannot imagine,' she told her eldest daughter, 'what agonies, what despair it caused me and what a fearful shock it was to me when I first heard of her wish! It

made me quite ill.'[12] The queen was reconciled in part only when
Beatrice's fiancé assured her that the couple would remain at court
with her and would continue to provide the companionship and care
that she felt her due. In his wedding poem, Tennyson wrote 'The
mother weeps / At that white funeral of the single life.' Beatrice
found the phrase distressing; her mother thought it *apropos*.[13] As
things stood, the queen continued to look on the wedding as 'a great
trial' and to 'hope and pray there may be no *results*! That would aggra-
vate everything and besides make me terribly anxious.'[14] Despite the
queen's apprehensions, there *were* results; Beatrice bore four children
during the ten years of married life that were allotted to her before
her husband died. Beatrice's only daughter was to grow up to
become the grandmother of the current King of Spain, and Beatrice
was to survive her husband by almost five decades.

In 1886 the start of the celebration of the Queen's Jubilee was
announced. It would conclude with a grand procession through
London on June 21, 1887, to mark the fiftieth anniversary of her accession to the throne and the completion of her jubilee year. The roots of
the word *jubilee* may be found both in Hebrew and in Latin. The
Hebrew word *Yobel* stood for the ram's horn that, after every forty-
nine years (seven multiplied by seven), would, according to the Book
of Leviticus, announce a time of emancipation for Hebrew slaves and
of restoration for Hebrew property-owners. At the same time the
Latin word *jubilum* meant a wild cry or shout of the type encountered
in a modern football stadium. The person who, during the Middle
Ages, gave a new lease on life to the concept of a *jubilee* as both 'emancipation' and 'celebration' was Pope Boniface VIII who decreed the
year 1300 to be a Jubilee year. That year sinful Christians might obtain
a remission of the punishment that awaited them in purgatory if they
undertook a pilgrimage to Rome in order to visit churches, fasted, and
gave alms. At first the Church decreed a one-hundred-year interval
between Jubilee years, but later popes reduced that number to fifty,
then thirty-three, then twenty-five.

Although two medieval English kings, Henry III and Edward III,
managed to last on the throne for fifty years or more, neither ever celebrated a Jubilee. The first usage of the phrase in a fashion that anticipated Queen Victoria's came in 1809 when some of the English,

Indian, and West Indian subjects of King George III celebrated his Jubilee, the completion of his forty-ninth year on the throne. No further royal anniversaries were marked during the next half-century, however, and the celebration of the Golden Jubilee in 1887 and the Diamond Jubilee ten years later constituted therefore less a link with an ancient tradition than an essentially novel phenomenon.

The queen did agree early in 1887 that it would be proper to mark the completion of her Jubilee year with a national holiday and an appropriate procession and ceremony of thanksgiving in Westminster Abbey, a building that she had not entered formally since her coronation forty-nine years earlier. She also agreed to open the state dining-room in Buckingham Palace for the first time since Albert's death.[15] Because she considered herself even in 1887 to be in a position of semi-mourning, she refused point-blank, however, to go 'in state' and to wear the robes of purple velvet with the sceptre, the orb, and the ceremonial crown. The Salisbury ministry was aware, at the same time, that MPs belonging to the Irish Home Rule Party and to the radical wing of the Liberal Party were eager to criticise as 'reckless extravagance' any large appropriations bill for Jubilee expenses. When Jubilee plans were first announced, one London paper therefore complained that the occasion 'promises to be a very shabby and tenth-rate affair' and another expressed analogous unhappiness with the prospect of a Jubilee procession that was 'utterly inadequate, mean, pinched, and narrow, and [that] appears to be dictated by a parsimonious spirit unworthy of a rich and powerful state.'[16]

In the meantime Victoria bombarded Lord Salisbury with one objection after another. Her private secretary was informed that he should tell her ministers that 'she will not be teazed & bullied ab[ou]t the Jubilee . . . w[hich] seems to be considered only for the *people* and their *convenience* & amusement while the Queen is to do the public and newspaper bidding. She will do *nothing* if this goes on.'[17] She vetoed her prime minister's suggestion that the Jubilee parade be timed for Monday, June 20, thereby providing Londoners with a three-day weekend; it would have served, Salisbury noted wistfully, 'a very convenient holiday for all working men.'[18] Even in her later years, the queen gave a low priority to ceremonial occasions, and she was as reluctant as ever to spend even one extra day in London.

Circumstantial evidence strongly suggests indeed that to Queen Victoria the Golden Jubilee of 1887 meant less a public celebration than a private day of remembrance. She preferred to celebrate it on the fiftieth rather than the forty-ninth anniversary of her accession because she visualised the occasion as the golden wedding anniversary that fate had denied her. In nineteenth-century Germany, unlike Britain, it had indeed become the custom to refer to the fiftieth wedding anniversary as a *Jubilaeum*. As her Jubilee year began, she was troubled by 'the thought of those no longer with me, who would have been so pleased and happy, in particular my beloved husband, to whom I owe everything.'[19] A *Te Deum* composed by the prince was therefore given pride of place in the Abbey service, and the queen replaced her customary black bonnet with a white bonnet, to which she added her wedding veil and her wedding lace.

When a large group of British women decided to present the queen with a Jubilee gift, the only idea she could come up with was yet another statue of Prince Albert. The organiser candidly told the queen's secretary that if such a purpose were publicly mentioned before the funds had been collected, then 'we have no more chance of obtaining the money for it, than of getting the moon out of the sky.' Eventually, the Women's Jubilee Offering was to involve almost £90,000 – worth about £9,000,000 in 2003. It also involved a congratulatory address to which almost three million female contributors affixed their signatures. Of that amount, £10,000 was indeed used to erect a new equestrian statue of Prince Albert on the Windsor Castle lawn. Another £4,000 was used, at Victoria's request, to purchase for her a jeweled brooch. More than four-fifths of the total amount raised was devoted to the Queen Victoria Jubilee Institute for Nurses, a brand new organisation designed to aid poor, sick people in their own homes.[20]

The queen's most immediate Jubilee concern was with the horde of relations who seemed intent on crossing the English Channel to do her honor. 'Altogether the Queen is appalled at the prospect of these endless visitors,' she told her private secretary. Her son and heir might delight at the presence of 'such a mob of royalties' but 'she owns she knows not she ever can live through it all.' Ultimately she not only endured them, but she filled ten state carriages with them, each pulled by six cream-colored horses, carriages that preceded her own in the two-mile Jubilee procession. They included the kings of Denmark, Belgium, Greece, and Saxony, the Queen of Hawaii, the crown princes of Germany, Austria, and Portugal, and scores of other luminaries from around the globe. Grudgingly she also served them breakfast in Buckingham Palace, a decision for which her prime minister thanked her in so fulsome a manner that one might have imagined that she had cooked the bacon and eggs in person.[21]

As matters turned out, the queen very much enjoyed the 'jubilee breakfast,' which was actually a late-afternoon post-procession meal, just as she enjoyed the grand extended-family meals at Buckingham Palace on the following day. She was also persuaded to add numerous other activities to the Jubilee calendar such as reviews of the army, the navy, and the Volunteers. Almost every city utilised the Jubilee to raise new buildings, to complete public improvements, to erect statues, and to inaugurate new philanthropic institutions. British manufacturers freely used Victoria's picture to advertise perfumes, soaps, pills, cocoa, and fabrics.[22] On sale in London were walking sticks featuring the queen's head as a knob, teapots in the shape of the queen's head with the lid shaped like a crown, and automatic musical Jubilee bustles that played 'God Save the Queen' whenever the wearer sat down.[23] Ultimately Victoria survived all the festivities without undue difficulty, and she publicly thanked her people for their faithful support.

> I was amply repaid [she conceded] for my great exertion and fatigue, by the unbounded enthusiastic loyalty and devotion evinced from all parts of my vast Empire, by high and low, rich and poor, from far and near, which has sunk deep into my heart![24]

The queen even attended a party that had brought 30,000 school children into London's Hyde Park. When a great colored balloon labeled 'Victoria' went aloft, one little girl was heard to remark: 'Look! There's Queen Victoria going to Heaven!'[25] The assessment proved premature.

The queen remained pre-eminently down-to-earth when it came to one monarchical function that political scientists neglected in the nineteenth century and that royal biographers were to overlook during most of the twentieth – the queen as philanthropic patron. Biographers have been keenly conscious of the admitted truth that

Queen Victoria was not a 'social reformer,' in the sense that (like most other Victorians) she did not favor social welfare services paid for by high rates of income tax and administered by a large central government bureaucracy. She strongly believed, however, as did a majority of her subjects, that the locally administered English Poor Law should be supplemented by a multitude of voluntary organisations whose purpose it was to help educate, help medicate, and help house the poorer classes of society and to relieve the victims of natural and man-made disasters. A voluntary charity not only helped its intended recipients but also gave meaning to the lives of the charity organisers: it expressed their religious convictions; it advanced a useful cause; it enhanced their sense of respectability and civic pride; it enabled members of distinct social classes to cooperate for a common purpose. In consequence, by the 1860s, 'most large towns and cities could take satisfaction in voluntary hospitals, infirmaries or dispensaries, asylums, benefit societies, lying-in and maternity charities, ragged schools, national schools, domestic missions, temperance societies and district visiting charities.' Even small villages could boast of their clothing and boot clubs, their mothers' meetings, and their Sunday schools. In 1885 *The Times* marveled that the monies collected that year for London charities alone exceeded the annual budgets of several European nations.[26]

During the Victorian years, philanthropy came to be seen as the particular province of middle-class and upper-class women, who (with rare exceptions) were not expected to engage in paid employment outside the home. It provided them with an opportunity both for self-expression and for the wielding of social influence. Nothing gave greater encouragement to any charitable organisation and nothing caused subscribers to reach for their chequebooks with greater alacrity than did the formal patronage and, ideally, the personal involvement of the queen. Victoria was fully in accord with this prevailing ethos, and in the course of her reign she became the personal patron of 150 institutions, three times as many as her uncle, King George IV, had supported during the 1820s. She not only contributed to permanent charities but she also responded to appeals for victims of earthquakes and storms, fires and shipwrecks, famines and mine disasters. By royal tradition she presented £3 to every mother of triplets (in a single year, 1867, eighty-two mothers requested such a payment). Each year more than 10 percent of Victoria's Privy Purse went for philanthropic purposes – at least £650,000 in the course of her reign – worth some £65,000,000 in 2003.

Albert may have been more systematic and statistically minded in his approach to charitable giving, but after his death the queen remained fully involved, especially in causes that concerned women, children, and wounded soldiers. The monarch's interest led to the construction of 'Queen Victoria hospitals, infirmaries, almshouses, maternity homes, memorial cottages, lunatic asylums, pension funds, schools of industry and institutions for every other cause imaginable' throughout Great Britain, Canada, Australia, and even India.[27] In her years of widowhood she derived more satisfaction from inaugurating a hospital than from opening Parliament. She always preferred the visible and the concrete to the abstract, and when she opened a new extension of the London Hospital in 1876 and comforted sick children there, she was greeted with banners reading 'Welcome Victoria, the Friend of the Afflicted' and 'I was sick & Ye visited me.'[28] Although its creation may have been coincidental, the Queen Victoria Jubilee Institute for Nurses built on the foundations laid down by Florence Nightingale and confirmed the establishment of nursing as a distinct, comprehensive, and highly respectable profession for women.[29]

In matters of philanthropy, the queen's children and their spouses duly and dutifully followed the parental example. From the time of his severe illness in 1871, the Prince of Wales took a special interest in the building and improvement of hospitals – and also in the establishment of orphanages. Princess Helena founded the National School of Needlework and organised the British Nurses' Association. Princess Louise became the first president of the National Union for Higher Education of Women and gave her name to a Salvation Army home for unwed mothers. The Duke of Connaught helped institute the British Red Cross. All members of the royal family supported and attended bazaars designed to raise funds for good causes. As Canon Henson in a Westminster Abbey sermon reminded his listeners after the queen's death, 'Every clergyman, philanthropist and social reformer has had, these sixty-three years past, an ally and sympathizer on the throne of his country.'[30]

One advantage that the queen had in advancing the cause of charitable giving was that she could reward philanthropists as well as generals and statesmen not only with words of praise but also with honors. They came in the form of knighthoods and of membership in the prestigious medieval English Order of the Garter, the Scottish Order of the Thistle, the Irish Order of St Patrick, and numerous others. For the truly eminent, there was even the possibility of a hereditary peerage in the form of a barony, or an upward movement in the peerage from baron to viscount to earl to marquess to duke. Retiring prime ministers merited earldoms – even when the monarch disapproved of their policies – and the queen would have been delighted to promote Salisbury from marquess to duke – had he been willing to accept that distinction. Much of Victoria's correspondence with her ministers involved such honors and their appropriateness: Time and again the queen would turn down, or at the very least delay, a prime ministerial recommendation. It was during Victoria's reign also that the practice was systematised whereby particular shops and manufacturers of jams, cheeses, soaps, and other goods received the cherished right to display the royal coat of arms and the words 'By Appointment to Her Majesty, the Queen.'

Queen Victoria came to see herself as not only the formal fount of honor but also as an expert on the entire system. In the course of her reign, she instituted personally at least three new forms of distinction. During the Crimean War she designed the Victoria Cross for acts of conspicuous military valor. After India became a Crown Colony in 1858, she instituted the multi-rank Order of the Star of India as a new 'high order of chivalry' to be presented to loyal Indian princes as well as to members of the Indian Civil Service. Late in her reign, she initiated the Royal Victorian Order to be conferred on 'such persons, being subjects of the British Crown, as have rendered extraordinary, or personal, or important services to Her Majesty, her heirs or successors.' All honors were conferred in her name, and the Royal Victorian Order was conferred solely at her personal behest.[31]

From time to time the queen found it expedient to confer honors on foreign dignitaries as well as on British subjects. There was no foreigner of whom the queen thought more highly than her German son-in-law, the Crown Prince of Prussia. No foreign participant in the

Golden Jubilee procession looked more imposing or was cheered more loudly than the bearded, ramrod-straight soldier-prince on horseback. Very few of the tens of thousands of procession spectators were aware that – notwithstanding intermittent wishful thinking by doctors and family members – that prince's fate was sealed; he had contracted cancer of the throat, and he had but one more year to live. Thus, when in March 1888 the 90-year-old German emperor, William I, died at long last, it was for the queen at best a bitter-sweet moment. At last Albert's dream had been realised: his cherished son-in-law had become King Frederick III of Prussia and Emperor of a united Germany, and his favorite daughter had become German empress. The couple prepared to reign in a truly enlightened, liberal, and con-stitutional manner over a land that, in partnership with Britain, would promote the peace of the world. Those were indeed the very senti-ments that Frederick included in the first telegram that he sent to Queen Victoria: '[M]y feelings of devoted affection to you prompt me, on succeeding to the throne, to repeat to you my sincere and earnest desire for a close and lasting friendship between our two nations.'[32]

In Berlin, the new emperor was, however, a bed-ridden invalid who could no longer speak, and if he had any notion of dismissing the vet-eran 'blood and iron' chancellor, Prince Bismarck, the time was obvi-ously not right. In April, Queen Victoria made a special journey to Berlin to comfort her daughter, to visit her son-in-law, and to hold a private summit conference with a visibly nervous Bismarck. She dis-cussed Great Power relations with him, and she pleaded with him to stand by her daughter and to resist the institution of a regency to take the place of the ailing Frederick. Bismarck duly promised. As she and her daughter traveled through Berlin in an open carriage, the friendly crowds cheered, threw flowers, and shouted 'Long Live the Empress.'[33]

Victoria's visit proved to be a brief happy interlude in a hapless reign that ended after only ninety-nine days. The queen was deeply saddened: 'My poor dear Vicky. God help her! . . . None of my own sons could be a greater loss. He was so good, so wise, and so fond of me!'[34] The death of Frederick III brought the accession, at the age of twenty-nine, of his and Vicky's eldest son (and Queen Victoria's eldest grandchild), the new Emperor William II. Vicky had proved a devoted but demanding mother, and during his teens, young William increasingly rebelled against his parents and their political views. Instead he identified himself with Prussian soldiers and military traditions and with a hard-boiled and intolerant form of German nationalism. Upon his accession, he scarcely took time to mourn his father. Instead he exulted in his new authority, and he soon began a frenetic round of theatrical military reviews and state visits. He found no time to comfort his widowed mother; instead he sympathised with those German critics who blamed her for the fact that he had been born with a withered arm and that she had sought assistance from English doctors in the treatment of her husband. William even had his father's writing-desk ransacked in his mother's presence in a vain hunt for 'secret papers.' A year later he publicly announced: 'An English doctor killed my father, and an English doctor crippled my arm – and this we owe to my mother who would not have Germans about her.' Thus Vicky was viewed by many Germans not as the dutiful Dowager Empress Frederick but as a foreign spy and 'a danger to the state.'[35]

Although the new German emperor behaved callously to his mother and happily snubbed his Uncle Bertie, the Prince of Wales, he continued to behave respectfully toward his grandmother, Queen Victoria. He always wrote to her in English, and he signed his letters, 'Your devoted and affectionate grandson, WILLY I. R.'[36] Queen Victoria was at her maternal best as she comforted her eldest daughter at Windsor during the winter of 1888-9. She described as *perfect madness* the notion that the youthful William II was 'to be treated *in private* as well as in public as "His Imperial Majesty". '

Lord Salisbury eventually facilitated a *modus vivendi* between the queen and her new fellow monarch, and she even agreed to appoint him an honorary Admiral of the Fleet in the British Navy. 'Fancy wearing the same uniform as . . . Nelson,' exulted William, 'it is enough to make one quite giddy.'[37] The delight that William took in greeting his grandmother at Osborne in 1889 and the pleasure that he took in succeeding years in participating in British naval reviews and in yacht races at Cowes reflect the love–hate attitude toward Britain that was to characterise his behavior for the rest of his life. In 1886, Prince William had announced that 'one cannot have enough hatred for England,' but after a successful state visit to England in 1891, the new emperor thanked his grandmother for her great kindness and noted that he was, after all, 'a good deal of an Englishman myself.'[38]

As German Emperor, he had by then forced the resignation as chancellor of his long-time hero Prince Bismarck. During the years that followed, his policies were to alienate first the world's largest land empire, Russia, and then the world's largest maritime empire, Great Britain. If only her husband had survived a few years longer, lamented the Empress Frederick in 1896, there would not be those 'fits and starts and incoherencies and inconsistencies' that promoted Anglophobia in the German press and that evoked a distrust of Germany among its neighbors.[39] By the time that the German Empire went to war against both Russia and Britain in 1914, William's grandmother and his mother were both dead.

The throne of Germany was not the only one that Queen Victoria's grandchildren were destined to occupy. The queen strongly objected to having one of her Hesse granddaughters marry Tsar Nicholas II of Russia, if only because the 'state of Russia is *so bad*, so rotten that at any time something dreadful might happen.'[40] Yet young Alexandra did convert to the Eastern Orthodox Church, and in 1894 she did marry Nicholas II soon after his accession. The queen became fully reconciled to the union during the summer of 1896 when the youthful czar and czarina and their giant entourage paid a visit to Victoria at Balmoral and turned out to be 'quite unspoilt and . . . as dear and simple as ever and as kind as ever'. They even accompanied the queen to the Sunday service at the local Presbyterian kirk, and they appeared in the first home movies ever made of Queen Victoria. On his departure the czar left a £1,000 tip for the Balmoral servants.[41]

By the 1890s, the queen's granddaughters were marrying not only into the Russian royal family and into numerous German princely families but also into almost every other royal family of Europe. One became the wife of the King of Spain, and others married the future kings of Greece and of Romania. Another granddaughter married the future king of Sweden, and yet another wed the Danish prince who in 1905 became the king of a newly-independent Norway. In the meantime, a first cousin occupied the throne of Belgium, and a niece served as Queen of Romania; another cousin was the monarch of Bulgaria, and the Prince of Wales's brother-in-law occupied the throne of Greece. A large share of the queen's correspondence was occupied with helping her granddaughters find suitable royal or princely husbands and suitable English nannies once they had become mothers. The queen was at the center of a monarchical epistolary network that was often better informed than was the British Foreign Office.

If the queen's correspondence was primarily concerned with European affairs, that did not mean that she ever lost interest in her expanding empire. Her concern with the self-governing settlement colonies, such as Canada, Australia, and New Zealand, was intermittent at best, but she was delighted that her son-in-law, the Marquess of Lorne, had been able to serve as Governor-General of the Dominion of Canada from 1878 to 1882. Back in 1858, it was the queen who had decided that 'British Columbia' should be the name of Canada's westernmost province.[42] In 1888, on the occasion of the centenary of the onset of English colonisation in Australia, the queen congratulated the Australians on 'the splendid material and social progress' that they had achieved and on the loyalty to the mother country that they continued to exhibit. The royal telegram was read at a giant celebratory banquet amidst 'great cheering,' and in Sydney a statue of the Queen was unveiled amidst 'great enthusiasm.'[43] In New Zealand, where the first avowedly Labour ministry took office in 1890, the Governor-General assured Queen Victoria that the photographs she had sent 'have served to keep alive the never-failing interest which is taken by all your Majesty's subjects at the other end of the world, who have never visited England, in all that concerns your Majesty and the Royal family personally.' That sense of loyalty was buttressed by Queen Victoria's willingness to serve as godmother to the Governor-General's new-born son.[44]

During the final decades of the nineteenth century, Britain's influence in Africa was exercised not only in the protectorate of Egypt in the north and in what (south of Egypt) became the Anglo-Egyptian Sudan, but also in Cape Colony and Natal at the southern tip of the continent. Along the west coast of Africa, Britain laid claim to Nigeria and the Gold Coast, along the east coast, to British Somaliland and Uganda and Kenya. And in the center of southern Africa was planted the new colony of Rhodesia, named after the dynamic Cecil John

Rhodes, the hugely successful mining company director who had become prime minister of Cape Colony. At a dinner with Queen Victoria in 1891, he assured her that 'Great Britain was the only country fit to colonise,' a task at which no other nation had truly succeeded. He dreamt of the construction, under British auspices, of a Cape-to-Cairo railway.[45] The queen agreed that colonisation could be justified only if it promoted the abolition of slavery where that institution yet existed and if it bettered the lives of subject peoples. When three African kings from the Bechuanaland Protectorate toured England in 1895, they expressed their appreciation for the work of missionaries in their land and appealed to temperance societies to curb the activities of unscrupulous white liquor traders. They also persuaded the Colonial Office that most of their lands should not be incorporated into Cecil Rhodes's private colonial empire but be kept 'under the Queen.' The climax of their tour was a ceremonial lunch in November 1895 with Queen Victoria at Windsor.[46] Two decades earlier, when the European 'scramble for Africa' was first getting under way, she had given strong support to Dr John William Colenso, the Anglican Bishop of Natal, who championed the cause of black Africans. She applauded

his noble, disinterested conduct in favour of the natives who were so unjustly used, and in general her very strong feeling (and she has few stronger) that the natives and coloured races should be treated with every kindness and affection, as brothers, not – as, alas! Englishmen too often do – as totally different to ourselves, fit only to be crushed and shot down! . . . [I]n general, all her Colonial Governors should know her feelings on this subject of the native races.[47]

The queen took the greatest pride in the Crown Colony of India, of which she had been formally proclaimed empress in 1877. As the historian W. E. H. Lecky observed in 1893:

Remember what India had been for countless ages before the establishment of British rule. Think of its endless wars of race and creed, its savage oppressions, its fierce anarchies, its barbarous customs, and then consider what it is to have established for so many years over the vast space from the Himalayas to Cape Comorin a reign of perfect peace; to have conferred upon more than 250 millions of the human race perfect religious freedom, perfect security of life, liberty, and property; to have planted in the midst of these teeming multitudes a strong central government, enlightened by the best knowledge of Western Europe, and steadily occupied in preventing famine, alleviating disease, extirpating savage customs, multiplying the agencies of civilisation and progress. . . . Whatever misfortunes, whatever humiliations, the future may reserve to us, they cannot deprive England of the glory of having created this mighty empire.[48]

Queen Victoria very much sympathised with such a verdict, even though she was fully conscious of the fact that 'the natives (though they are very loyal to the Queen-Empress and Royal family) have no affection for the English rule, which is one of fear not of love.'[49] For that reason only the ablest and most fair-minded Britons were to be sent to govern the Crown Colony; for that reason also there should be no interference with religious practices in India, whether Moslem or Hindu. A significant portion of the queen's correspondence with her prime minister (and necessarily with successive Viceroys and Secretaries of State for India) reminded them that such lofty standards should be upheld.

Although the queen never traveled to India, she was delighted to meet Indians who, in increasing numbers, visited London. She encountered many at the Colonial and Indian Exhibition of 1886 and at the Jubilee receptions and procession of 1887; in her journal she was to record meetings with many others during the years that followed. Although she was pleased when they spoke English, she preferred them not to be dressed in European fashion: the more exotic their appearance, the more picturesque their garb, and the more magnificent their jewels, the better the queen liked them.[50] At the same time she was delighted to learn of the hundreds and thousands of Indians who shared in the magnificent Golden Jubilee celebration in India itself. 'The natives of India are passionately fond of pyrotechnic displays', the Viceroy reported from Calcutta, and they were dazzled by 'the outline of your Majesty's head, traced in lines of fire, which unexpectedly burst on the vision of the astonished crowd . . . and caused an enormous shout of pleasure and surprise.'[51] In India even more than at home, the queen very much approved of that aspect of empire that involved neither economic exploitation nor the construction of railway lines and steamship routes nor a sense of racial superiority, but what one modern historian has called *Ornamentalism*, a preoccupation with theatre in the form of uniforms, badges, emblems, titles, anthems, and ceremony.[52]

In the aftermath of the Jubilee of 1887, Queen Victoria acquired two Indian servants of her own who were always to wear their turbans and Indian garb. One of them, Abdul Karim, was soon promoted from the role of dining-room waiter to that of the Queen's Munshi, her teacher both in the Hindustani language and in the social and religious customs of India. During the next decade, her exercises in that language filled at least twelve large lesson books, and she came to look on herself as a good example to those British women who moved to India (as the wives of administrators or as nurses) and yet remained studiously monolingual.[53] In due course, Karim became, first, Personal Indian Clerk to the Queen, and then her Indian Secretary, in charge of a growing number of Indian servants at court. At Balmoral he was given John Brown's old room, and to an ever greater degree he came to occupy the Highlander's place in the queen's heart.

In the queen's eyes, the Munshi could do no wrong; thus if he told her that his father had served as Surgeon-General in the Indian Army, she believed him, even if the prosaic truth was that the father's job had been that of apothecary in an Indian gaol. In due course the Munshi brought his wife, his mother-in-law and their female relations to England and the court; there they set up their own secluded Moslem quarters. Most members of her household took less delight in the exotic than did the queen, and they increasingly resented the Munshi's power and pretensions. Her private physician, a Scot, found his talents as diplomat stretched to the full, and the prime minister became fearful that Karim might reveal the contents of the government despatch boxes that crossed the queen's desk. Apparently he did not, but in the Hindu–Moslem disputes that intermittently beset British administrators in India, he understandably favored the Moslem point of view. Ultimately, Queen Victoria resisted successfully all efforts by her children and courtiers to persuade her to dismiss Karim, and he remained by her side until the day she died.[54]

Her obsession with the Munshi did not prevent Queen Victoria in her later years from taking an often intense interest in the cultural life of Britain. Numerous command performances by the great musicians of the day took place at Windsor. They included brilliant singers such as Emma Albani and Emma Calvé and distinguished pianists such as the aging Franz Liszt, who played four pieces at Windsor 'with such an exquisite touch,' and the youthful Ignaz Paderewski, who played 'quite marvellously' and who was one day to become the President of an independent Poland.[55] The brilliant Spanish cellist Pablo Casals, who played for Queen Victoria at Windsor in 1898, was to live long enough to perform for President John F. Kennedy in the White House in 1961.

In the meantime, in 1893 Pietro Mascagni came to Windsor in person to conduct a fully-staged performance of his new opera, *Cavalleria Rusticana*.[56] Even earlier, the D'Oyly Carte Opera Company had performed Gilbert and Sullivan's *The Mikado* at Balmoral and *The Gondoliers* at Windsor. The queen had known Sir Arthur Sullivan since the 1860s, when she had asked him to edit Prince Albert's music. She had also asked him to play at the wedding of her youngest son, and she had conferred a knighthood on him in 1883 in recognition of his 'distinguished talents as a composer' and as a promoter of 'the Art of Music generally in this Country.'[57] The queen was enchanted with both the words and the music of *The Gondoliers*, and she beat time with the chorus as it sang

> Oh, 'tis a glorious thing, I ween
> To be a regular Royal Queen
> No half-and-half affair, I mean
> But a right-down regular Royal Queen!

The queen asked impresario Richard D'Oyly Carte why some of the actors had added bits of comic business to the text. 'Those, Your Majesty', replied Carte, 'are what we call gags.' 'Gags?' countered Queen Victoria, 'I thought gags were things that were put by authority into people's mouths.' 'Those gags, Your Majesty,' rejoined Carte, 'are things these people put into their own mouths without authority.'[58]

Americans were well represented among those who entertained the queen. When Buffalo Bill's Wild West Show performed at London's Earls Court in 1887, Victoria was an admiring attendant at what she called 'a very extraordinary' spectacle involving cowboys and Indians. A mock attack on a coach and a ranch involved an 'immense amount of firing' and 'was most exciting.' She found the Red Indians 'with their feathers, & wild dress (very little of it) rather alarming' and 'their war dance quite fearful.' Colonel Cody himself was, however, 'a splendid man, handsome & gentlemanlike in manner.' The queen was so impressed with the performance that when the troupe returned to England five years later, she imported the entire company for a performance on the lawn adjoining Windsor Castle.[59] In the meantime, she had visited London's Olympia in order to revel in P. T. Barnum's spectacle, *Nero, or the Burning of Rome*, with its cast of more than 1,200 performers and almost as many animals.[60]

During these same years, by a combination of sticks and carrots, Salisbury's second ministry was restoring a greater degree of public order to Ireland. At the same time, the leader of the Home Rule Party, Charles Stewart Parnell, briefly gained in stature. A journalist who had accused Parnell of condoning the assassination of government officials in Ireland publicly admitted that he had forged an incriminating letter. Only a year later came Parnell's downfall after he was named, in a divorce suit by a fellow MP, as an adulterer, and put up no defence. The Home Rule Party divided into Parnellites and anti-Parnellites, and the prospect faded of a Liberal/Irish Nationalist resurgence under Gladstone's leadership. Queen Victoria remained fearful that Salisbury would be defeated in the general election and that Gladstone would again attempt to push a Home Rule Bill through Parliament. As she lamented to her eldest daughter, 'Ireland has recovered its quiet and prosperity so wonderfully, that it is very wicked to try and upset everything again.' In the general election of 1892, the Liberal/Home Rule alliance *did* defeat the Conservative/Liberal Unionist alliance by a narrow margin, 354 votes to 315. It appeared to the queen 'a defect in our much famed Constitution, to have to part with an admirable Gov[ernmen]t like L[or]d Salisbury's for no question of any importance, or any particular reason, merely on account of the number of votes.'

She had no choice, however, but to name 'the half crazy, half silly' Gladstone, at the age of eighty-two, prime minister for the fourth time.[61] The queen's influence helped deny a cabinet post to the radical

Henry Labouchere, whose journal *Truth* had regularly criticised the royal family and who had lived with his wife prior to marriage. At the same time, the queen strongly encouraged the Liberal whom she liked most, Lord Rosebery, to resume the role of foreign secretary. Gladstone remained as certain as before that only Home Rule would truly reconcile the Irish to remain part of the United Kingdom and the British Empire, and in 1893 his passionate oratory persuaded the House of Commons, after eighty-three days of debate, to agree not merely to the principle but also to a fully developed scheme of government in Ireland. By then the Liberals constituted only a small minority in the House of Lords, however, and after a scornfully brief debate, that chamber rejected the measure by a vote of 419 to 41. Early in the next year, after giving the upper House a stinging lecture warning it that its days were numbered, Gladstone retired at last from both the prime ministership and the leadership of the Liberal Party.

The Liberal cabinet was badly divided, and without bothering to consult any of its members, Queen Victoria asked Lord Rosebery to take over as prime minister. That brilliant but enigmatic Scottish earl reluctantly agreed. She liked Rosebery personally, and she had provided him with maternal comfort four years earlier on the death of his beloved wife Hannah, the Rothschild heiress, but she remained suspicious of his supporters. She therefore warned Rosebery not to 'destroy well tried, valued, & necessary institutions for the sole purpose of flattering useless Radicals,' and she persuaded him to rephrase the 'Speech from the Throne' that promised to enact the new Liberal program of Church disestablishment in both Scotland and Wales.[62] When the queen rebuked Rosebery on yet another issue, his associate Sir William Harcourt remarked: 'The spirit of George III survives in his descendant.'[63] Harcourt had dearly wished to become prime minister himself, and while he was government leader in the House of Commons, he and Rosebery disagreed on many matters. As Chancellor of the Exchequer, Harcourt pioneered a budget innovation that disquieted Rosebery, introducing the principle of progressive taxation to 'death duties' (inheritance taxes)and raising the maximum to 8 percent of each estate. In June 1895 Rosebery almost welcomed a parliamentary defeat on another budget issue; it provided an excuse to resign the prime ministership.

The queen quickly summoned Lord Salisbury. The latter not only agreed to form a government, but he was also pleased to include the two most eminent Liberal Unionists, the Duke of Hartington and Joseph Chamberlain. In the general election that followed, the Conservative/Liberal Unionist coalition, now known as Unionist, obtained a large majority of parliamentary seats over the Liberal/ Home Rule alliance, 411 to 259. The reliable Lord Salisbury was to remain prime minister for the remainder of the queen's reign.

During her last years, the queen was increasingly plagued by failing eyesight, but that disability did not stop her from taking as intense an interest as ever in events both at home and abroad. Sympathetic as she generally was both to Prime Minister Salisbury, who also served as foreign secretary, and to his nephew Arthur Balfour, who led the government in the House of Commons, she remained ever ready to criticise. Thus it seemed 'incredible' to the queen that a government that had officially announced a major Education Bill in her 'Speech from the Throne' should abruptly abandon it a few months later. At the same time, she did not object to the Automotor Car Bill of 1896, which ended the requirement that all horseless carriages on British roads should be preceded by a man waving a red flag.[64]

During the same year, planning began for a celebration of the sixtieth anniversary of Victoria's accession, the longest reign in all of England's or Scotland's history. The queen agreed to participate in what was to become the grandest parade in her kingdom's history only after three conditions had been met: that state ceremonial not be used, that she not be compelled to get out of her carriage on Jubilee Day, and that the entire occasion not involve a single penny from her Privy Purse. The Golden Jubilee had cost her £50,000. But what ought this sixtieth anniversary of her accession to be called? The fiftieth had been a Jubilee; let the sixtieth be the Jubilissimee, so went one suggestion. There was no precedent for calling a sixtieth anniversary of any kind a Jubilee. As her scholarly home secretary observed, ' "Jubilee" has got its meaning from the old Jewish law & is certainly inseparably connected with a notion of 50 years. "Diamond" is understood to mark the completion of 60 years of married life.' Her new private secretary felt certain that 'Diamond' was a title that 'Your Majesty would not approve of.'[65] To the contrary, the queen was much taken with the title because, one suspects, it served as the substitute for that truly momentous wedding anniversary that she and Albert might have celebrated had he not died young.

The 78-year-old queen was not prepared to take on again the feeding and housing of what would have proved a yet larger gathering of European royal relations. A ban on all crowned heads would make it unnecessary for her to entertain Kaiser Wilhelm II of Germany, who was once again proving difficult. Grudgingly her cabinet agreed to such a ban, and the prospective celebratory vacuum inspired the enterprising colonial secretary Joseph Chamberlain to transform the Diamond Jubilee into a true celebration of empire. As he pointed out to Salisbury, 'there has never been in English territory any representation of the Empire as a whole, and the Colonies especially have, hitherto, taken little part in any ceremony of the kind.'[66] All eleven prime ministers of the Empire's self-governing colonies were therefore invited as guests of the government along with representative military escorts. And so contingents from Canada, Cape Colony, Natal, New Zealand, and the several Australian colonies – along with Indian Army troops and detachments from Malta and Trinidad and other dependencies – all became part of the gigantic procession. Joseph Chamberlain took the opportunity to preside over the first conference that enabled all of the prime ministers of the self-governing states within the British Empire to talk to one another, a tradition that, in the form of regular Commonwealth conferences, continues into the twenty-first century.

The procession of June 22, 1897, which took place in brilliant sunshine, was climaxed by a religious service outside St Paul's Cathedral where a grandstand had been set up for thousands of dignitaries and where Victoria remained in her carriage. The Mother of the Empire, reported London's *Daily Mail*, had gone to do homage to the One Being 'MORE MAJESTIC THAN SHE.' At the end of the service there was a brief lull. The Archbishop of Canterbury intervened with a spontaneous cry, 'Three cheers for the Queen.' The spectators responded with delight, and the band and chorus burst into 'God Save the Queen.'[67] The return journey to Buckingham Palace was deliberately routed through the poorer sections of the metropolis south of the Thames. It turned out to be the greatest ceremonial occasion in the history of London and in the life of the queen. 'A never-to-be-forgotten day,' wrote the queen in her daily journal. She went on:

> No one ever, I believe, has met with such an ovation as was given to me, passing through those six miles of streets. . . . The crowds were quite indescribable, and their enthusiasm truly marvellous and deeply touching. The cheering was quite deafening, and every face seemed to be filled with real joy.[68]

Like its predecessor, the Diamond Jubilee served as a catalyst for civic improvements and philanthropic bequests throughout the British world.

The queen's final decade involved international crises as well as celebrations. Thus late in 1895 a dispute broke out with the United States. There the second Grover Cleveland administration sought to restore its waning popularity at home by loudly trumpeting its support of Venezuela in a long-simmering dispute about the jungle boundary between that country and British Guiana. In a public letter to Joseph Pulitzer's *New York World*, the Prince of Wales appealed for a peaceful solution and the restoration of a 'warm feeling of friendship' between the two countries.[69] Eventually the dispute was referred to an independent arbitration commission that largely upheld the British case. Not long after, Victoria's niece, the Queen Regent of Spain, appealed in vain to Britain for support against the manner in which the American government was preventing the Spaniards from suppressing an insurgency in Cuba.[70] When the Spanish–American War broke out in 1898, the American ambassador in London, John C. Hay, found indeed that Britain was 'the only European country whose sympathies are not openly against us.'[71] Privately, the queen was highly dubious. As she wrote to her daughter, 'this Spanish war distresses me very much. . . . No doubt Cuba was dreadfully governed, but that does not excuse America and the principle is dreadful. They might as well say we governed Ireland badly and they ought to take possession of it & free it.'[72]

One of the other events of 1898 was the death of William Ewart Gladstone at the age of eighty-eight. In the eyes of Queen Victoria's eldest daughter, he was 'a great Englishman.' 'I cannot say that I think he was "a great Englishman",' the queen responded.

He was a clever man, full of talent, but he never tried to keep up the *honour* and *prestige* of Great Britain. He gave away the Transvaal, he abandoned Gordon, he destroyed the Irish Church and tried to separate England from Ireland and to set class against class. The harm he did cannot easily be undone. But he was a good and very religious man.[73]

During the 1890s the queen was generally on good terms with the Prince of Wales, who treated her with both respect and affection, but she was very much annoyed with him for serving as one of Gladstone's pallbearers along with his own son (the future King George V). She was in much closer accord with both her eldest son and her eldest daughter when it came to the *cause célèbre* of Alfred Dreyfus, the French army captain whose conviction for treason (on the basis of forged evidence) had aroused a storm of anti-semitism in France. His second conviction on the basis of perjured testimony impressed the queen as 'the greatest disgrace to France and the army which could take place.'[74] Victoria practiced what she preached; in 1884 she had become the first British monarch to award a hereditary peerage to a professing Jew.

On the occasion of her eightieth birthday in 1899, she thanked God for having preserved her for so long for her children, her friends, and 'the whole nation. . . . May God still mercifully preserve me to work for the good of my country!'[75] That opportunity would come only four months later with the outbreak of the Anglo-Boer War. In the course of the 1880s, the Boers (the descendants of Dutch settlers who had moved into the Transvaal as patriarchal farmers) found that they lived atop some of the richest gold and diamond deposits in the world, and during the 1890s Johannesburg became the world's great 'gold rush' boom town. Foreigners, many of them British, poured into the Transvaal, where they ended up paying three-quarters of the taxes but exercising almost no political power. The Britons, who controlled Cape Colony and Natal, soon found themselves in a state of Cold War with the Boers. In May 1899, more than 20,000 foreign residents of the Transvaal sent a petition to Queen Victoria asking for her aid against the arbitrary Boer government, which had violated its treaties with Britain. 'There is no way out of the political troubles of South Africa,' declared Sir Alfred Milner, the British High Commissioner there, 'except reform in the Transvaal or war.'[76] The rapidly arming Boers ordered Britain to stop interfering with the domestic affairs of the Transvaal and to withdraw its troops from the Transvaal frontier. Milner refused, and in October 1899, the Transvaal and the Orange Free State (also under Boer control) declared war on the British Empire.

The queen had no doubt as to the justice of Britain's cause. As she explained to the youthful Queen Wilhelmina of the Netherlands, 'I cannot abandon my own subjects who have appealed to me for protection.'[77] Besides, it was not the British who had declared war, but the Boers, and they were 'horrid people, cruel & over-bearing.'[78] In the short run, the outnumbered British forces in Cape Colony and Natal suffered a series of stinging defeats at the hands of the Boers, but in response – with Victoria's enthusiastic support – the British government sent a force of 70,000 men to South Africa to counter-attack. She 'felt quite a lump in [her] throat' as she bid a personal farewell to regiment after regiment, aware that 'these remarkably fine men might not all return.'[79]

As the conflict continued, the octogenarian queen 'became the embodiment of the national spirit.'[80] She wrote to the widows and mothers of fallen heroes, and she began an album displaying a photograph of every officer killed in the war. The date and the circumstances of the death were inscribed beneath each picture. One of the dead (of tropical fever) was her grandson, Prince Christian Victor, the son of her daughter Helena.[81] She worked on woolen comforters and caps for the troops, and at Christmas time, Queen Victoria ordered a box of chocolates with her effigy on the lid shipped personally to every single British soldier and officer fighting in South Africa.[82]

When the tide of war turned, early in the year 1900 – with the relief of the besieged cities of Kimberley and Ladysmith and the capture of a major Boer army leader – the queen sent telegrams of congratulation to her victorious generals and celebrated with her people. On March 8, 1900 the queen made a triumphant circular tour through London – from Paddington Station to Buckingham Palace and then up the Mall and along the Thames Embankment all the way to Blackfriars where she was formally greeted by the Lord Mayor and the Aldermen of London. Along the way, she was cheered by hundreds of assembled members of the House of Commons and the House of Lords. In addition, the queen reported, 'I received a perfect ovation from thousands and thousands of people assembled along the whole route.' Their cheers were deafening, and with enormous enthusiasm they waved handkerchiefs and flags and sang 'God Save the Queen.'[83] 'It was like a triumphal progress,' Victoria went on, and the number of people in the streets exceeded even the number who had cheered the Diamond Jubilee procession less than three years before.[84]

A month later came the queen's equally triumphant visit to Dublin. Although two of her sons had paid ceremonial visits, not since 1861 had Victoria herself set foot in the Emerald Isle, but pro-Boer sentiment voiced in France and Italy seemed to argue against the queen's now customary visit to the French Riviera. She had become deeply impressed, however, by the gallantry and the bravery that her Irish soldiers had displayed in the Anglo-Boer conflict. She was greeted at Kingstown with renditions of 'God Save the Queen' and 'Soldiers of the Queen,' and she entered an elaborately decorated Dublin beneath banners that read: 'Blest for ever is she who relied/On Erin's honour and Erin's pride.' As one of the Queen's equerries was to recall, 'Although I had seen many visits of this kind, nothing had ever approached the enthusiasm and even frenzy displayed by the people of Dublin.'[85]

In the course of the year 1900, British forces conquered Johannesburg and Pretoria (the Transvaal capital), but, at the end of the year, fighting in the form of guerrilla warfare still dragged on. In the meantime, the queen was still handing out medals and visiting military hospitals and corresponding with the families of soldiers. As she wrote to her eldest daughter, 'I am constantly [receiving the] most touching professions of loyalty & many very sad ones, but even these [are] full of devotion & pride that these sons & husbands have died for me. I feel deeply *touched* at the extraordinary personal devotion to me.'[86] When the queen lay gravely ill at Osborne on January 14, 1901, her final non-family visitor was Field Marshal Lord Roberts; she talked to him for an hour about the war and then she raised him in the ranks of the peerage from a baron to an earl.[87] Five days later, on her deathbed, she was able to take comfort in the thought that, as she murmured to her doctor, '[t]here is much better news from South Africa today.'[88]

By then members of her family were gathering, including the self-invited Emperor William II of Germany, who on this occasion behaved in exemplary fashion. It was while he was supporting one side of her pillow and her doctor the other – with numerous other family members in attendance – that the queen glanced at her eldest son, whispered 'Bertie' and closed her eyes forever.[89] The time was 6.30 p.m., the date Tuesday, January 22, 1901.

Long before the Boer War, in keeping with the belief that she remained the leader of the kingdom's armed forces, Queen Victoria had insisted on a military funeral for herself. Tens of thousands of soldiers and sailors were therefore recruited to help convey the queen's coffin all the way from Osborne House to Windsor on February 1, the day of the funeral. Across the Solent from the Isle of Wight to Portsmouth, eighteen battleships and twelve cruisers lined the naval route. From Portsmouth the coffin went by train to London's Victoria Station while tens of thousands of spectators packed the platform of every station through which the funeral train passed. The burnished two-and-a-half-ton gun carriage that bore the coffin was accompanied on its two-hour journey through London from Victoria Station to Paddington Station by carriages filled with members of the royal family. They were followed by 32,000 slow-marching infantrymen. The entire route was jammed with well-behaved and eerily quiet spectators. Another train brought the coffin to Windsor station. When the horses rebelled that had waited in the bitter cold to move the *caisson* up the hill to the castle, Prince Louis of Battenberg recommended that the sailors of the naval guard take over the task. The bluejackets therefore cut away the horses and grasped the reins themselves. They pulled the *caisson* with dignity and precision through the crowded streets of the royal borough all the way to the Windsor Castle grounds for the formal funeral service at St George's Chapel and the subsequent burial next to Albert at Frogmore. The queen had come home.[90]

10 *The Tomb of Queen Victoria*

The effigy of the monarch fashioned by Baron Carlo Marochetti soon after the death of Prince Albert in 1861 was placed four decades later on her sarcophagus in the Royal Mausoleum at Frogmore in the Windsor Castle grounds. (Courtesy of The Royal Archives; © Her Majesty Queen Elizabeth II 2003)

10 The Paradoxical Monarch

News of the birth of Princess Victoria on May 24, 1819, was reported, in the course of the next few days, in but a handful of British newspapers. News of the death of Queen Victoria on January 22, 1901, was spread within half an hour by telegraph and cable to every major city in the British Empire and to world capitals as distant as Washington DC and Tokyo. An hour or two later there appeared on the streets of these cities black-bordered newspapers featuring lengthy obituaries of the most famous woman in the world. Throughout metropolitan London, church bells tolled dolefully while theatres and music halls shut down until after the funeral. In Dublin too the streets fell silent. In Berlin, a period of official mourning was immediately decreed for all branches of the government. In Washington DC, Congress adjourned early and President William McKinley ordered the White House flag lowered to half-staff as a national sign of respect for the granddaughter of King George III.

On Saturday, February 1, the day of the funeral, special church services throughout the United Kingdom were packed with worshippers, and a ten-minute period of silence was decreed for every city and village, during which all business ceased. In New York City, the stock exchange canceled its customary half-day session, while in Washington DC, the President and the entire Cabinet attended a memorial service at St John's Episcopal Church. Such services took place on every other continent as well. 'From Dresden and Trieste and Tangier, Port Said and Copenhagen and Bombay, from the meanness of Calcutta to the splendors of St Petersburg . . . Victoria, and the serenity she represented, were mourned.'[1] Even Henry Labouchere, the Radical MP whom the queen had barred from cabinet office, felt compelled to pay tribute. In his journal *Truth*, he wrote:

Among her millions of subjects, there are few who will not mourn her as
for one of their own household. Nor will the mourners be found among
her own subjects alone. It is not too much to say that never in the history
of the world has a single death caused such universal grief.[2]

In the judgment of London's St. *James's Gazette*, Victoria had 'figured in
our imagination less as a Person than as an Institution – an
Institution immovably fixed in the political and social Order of our
age.' For those who mourned her passing in 1901, the pre-Victorian
era had become so 'remote as to seem to belong to a different epoch,
a different civilisation.'[3] Arthur J. Balfour, the government leader in
the House of Commons, concurred: 'We feel that the end of a great
epoch has come upon us.'[4]

Balfour's sentiments were to be echoed by many other observers
during the days and years that followed, but more than one hundred
years have now elapsed since the death of Queen Victoria. How
should we think of her today? How can we best understand the status that she attained and the roles that she played in her world and in
her century? It seems most appropriate to conclude this volume with
a series of paradoxes.

**The queen saw herself as a straightforward and down-to-earth
person with a penchant for truth-telling and a devotion to
practical common sense, and yet her character also partook
of a romantic streak that time and again made her a creature of
passion.**
Thus she saw Lord Melbourne not merely as a wise and experienced
political mentor but also as a romantic figure who linked her directly to the distant world of her royal paternal grandparents. In his personal life, Melbourne had also been compelled to cope with a deeply
unstable spouse and a mentally unbalanced child. Victoria visualised
Prince Albert not as a German 'professor' who wrote long and sometimes stultifying memoranda but as a handsome knight in shining
armor who became her partner in the grandest love match in all of
recorded history. Although at times the Emperor Napoleon III of
France appeared to be an upstart politician who threatened the peace
of Europe, he also impressed Victoria as the epitome of French style

and *savoir faire*, as a ruler who provided her with the most elegant ceremonial reception that she ever experienced in a foreign capital. When his star and his empire fell abruptly in 1870–1, she found admirable the spirit of stoic nobility with which he accepted his fate. Benjamin Disraeli, in turn, became for her not merely another of her ten prime ministers, but also a character in a romantic novel. Both in actions and words, he transformed himself from a Victorian politician into an Elizabethan courtier. Even before she encountered John Brown, the queen had come to look on Scottish Highlanders as the most rugged, honest, and trustworthy of the numerous 'races' that populated her multi-ethnic empire, and for two decades John Brown became for her the personal embodiment of all these virtues and more. In her later years, Queen Victoria looked on her title Empress of India not solely as an honor but also as a responsibility, and in her eyes Abdul Karim, the Munshi, became the respected personal embodiment, ever at her side, of that exotic Jewel in her Crown with all its varied languages and peoples.

The queen is so often associated with what has been called the Victorian 'celebration of death' that we readily forget that for most of her life she was an exceptionally healthy and vital individual.
She beat the nineteenth-century demographic odds in that all nine of her children grew to adulthood, and she did not experience the death of an immediate member of her household until the demise of her mother in March 1861 and that of her husband nine months later. Her mother's passing did indeed afflict her to an unexpected degree, and Albert's death marked her for the rest of her life. She did thereafter take that intense interest in memorials and in the details of deathbed scenes that later generations have found obsessive, and according to her private secretary she took a special satisfaction in the arrangement of funerals.[5] Yet, unlike Albert, she was blessed with a healthy constitution; by nineteenth-century standards, she was afflicted by few serious diseases, and for most of her life she possessed an excellent appetite. Her own death came as much of a shock to her subjects as it did because, despite her lameness and failing eyesight, until the later months of 1900 she continued to exhibit remarkable stamina.

The statement by the queen that is cited most often is 'We are not amused!' and yet the implication of unbroken royal sobriety is equally misleading.[6]
When the portrait painter Heinrich von Angeli suggested that Victoria was posing in 'too earnest' a fashion, she admittedly replied that such seriousness was altogether proper because 'it represents the Queen.'[7] Yet the shortage of photographs displaying the dazzling royal smile is attributable to the fact that, for most of her reign, sitters had to hold still for a minute or two, and a smile turned too readily into a grimace. In private, she could derive enormous enjoyment from music and dancing as well as from the theatre, the circus, and a Wild West show – and also from excursions in the Scottish Highlands and carriage rides near her holiday home on the French Riviera.[8]

The queen was both an exemplar and proponent of such Victorian virtues as character, duty, domesticity, and modesty, and yet she was fully aware that in this world, precept and reality did not necessarily accord.
In some respects, the queen was a prude: for most of her reign she barred divorced women from her court; she frowned on public discussions of pregnancy; she disliked the 'modern' custom of the 1870s whereby engaged couples went about unchaperoned.[9] At the same time, her birthday gifts to Prince Albert included paintings displaying female nudes, and her sense of modesty did not extend to her own marriage bed. The queen was very much aware that the world was replete with corruption and crime; she was quite willing, after all, to advise the home secretary as to how best to catch Jack the Ripper.[10] She was also conscious of the fact that few marriages were as blessed as hers had been. On one occasion she compared the giving of a daughter in marriage to 'taking a poor lamb to be sacrificed.' Most marriages were lotteries, she concluded, and often 'the poor woman is bodily and morally the husband's slave. That always sticks in my throat.'[11] As has been noted earlier, Queen Victoria deeply resented the burdens of pregnancy and the pains of childbirth, and she avoided altogether the practice of breast-feeding, for which she felt a 'totally insurmountable disgust.'[12] She became dependent on her eldest

daughter as an epistolary confidante and on her youngest daughter as a constant companion, and she became a matriarchal symbol not only for her empire but also for the entire European world. Yet she retained grave doubts about the suitability of most marriages and about the gratitude of most children.

The era to which Queen Victoria gave her name has been called an age of serenity and complacency, but contemporaries viewed it as the most dynamic century of change in all human history. It was the social and the technological alterations that impressed contemporaries most of all. Thus, in describing the Diamond Jubilee procession of 1897, the American ironist Mark Twain noted unironically that 'British history is two thousand years old, and yet in a good many ways the world has moved further ahead since the Queen was born than it moved in all the rest of the two thousand years put together.' There were, first of all, the innumerable inventions that made the later 1890s so different from the later 1810s: the railway and the steamship, the telegraph and the telephone, the sewing machine and the electric light, the typewriter and the camera. 'She has seen more things invented than any other monarch that ever lived.'

Some of those material inventions, Mark Twain conceded, may have added burdens as well as comforts to life, but enormous 'moral advancement' had also taken place. Two hundred crimes once subject to capital punishment had been swept from England's statute book. 'She has seen English liberty greatly broadened – the governing and law-making powers, formerly the possession of the few,' had been 'extended to the body of the people.' That 'public educator,' the modern newspaper, had been created 'and its teachings placed within the reach of the leanest purse.' She had seen the 'world's literature set free' by means of the institution of international copyright. She had witnessed how anesthetics could 'for all time banish the terrors of the surgeon's knife,' and she had herself pioneered the use of such a balm in childbirth. In the cities of civilised lands medical science and improved sanitation had cut the death rate in half.

Queen Victoria, Mark Twain continued, had also 'seen woman freed from the oppression of many burdensome and unjust laws;

colleges established for her . . .; in some regions rights accorded to her which lift her near to political equality with man, and a hundred bread-winning occupations found for her where hardly one existed before – among them medicine, the law, and professional nursing.' The queen had also seen 'the right to organize trade unions extended to the workman,' and she had witnessed a reduction of working hours from twelve or fourteen hours a day to eight, 'a reform which has made labor a means of extending life instead of a means of committing salaried suicide.' In the course of her life, she had witnessed a quintupling in the number of people in the world who spoke the English language. [Whereas her predecessor Queen Elizabeth had ruled a land of less than one hundred thousand square miles with fewer than five million people, Queen Victoria's 'estate covers a fourth part of the habitable area of the globe, and her subjects number about 400,000,000.']

Although Queen Victoria may have neither sponsored nor sanctioned all these changes, she very much approved of both the railway and the camera, and of the cypher telegraph, which she had increasingly employed in order to communicate with her ministers – especially when they were in London and she at Balmoral. For Mark Twain, in any case, it was Queen Victoria herself who had given true meaning to the Jubilee procession.

> She was received with great enthusiasm. . . . [S]he was the procession herself; . . . all the rest of it was mere embroidery. . . . She was a symbol, an allegory of England's grandeur and the might of the British name. . . . The procession stood for sixty years of progress and accumulation, moral, material and political.[13]

It was only in distant retrospect that the Victorian era came to be remembered by some memoirists as stable and complacent.

Queen Victoria lived during an age of relative international peace, and yet by temperament she was a warrior queen.

The queen's reign did indeed coincide with what has sometimes been called the Ninety-Nine Year Peace, the era between the world war that we associate with the French Revolution and Napoleon and that ended in 1815 with the Battle of Waterloo, and the onset in 1914 of what is misleadingly called the First World War. It is also true that, most of the time, Britain's all-volunteer army was surprisingly small: little more than 100,000 troops in a kingdom of well over 30 million people. Of the wars that did occur in Europe during those years, Britain was directly involved only in the Crimean War of 1854–56.

In other parts of the world Britain was frequently preoccupied, however, with what one historian has aptly dubbed *Queen Victoria's Little Wars.*[14] In Asia, Britain participated in two wars with China, and in India, British-led forces were involved not only with the suppression of the Great Mutiny of 1857–58 but also with intermittent fighting along India's North-west Frontier. Military conflict took place in late nineteenth-century Africa as well, but only the Anglo-Boer War of 1899–1902 involved for Britain a large army and a significant death toll (about 22,000). The enemy then was another people of European origin; native Africans played a secondary role, though 10,000 of them too became victims of the conflict. As has been noted above, Queen Victoria always looked upon herself as a soldier's daughter, and she took an intense interest in every campaign, however distant the setting. In her later years, she found numerous excuses for failing to open Parliament in person, but she did make time to review troops, to visit the wounded, to write directly to senior generals, and to award medals. In 1880 a British force in Afghanistan successfully marched from Kabul to Kandahar to relieve a British garrison there. When a participating regiment traveled to Osborne in 1881 to receive campaign awards directly from the queen, she was happy to pin a medal even on the collar of Bobbie, the small white mongrel dog that had accompanied the regiment throughout the conflict.[15] As Alfred Austin, her last poet laureate, recognized,

> Yet while for peace she wrought and prayed,
> She bore the trident, wore the helm,
> And, mistress of the main, she made
> An empire of her island realm.[16]

For Queen Victoria, national defense was ever a priority, and soldiering remained the noblest of professions. It is hardly surprising that she decreed a military funeral for herself.

In her later years the queen became a staunch imperialist. At the same time she became a fervent champion of religious and racial diversity.

At first glance, these statements may seem contradictory, but on further examination they are far less so. Queen Victoria did possess an underlying belief in the superiority of European civilisation and of British civilisation above all others, and she felt sure that people under British rule or protection were more likely than others to become peaceful, humane, law-abiding, and economically prosperous. She might criticise territorial expansion *per se*, but once a territory had fallen under British jurisdiction she strongly opposed the end of such rule. British abdication meant not native independence, after all, but rule by the French or the Germans or the Russians – hardly an improvement in the eyes of the queen. Victoria saw herself far less as the head of a homogeneous nation-state than as the head of a multi-ethnic and multi-religious Empire. As such, she insisted time and again that other traditions and religions and even rulers in that Empire deserved respect. She therefore opposed the forcible Christianisation of India. At the same time, she saw no reason why a qualified black African should not be ordained a bishop in the Church of England or why a Moslem from India should not serve as her right-hand man at court. Analogously, even as she took for granted Britain's prevailing social structure, she deplored all talk of class conflict; and she welcomed examples of upward social mobility in her realm – such as the son of a butcher who became the Archbishop of York, and the prime minister (Benjamin Disraeli) who had directly 'risen from the people.'[17]

She was a female ruler in a patriarchal society, and she accepted the widespread belief that men and women occupied 'separate spheres' in society. Yet her very presence as queen ultimately strengthened the modern women's movement.

Victoria concurred in the belief that the public world, that of business and of politics, was predominantly masculine whereas the domestic world – the management of the household, the raising of small children, the upholding of standards of morality and rules of etiquette, and match-making – was fundamentally feminine. The doctrine of separate spheres was undermined in part by changes in the legal status of Victorian women – such as the Child Custody Act of 1839, the Divorce Act of 1857, the Married Women's Property Acts of 1870 and 1882, and the acts that gave women householders the right to vote in local government elections. Queen Victoria approved of some of these changes, just as she admired numerous women novelists and painters, and she looked on Florence Nightingale as 'one who has set so bright an example to our sex.'[18] She opposed, however, the later Victorian movement working towards complete legal, educational, and professional equality for all women. In 1872, the queen privately protested, indeed, against 'this mad, wicked folly of "Women's Rights", with all its attendant horrors. . . . It is a subject which makes the Queen so furious that she cannot contain herself. God made men and women different – then let them remain each in their own position.'[19]

Although the queen sometimes described her own position as 'anomalous,'[20] in practice she was compelled to concede that that position, and the spirit of responsibility that she brought to it, undermined the contention that women were by nature disqualified from exercising political authority. (And if the Salic Law barred reigning queens from German lands such as Prussia and Austria, it did not exclude them from the thrones of Spain, Portugal, Belgium, the Netherlands, Denmark, Sweden, and Russia as well as Great Britain.) During her long years of widowhood, at no time did the queen consider seriously the possibility of abdicating in favor of her eldest son. Members of Parliament who during the 1870s annually contended that the parliamentary franchise should be granted to women householders therefore often cited the eminent position occupied by Queen Victoria as a decisive argument in favor of their cause. In some respects her sex enhanced the queen's authority. The code of Victorian chivalry that placed women on a moral pedestal made it more difficult for her ministers to argue with their monarch than if she had been a man. She was thus able to display her spirit of determination, and even her idiosyncracies, in a manner that during those same years might not have been tolerated in a male monarch. She remained to the last, therefore, an active player as well as a symbol in Her Majesty's Government. The only woman in Britain during these past two centuries to exercise more political power than did Queen Victoria was Margaret Thatcher during her eleven-year prime ministership (1979–1990).

By the standards of our day, Queen Victoria often behaved in an 'unconstitutional' manner, but by the standards of her own era she did not.
It was only after the publication, three decades after her death, of many of her post-1861 letters that scholars (such as the historian Frank Hardie) became conscious of how deeply involved 'the widow at Windsor' had been in day-to-day politics and in the choosing of cabinet ministers, diplomats, and bishops – at times even prime ministers. She was intermittently willing to participate in public spectacles, but she did not see the ceremonial as her primary role in government. In a number of respects, she was, as David Cannadine has suggested, 'The last Hanoverian sovereign.'[21] How Britain's 'constitution' operated at any given time was in part a matter of statute law and in part a matter of slowly changing convention, and no step that the queen took either violated the law or lacked earlier precedent.

Why did her ministers accept a system in which the monarch not merely reigned but also participated, at least intermittently, in the process of ruling? One reason is that monarchs had always been involved in politics. Neither political party had in place, after all, a procedure whereby it could systematically choose a new leader if an old one died or retired, and political leaders approved of, or acquiesced in, a system whereby the monarch contributed to the process of selection. They also agreed that, if no party possessed an overall majority in the House of Commons, then an individual above the immediate party battle was necessary to arrange the consultations that might lead to a workable ministry. In his *English Constitution,* Walter Bagehot had prescribed but three 'rights' for a monarch once a ministry had been formed that was supported by a majority in the House of Commons: 'the right to be consulted, the right to encourage, and the right to warn.' As almost all her ministers discovered, such rights were far more than symbolic. They could prove immensely time-consuming; on occasion they even persuaded prime ministers to alter their policies.

Why did even Liberal champions such as Gladstone, who was often frustrated by the queen's attitudes, believe in the continuation of Britain's royal order? They had come to the conclusion that a stable constitutional monarchy remained superior to a republic. Ever since the establishment of its First Republic in 1792, after all, France had been a by-word in Europe for governmental instability, and even the Third French Republic (set up in 1871) seemed likely to be overthrown before long. The other large republic with which Britons were familiar was the United States, and between 1861 and 1865 it had engaged in a Civil War far more bloody than any conflict that took place in Europe between 1815 and 1914. The republics of South America had proved even less stable.

By contrast, the queen was a living symbol both of the state and of its long history. Ministries might form and ministries might fall, but the queen lived on as a symbol of the longevity of her country's permanent institutions. In an age deeply fascinated by historic origins, Queen Victoria was the direct descendant of King George I (1714–27), the first of the Hanoverians, and of King James I (1603–25), the first of the English Stuarts and a descendant of the prime medieval Scottish dynasty. In consequence, she was also a direct descendant of King Henry VII (1485–1509), the first of the Tudors, and therefore of England's great medieval monarchs King Edward I (1272–1307) and before him King Henry II (1154–89) and, even earlier, the Norman William the Conqueror (1066–87) and the Anglo-Saxon Alfred the Great (877–99). Flags and anthems had their virtues, no doubt, but for a nation or an empire to possess a personal symbolic head was better still. The existence of the monarch as a focus of loyalty also helped to disguise the possible confusions implicit in the fact that a Victorian might somehow, at the very same time, be a Yorkshireman, an English subject, an inhabitant of the United Kingdom, and a participant in the worldwide British Empire, allegiances that overlapped, no doubt, but that might on occasion come into conflict. In any event, when Queen Victoria compared herself to other rulers, she placed herself in the context of the Czar of Russia, the German Emperor, the Emperor of Austria–Hungary, the Sultan of the Ottoman Empire, and the king or queen of such lands as Italy and Spain. In the eyes of her ministers, even when at her (privately) most obstinate, Queen Victoria compared favorably with her Continental counterparts – as the head of a remarkably stable and surprisingly unrevolutionary constitutional monarchy.

Although some of Queen Victoria's private letters and journals have been destroyed, quite enough remain to make possible a multi-dimensional account of both her private and public life far longer than this biography – which has been designed to whet rather than to sate the reader's appetite. We can know Queen Victoria in her various roles – as monarch and as matriarch, and as symbol of an age – as well as we can know any person who lived in her century. In the words of the British critic Raymond Mortimer, 'Few letter writers have revealed their feelings more openly. Her pen made everything personal and expressive.'[22] In that personality, a spirit of romance was at war with an underlying penchant for truthfulness and common sense. On occasion she could behave in a manner both stuffy and ornery, and selfish; at the same time she had the ability to epitomize grace and to attract both awe and devotion. In her quest for respectability and her spirit of self-improvement, she reflected as well as helped mould her age. So did the strong sense of right and wrong that from childhood on she affirmed in both private and public affairs. In her attitudes toward race and religion she was generally less parochial than were most of her subjects. Whatever her errors of judgment, none proved fatal to her influence or to the dignity of her office. And by the time of her death, books and articles, pictures and engravings, coins and postage stamps had transformed the solitary princess into the single best-known person on earth as well as into an adjective that dictionaries are unlikely to define as 'archaic' for some generations to come. More than one hundred years after her death, her personality continues to fascinate and her image remains engraved on our collective memory.

Appendix 1: Queen Victoria's Maternal Relations

(simplified)

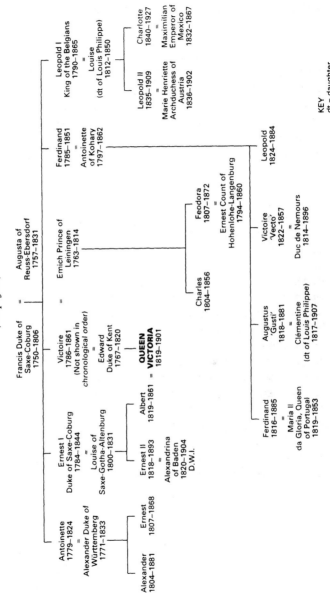

KEY
dt = daughter
D.W.I. = Died without issue

Appendix 2: Queen Victoria's Paternal Relations

(simplified)

George III 1738–1820 = Charlotte of Mecklenburg-Strelitz 1744–1818

George IV 1762–1830 = Caroline of Brunswick 1768–1821
- Charlotte 1796–1817 = Leopold of Saxe-Coburg 1790–1865

William IV 1765–1837 = Adelaide of Saxe-Meiningen 1792–1849 D.W.I.

Edward Duke of Kent 1767–1820 = Victoire of Saxe-Coburg 1786–1861
- **QUEEN VICTORIA** 1819–1901 = Albert Prince of Saxe-Coburg 1819–1861 →

Ernest Duke of Cumberland King of Hanover 1771–1851 = Frederica of Mecklenburg-Strelitz 1778–1841
- George V King of Hanover 1819–1878 = Mary of Saxe-Altenburg 1818–1907 →

Adolphus Duke of Cambridge 1774–1850 = Augusta of Hesse-Cassel 1797–1889
- George Duke of Cambridge 1819–1904
- Augusta 1822–1916 = Frederick Duke of Mecklenburg-Strelitz 1819–1904 →
- Mary Adelaide 1833–1897 = Francis Duke of Teck 1837–1900
  - Mary 1867–1953 = George V 1865–1936

Mary 1776–1857 = William Duke of Gloucester 1776–1834 D.W.I.

Sophia 1777–1848

Appendix 3: Queen Victoria as 'Grandmother of Europe'

(a simplified genealogy)

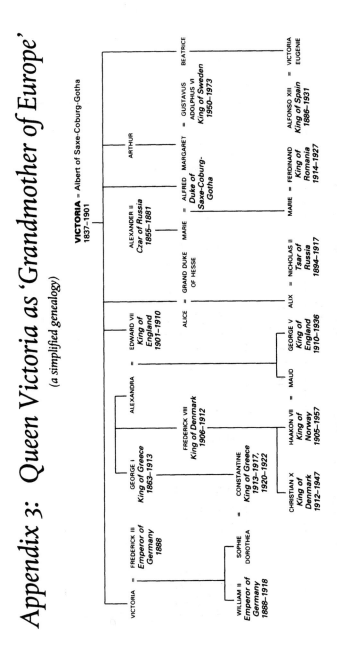

Notes

Notes to Chapter 1 : Introduction

1. H. C. G. Matthew, *Leslie Stephen and the New Dictionary of National Biography* (Cambridge: Cambridge University Press, 1995), p. 4.
2. Sidney Lee, *Queen Victoria: A Biography*, new and revised edn. (London: Smith Elder, 1904), pp. ix–x.
3. Ibid., p. ix.
4. Lytton Strachey, *Eminent Victorians* (Harmondsworth: Penguin Modern Classics), p. 9.
5. Frank Hardie, *The Political Influence of Queen Victoria, 1861–1901* (London, 1935), p. 30.
6. Lytton Strachey, *Queen Victoria* (New York: Harcourt Brace, 1922), p. 65. According to David Cecil, *Melbourne* (London, 1955), Victoria 'became at once his sovereign, his daughter, and the last love of his life' (p. 277).
7. *New Republic*, cited on back cover of Lytton Strachey, *Queen Victoria* (New York: Harbrace Paperback, n.d.).
8. Walter Bagehot, *The English Constitution* (first published in 1867; Ithaca, NY: Cornell University Press, 1967), p. 94.
9. Ibid., p. 111.
10. Kenneth Rose, *King George V* (London: Macmillan, 1983), p. 35.
11. Hardie, *Political Influence*, p. 26.
12. Ibid., p. 245.
13. Ibid., p. 238.
14. Elizabeth Longford, *Victoria R.I.* (London, 1964), p. 336.
15. Giles St Aubyn, *Queen Victoria: A Portrait* (London, 1991), p. 623.
16. David Cannadine, *The Pleasures of the Past* (London, 1989), pp. 27–9. Cannadine has written about Queen Victoria also in 'The Context, Performance and Meaning of Ritual: the British Monarchy and the "Invention of Tradition" *c.* 1820–1977,' in Eric Hobsbawm and Terence Ranger (eds), *The Invention of Tradition* (Cambridge, 1983), pp. 101–64, and 'The Last Hanoverian Sovereign? The Victorian Monarchy in Historical Perspective, 1688–1988,' in James Rosenheim (ed.), *The First Modern Society:*

Essays in English History in Honour of Lawrence Stone (Cambridge, 1989), pp. 127–65.

17. Marie Corelli, *The Passing of the Great Queen: A Tribute to the Noble Life of Victoria Regina* (New York, 1901).

18. Cf. W. L. Burn, *The Age of Equipoise: A Study of the Mid-Victorian Generation* (London, 1964), p. 36.

19. St Aubyn, *Queen Victoria: A Portrait*, p. 1

20. See Dorothy Thompson's review of Carolly Erickson, *Her Little Majesty: The Life of Queen Victoria* (London, 1997) in *Victorian Studies*, 42: 1 (Autumn 1998/99), p. 138.

21. Christopher Hibbert, *Queen Victoria: A Personal History* (New York: Basic Books, 2000). Christopher Hibbert is also the compiler and editor of that highly useful compilation, *Queen Victoria in Her Letters and Journals* (London: John Murray, 1984).

22. Cited in St Aubyn, *Queen Victoria: A Portrait*, p. 219.

23. Sir Theodore Martin, *Queen Victoria As I Knew Her* (London, 1908), p. 69.

24. Dorothy Thompson, *Queen Victoria: Gender and Power* (London: Virago Press, 1989). The book was published in the United States as *Queen Victoria: The Woman, the Monarchy, and the People* (New York, 1990). The fullest account of the relationship may be found in Tom Cullen, *The Empress Brown: The True Story of a Victorian Scandal* (Boston, 1969). See also Theo Aronson's *Heart of a Queen: Queen Victoria's Romantic Attachments* (London, 1991). It includes essays on Melbourne, Albert, Napoleon III, Benjamin Disraeli, and Abdul Karim as well as Brown.

25. Adrienne Munich, *Queen Victoria's Secrets* (New York, 1997), p. 2.

26. For a detailed review by Walter L. Arnstein, see *Pre-Raphaelite Studies; New Series* 6 (Spring 1997), pp. 102–03.

27. Margaret Homans, *Royal Representations: Queen Victoria and British Culture, 1837–1876* (Women in Culture and Society) (Chicago, 1998), p. xxxii.

28. Ibid., pp. 100–1. For a review by Walter L. Arnstein, see *Albion*, 31:4 (Winter 1999), pp. 680–1. In reviewing a related collection of essays, Margaret Homan and Adrienne Munich (eds), *Remaking Queen Victoria* (Cambridge, 1997), Dorothy Thompson notes that those essays are often 'divorced from the discipline of history,' in *Victorian Studies*, 42:1 (Autumn 1998/1999), p. 140.

29. William Kuhn, *Democratic Royalism: The Transformation of the British Monarchy, 1861–1914* (London, 1996).

30. Katherine Hudson, *A Royal Conflict* (London, 1994).

31. Lynne Vallone, *Becoming Victoria* (New Haven, CT, 2001).

32. Hannah Pakula, *An Uncommon Woman: The Empress Frederick* (London, 1996).

33. Noble Frankland, *Witness of a Century: The Life and Times of Prince Arthur Duke of Connaught, 1850–1942* (London, 1993); and Charlotte Zeepvat, *Prince Leopold: The Untold Story of Queen Victoria's Youngest Son* (Stroud, 1998).

34. Michaela Reid, *Ask Sir James: Sir James Reid, Personal Physician to Queen Victoria and Physician-in-Ordinary to Three Monarchs* (London: Penguin Books, 1987).

35. Richard Williams, *The Contentious Crown; Public Discussion of the British Monarchy in the Reign of Queen Victoria* (Aldershot, 1997).

36. Frank Prochaska, *Royal Bounty: The Making of the Welfare Monarchy* (New Haven, CT, 1995).

37. Ibid., p. 103.

38. Cited in Jerrold M. Packard, *Farewell in Splendor: The Passing of Queen Victoria and Her Age* (New York, 1995), p. 169.

Notes to Chapter 2: The Cloistered Princess

1. Although the Hanoverian dynasty is usually referred to as a German dynasty, just as the preceding Stuart dynasty may be described as Scottish, and the Tudor dynasty as Welsh, these successive dynasties were all interrelated. Thus George I was the great-grandson of King James I, the first Stuart king of England, and James I was in turn the great-great-grandson of King Henry VII, the first of the Tudor monarchs. Henry VII in turn was directly descended from Yorkist, Lancastrian, Plantagenet, Norman, and Anglo-Saxon predecessors.

2. See John Brooke, *King George III* (London, 1972), pp. 436–40. There was a proviso that any child over twenty-five could marry without such consent provided that he or she gave twelve-months' warning and that neither House of Parliament objected.

3. See Christopher Hibbert, *George IV: Regent and King* (Newton Abbot, 1975), pp. 92–101.

4. *Childe Harold's Pilgrimage*, Canto 4, cited in Dorothy Thompson, *Queen Victoria: The Woman, the Monarchy, and the People* (New York, 1990), p. 7.

5. Monica Charlot, *Victoria the Young Queen* (London, 1991), p. 11.

6. The Duke of Cumberland was the most socially disreputable and politically reactionary of the sons of George III. His wife, Princess Frederica of Mecklenburg-Strelitz, had already had two husbands, the second as the result of a shot-gun wedding.

7. See, for instance, Giles St Aubyn, *Queen Victoria: A Portrait* (New York, 1992), pp. 2–9. The description was provided by Baron Christian Stockmar, the long-time adviser of Victoria's uncle, Prince Leopold. In a

widely reviewed book, *The Victorians* (London, 2002), A. N. Wilson makes the sensational claim that the biological father of the princess was not the Duke of Kent but Sir John Conroy, a man who later became the financial adviser of the widowed Duchess of Kent. This highly implausible thesis assumes that Victoria's mother committed adultery with her husband's equerry less than three months after a marriage specifically contracted to assure a legitimate heir to Britain's throne. It is also undercut by the princess's strong physical resemblance to members of her father's family rather than to members of Conroy's.

8. Elizabeth Longford, *Victoria R.I.* (London, 1964), pp. 25–6.

9. Cf. St Aubyn, *Queen Victoria: A Portrait*, p. 17.

10. A few noted a German accent (see ibid., p. 16). A recording made of the Queen's voice, in extreme old age, was subsequently destroyed at Victoria's command. An earlier recording, made in 1888, survives in the Science Museum of London. All technological attempts to make it intelligible have failed, though one listener has discerned the word 'tomatoes.' See Paul Triton, *The Lost Voice of Queen Victoria: The Search for the First Royal Recording* (London, 1991).

11. Unpublished diary entry for May 24, 1899. I owe this citation to my friend Yvonne M. Ward of Latrobe University, Australia.

12. Cf. Charlot, *Victoria the Young Queen*, pp. 47–9. In *Becoming Victoria* (New Haven, CT, 2001), Lynne Vallone has provided the fullest and most meticulously documented account of the princess's education.

13. *Letters of Queen Victoria 1837–1861*, 1st ser., ed. A. C. Benson and Viscount Esher, 3 vols (London: John Murray, 1908), 1: 16–17.

14. Ibid., 1: 11.

15. Cited in Charlot, *Victoria the Young Queen*, p. 45.

16. *Letters*, 1st ser., 1: 46, 54.

17. Cited in Hibbert, *George IV*, p. 339.

18. *Letters*, 1st ser., 1: 52–3.

19. Cited in Cecil Woodham-Smith, *Queen Victoria: From her Birth to the Death of the Prince Consort* (New York, 1972), p. 172.

20. The most detailed exposition of Conroy's life, hopes, and delusions may be found in Katherine Hudson, *A Royal Conflict: Sir John Conroy and the Young Victoria* (London, 1994).

21. Longford, *Victoria R.I.*, pp. 44–6.

22. See, e.g., Charlot, *Victoria the Young Queen*, pp. 52, 55–61.

23. Letter to her eldest daughter, June 9, 1858. *Dearest Child: Private Correspondence of Queen Victoria and the Crown Princess of Prussia, 1858–1861*, ed. Roger Fulford (London, 1964), pp. 111–12.

24. Louis Auchincloss, *Persons of Consequence: Queen Victoria and Her Circle* (New York, 1979), p. 18.
25. Cited in Lynne Vallone, *Becoming Victoria*, p. 166.
26. *Letters*, 1st ser., 1: 38.
27. Longford, *Victoria R.I.*, pp. 53–4.
28. Cited in St Aubyn, *Queen Victoria: A Portrait*, p. 47.
29. Cited in Michael Joe Budds, 'Music at the Court of Queen Victoria: A Study of Music in the Life of the Queen and Her Participation in the Musical Life of Her Time' (unpublished PhD dissertation, University of Iowa, 1987), p. 120.
30. For the career of Lucy Anderson, see ibid., pp. 199, 214 and *passim*.
31. For numerous examples, see Marina Warner, *Queen Victoria's Sketchbook* (New York, 1979).
32. See Hudson, *A Royal Conflict*, pp. 2–3 and *passim*.
33. Longford, *Victoria R.I.*, pp. 50–2. For the details, see David Duff, *Victoria Travels* (New York, 1971), pp. 15–54.
34. Duff, *Victoria Travels*, pp. 39, 42–3.
35. Cited in Longford, *Victoria R.I.*, p. 59.
36. *Letters*, 1st ser., 1: 35–7, 41, 51–2, 53, 61, 70.
37. Cited in Lytton Strachey, *Queen Victoria* (London, 1921), p. 42.
38. Charlot, *Victoria the Young Queen*, p. 66.
39. Cited in ibid., p. 68.
40. Cited in Longford, *Victoria R.I.*, p. 71.
41. Cited in ibid., p. 73.
42. *Letters*, 1st ser., 1: 75.

Notes to Chapter 3: The Royal Teenager

1. *The Girlhood of Queen Victoria: A Selection from Her Majesty's Diaries Between the Years 1832 and 1840*, ed. Viscount Esher, 2 vols (New York, 1912), 1: 197.
2. Cited in Stanley Weintraub, *Victoria: An Intimate Biography* (New York, 1987), p. 99.
3. Elizabeth Longford, *Victoria R.I.* (London, 1964), pp. 144–8.
4. Dulcie Ashdown, *Queen Victoria's Mother* (London, 1974), p. 114.
5. Sidney Lee, *Queen Victoria: A Biography*, new and revised edn (London, 1904), pp. 62–3.
6. Weintraub, *Victoria: An Intimate Biography*, pp. 103–4, 116–17.
7. Cited in Sir Spencer Walpole, *Life of Lord John Russell*, 2 vols (London, 1889), 1: 284.

8. See, for instance, Geoffrey Finlayson, *Decade of Reform: England in the Eighteen-Thirties* (New York, 1970).

9. Lord Broughton [John Cam Hobhouse], *Recollections of a Long Life*, 6 vols (London, 1911), 5: 91.

10. Cited in Lee, *Queen Victoria: A Biography*, pp. 67–8.

11. Weintraub, *Victoria: An Intimate Biography*, p. 110; *Girlhood*, 1: 234. Nine years later Sir Moses Montefiore was granted the hereditary title of baronet. The official 'City of London' retained the boundaries of the walled medieval community even as geographically it had become only a small part of a metropolitan area of almost two million people.

12. The most reliable discussion of this subject may be found in chapters 2 and 3 of G. H. L. Le May, *The Victorian Constitution: Conventions, Usages and Contingencies* (New York, 1979).

13. The queen's journal as cited in *Letters of Queen Victoria, 1837–1861*, 1st ser., ed. A. C. Benson and Viscount Esher, 3 vols (London: John Murray, 1908), 1: 76.

14. *Girlhood*, 1: 221.

15. Ibid., 1: 301.

16. Ibid., 2: 14.

17. The six points of the People's Charter were: (1) universal manhood suffrage; (2) annual parliamentary elections; (3) voting by secret ballot; (4) equal electoral districts; (5) abolition of property qualifications for Members of Parliament; (6) payment of Members of Parliament.

18. *Girlhood*, 2: 148.

19. Chris Cook and Brendan Keith (eds), *British Historical Facts, 1830–1900* (New York, 1975), p. 139.

20. E.g. Louis Auchincloss, *Persons of Consequence: Queen Victoria and Her Circle* (New York, 1979), p. 27.

21. *Girlhood*, 2: 86, 89, 144.

22. For the details of Victoria's financial situation during her early years as queen, see Monica Charlot, *Victoria: The Young Queen* (Oxford, 1991), pp. 107–11.

23. The description of these events draws largely on chapter 7 of Charlot, *Victoria: The Young Queen.*

24. See ibid., pp. 128–40, and Richard Spall, Jr, 'The Bedchamber Crisis and the Hastings Scandal: Morals, Politics, and the Press at the Beginning of Victoria's Reign,' *Canadian Journal of History*, 12:1 (April 1987), pp. 19–39.

25. *Girlhood*, 2: 166–7.

26. 2: 171, 167–8.

27. *Letters*, 1st ser., 1: 162.

28. A comprehensive summary of the 'Bedchamber crisis' may be found in Charlot, *Victoria: The Young Queen*, pp. 140–6.
29. *Girlhood*, 1: 353, 355.
30. Ibid., 2: 154.
31. Ibid., 2: 188.
32. Ibid., 2: 153.
33. Charlot, *Victoria: The Young Queen*, pp. 164–6.

Notes to Chapter 4: The Model of Domesticity

1. Prime Minister Melbourne was distinctly uncomfortable with the idea of the marriage of first cousins. According to one report, he was privately assured by King Leopold of the Belgians that Albert – who differed markedly in personality from both his father and his elder brother – was not truly the son of Duke Ernest. Most of Albert's and Victoria's biographers continue to reject such a hypothesis. The most persuasive case on its behalf is made by David Duff in *Victoria and Albert* (New York, 1972), pp. 28–32, 66.
2. Cited in Paul Revere Frothingham, *Edward Everett, Orator and Statesman* (Boston, MA, 1925), pp. 193–4. Until 1856, Stockmar was often to serve as confidential adviser to both Albert and Victoria. He therefore plays a significant role in the television mini-series *Victoria and Albert* (2001). That series is successful in conveying the atmosphere of the courtship and of the early years of married life. It is less successful in conveying the manner in which, in the eyes of many of the queen's subjects, Albert remained a foreigner, and it only hints at the political concerns that came to occupy much of his daily routine.
3. Victoria's journal entries for October 10, 1839, cited in Monica Charlot, *Victoria: The Young Queen* (Oxford, 1991), p. 164.
4. Cited in Stanley Weintraub, *Uncrowned King: The Life of Prince Albert* (New York, 1997), p. 84.
5. The Greville *Memoirs*, cited in Charlot, *Victoria: The Young Queen*, p. 170.
6. Cited in Walter L. Arnstein, 'Queen Victoria and Religion,' in Gail Malmgreen (ed.), *Religion in the Lives of English Women, 1760–1930* (London, 1986), p. 93. See also Weintraub, *Uncrowned King*, p. 20.
7. Cited in Arnstein, 'Queen Victoria and Religion,' p. 94. The adviser was Dean (and subsequently Bishop and Archbishop) Randall Davidson.
8. Cited in Cecil Woodham-Smith, *Queen Victoria: From Her Birth to the Death of the Prince Consort* (London, 1972), p. 263. Albert was able to bring from Coburg a clerk, a librarian, and a stable master. See Stanley Weintraub, *Victoria: An Intimate Portrait* (New York, 1987), p. 137.

9. Cited in Charlot, *Victoria: The Young Queen*, pp. 180–1.
10. *Letters of Queen Victoria, 1837–1861*, 1st ser., ed. A. C. Benson and Viscount Esher, 3 vols (London: John Murray, 1908), 1: 269.
11. Cited in Weintraub, *Victoria: An Intimate Portrait*, p. 143.
12. Cited in Charlot, *Victoria: The Young Queen*, p. 189.
13. See ibid., pp. 220–1. This was to be the first of seven attempts to assassinate Queen Victoria. There were two attempts in 1842 and others in 1849, 1850, 1872, and 1882. All involved boys or young men described as loners or as insane. The most damaging attack took place in 1850 when an ex-soldier struck the queen violently with a cane and badly bruised her forehead. See Woodham-Smith, *Queen Victoria*, pp. 401–2.
14. Cited in Woodham-Smith, *Queen Victoria*, p. 285.
15. Cited in ibid.
16. Cited in Giles St Aubyn, *Queen Victoria: A Portrait* (New York, 1992), p. 168.
17. Sidney Lee, *Queen Victoria: A Biography*, rev. edn (London, 1904), p. 123.
18. *Letters*, 1st ser., 2: 27.
19. *Dearest Child: Private Correspondence of Queen Victoria and the Crown Princess of Prussia, 1858–1861*, ed. Roger Fulford (London, 1964), p. 186.
20. Cited in *Dear and Honoured Lady: The Correspondence between Queen Victoria and Alfred Tennyson*, ed. Hope Dyson and Sir Charles Tennyson (London, 1969), p. 32.
21. Cited in Sir Theodore Martin, *Life of the Prince Consort*, 5 vols (London, 1875–80), 5: 325.
22. Hector Bolitho, *Prince Albert* (London, 1938), p. 104.
23. The composer provided a detailed description of the occasion in a letter to his mother, which is cited (in translation) in George R. Marek, *Gentle Genius: The Story of Felix Mendelssohn* (New York, 1972), pp. 290–2.
24. The subject is treated in highly informative detail in Michael Joe Budds, 'Music at the Court of Queen Victoria: A Study of Music in the Life of the Queen and Her Participation in the Musical Life of Her Time' (unpublished PhD dissertation, University of Iowa, 1987). See also George Rowell, *Queen Victoria at the Theatre* (London, 1977).
25. *Dearest Child*, p. 112.
26. Ibid., pp. 94, 115.
27. *Darling Child: Private Correspondence of Queen Victoria and the German Crown Princess, 1871–1878*, ed. Roger Fulford (London, 1976), p. 159.
28. *Dearest Child*, pp. 143, 118; *Your Dear Letter: Private Correspondence of Queen Victoria and the Crown Princess of Prussia, 1865–1871*, ed. Roger Fulford (London, 1971), pp. 200–1.
29. In 'The Womanly Garb of Queen Victoria's Early Motherhood, 1840–42,'

in *Women's History Review*, 8:2 (1999), Yvonne M. Ward emphasises that the queen not only welcomed her first two children but visited the nursery several times a day and happily showed off her new family to domestic and foreign dignitaries (p. 288).

30. Cited in Robert Rhodes James, *Prince Albert* (London, 1983), p. 231.
31. *Dearest Child*, p. 68. See also Woodham-Smith, *Queen Victoria*, pp. 347–50.
32. Cited in Giles St Aubyn, *Edward VII: Prince and King* (London, 1979), p. 22. The often tempestuous relationship between Queen Victoria and her eldest son has been dramatized in a generally persuasive manner in the thirteen-part television mini-series, *Edward the King* (1986).
33. Cited in St Aubyn, *Queen Victoria: A Portrait*, pp. 202, 208.
34. Victoria cited in Greville *Memoirs*, entry for Jan. 22, 1848. Albert cited in Duff, *Victoria and Albert*, p. 232.
35. *Further Letters from the Archives of the House of Brandenburg-Prussia*, ed. Hector Bolitho (London, 1938), p. 74.
36. Daphne Bennett, *King without a Crown: Albert, Prince Consort of England, 1819–1861* (London, and Philadelphia, 1977), pp. 103–4; Duff, *Victoria and Albert*, pp. 213–15.
37. Bennett, *King Without a Crown*, p. 103.
38. Cited in Charlot, *Victoria: The Young Queen*, p. 283.
39. David Duff, *Victoria Travels* (New York, 1971), pp. 68–76.
40. *Letters*, 1st ser., 2: 35.
41. See Charlot, *Victoria: The Young Queen*, pp. 283–7, and St Aubyn, *Queen Victoria: A Portrait*, pp. 186–90.
42. See Charlot, *Victoria: The Young Queen*, p. 287, and John van der Kiste, *Children at Court, 1819–1914* (Stroud, 1995), pp. 55–7.
43. *The Scottish Diaries of Queen Victoria* (Newtongrange, 1980), entry for October 3, 1842. [The facsimile edition of an 1868 work, it is unpaginated.]
44. Ibid., entry for September 8, 1848.
45. Ibid., entry for August 30, 1849.
46. Simon Schama, 'Balmorality,' *The New Yorker*, August 11, 1997, p. 40.
47. Elizabeth Longford, *Victoria R.I.* (London, 1964), pp. 266–8. In *Queen Victoria's Secrets* (London, 1997), Adrienne Munich applies 'post-colonial theory' to the queen's love affair with Scotland. She contends that the construction of Balmoral Castle represented a 'colonizing masquerade' (p. 39) and she describes the adoption of Highland dress by the royal family as 'a way of colonizing through clothes' (p. 54). One could equally argue that the Scots were 'colonising' a queen who took enormous pride in being the closest surviving Protestant successor to King James VI

of Scotland, who in 1603 had succeeded Elizabeth as King James I of England. She found it easy, therefore, to visualise herself as what she was, the most direct Protestant descendant of the Stuart dynasty. At a time when Scotland was, in terms of population, over-represented in the United Kingdom Parliament, she also took increasing pride in cabinet ministers, soldiers, and administrators of the British Empire who were of Scottish origin.

48. Charlotte Zeepvat, *Prince Leopold: The Untold Story of Queen Victoria's Youngest Son* (Thrupp, Stroud 1998), pp. 2, 16–18, and *passim*. Leopold's case did much to advance the scientific study of hemophilia, the gene for which was probably transmitted by the queen from one of her maternal ancestors. The boy's full name was Leopold George Albert Duncan, the last 'as a compliment to dear Scotland.' Three of Queen Victoria's grandchildren and several great-grandchildren became hemophiliac. See chart in Zeepvat, *Prince Leopold*, pp. 206–7. See also *Further Letters*, p. 37.

49. See, e.g., Simon Schama, 'The Domestication of Majesty: Royal Family Portraiture, 1500–1850,' *Journal of Interdisciplinary History*, 17:1 (Summer 1986), pp. 155–83.

Notes to Chapter 5: The Reigning Partner

1. *Letters of Queen Victoria, 1837–1861*, 1st ser., eds A. C. Benson and Viscount Esher, 3 vols (London: John Murray, 1908), 1: 198.
2. Cited in Robert Rhodes James, *Prince Albert: A Biography* (London, 1984), p. 111.
3. The memoirs of Charles Greville, Clerk of the Privy Council, cited in Monica Charlot, *Victoria: The Young Queen* (Oxford, 1991), p. 262.
4. Cited in James, *Prince Albert*, p. 168.
5. *Letters*, 1st ser., 2: 367.
6. Cited in James, *Prince Albert*, p. 121.
7. Cited in ibid., p. 218.
8. Cited in ibid., p. 105.
9. Daphne Bennett, *King without a Crown: Albert, Prince Consort of England, 1819–1861* (London and Philadelphia, 1977), p. 169. See also James, *Prince Albert*, p. 153.
10. For the details of Peel's Irish policy, see Donal A. Kerr, *Peel, Priests and Politics: Sir Robert Peel's Administration and the Roman Catholic Church in Ireland, 1841–1846* (Oxford, 1982).
11. *Letters*, 1st ser., 2: 36–7.
12. Ibid., 2: 64.

13. Cited in James, *Prince Albert*, p. 164.

14. Cited in ibid., p. 151.

15. Cited in Walter L. Arnstein, *Britain Yesterday and Today: 1830 to the Present*, 8th edn (Boston, 2001), p. 46.

16. Cited in Elizabeth Longford, *Victoria R.I.* (London, 1964), p. 237.

17. The queen's journal for Jan. 10, 1847 and March 20, 1847 cited in Walter L. Arnstein, 'Queen Victoria's Other Island,' in Wm. Roger Louis (ed.), *More Adventures with Britannia: Personalities, Politics, and Culture in Britain* (Austin, TX and London, 1998), p. 48.

18. *Hansard*, 3rd Series, vol. 101, cols 792–3.

19. Arnstein, 'Queen Victoria's Other Island,' pp. 48–9. Cf. Cecil Woodham-Smith, *The Great Hunger: Ireland, 1845–1849* (London, 1962), p. 385. Curiously, Woodham-Smith makes no mention of Albert's contribution – nor do any of the historians who have relied on *The Great Hunger* for all their information about the reaction of the royal family to the famine.

20. Woodham-Smith, *Great Hunger*, pp. 151–2, 164–5. The records of the association 'disprove a legend, widely believed in Ireland' that the queen had limited her contribution to £5. Rothschild and the Duke of Devonshire each gave £1,000, Lord John Russell £300, and Sir Robert Peel £200.

21. See Arnstein, 'Queen Victoria's Other Island,' p. 49.

22. See ibid., pp. 49–50.

23. Ibid., p. 50. Albert conceded that the Roman Catholic hierarchy was also opposed to the plan to pay a salary to the clergy, but he felt certain that parish priests 'would gratefully accept it, if offered, but dare not avow it.'

24. *Letters*, 1st ser., 2: 199.

25. Cited in Woodham-Smith, *Great Hunger*, p. 386. That volume, on pp. 381–404, provides the fullest account of the royal visit of 1849.

26. Cited in ibid., p. 393.

27. *Letters*, 1st ser., 2: 226.

28. See Arnstein, 'Queen Victoria's Other Island,' pp. 51–2.

29. See Woodham-Smith, *Great Hunger*, p. 397.

30. Cited in Sir Theodore Martin, *The Life of His Royal Highness, the Prince Consort*, 5 vols (London, 1875–80), 2: 175.

31. Cited in ibid., 2: 175, 179. Nine months earlier he had recorded Lord Clarendon as reporting that there was not 'one *loyal* Roman Catholic in the Country.'

32. Woodham-Smith, *Great Hunger*, pp. 401–3. The Queen noted in her journal that the reception in Belfast was as 'hearty' but not 'quite so typically Irish' as it had been in Dublin. She noted also that 'the Protestants and

Roman Catholics are nearly equally divided in Belfast, and religious hatred and party feeling runs very high.' Martin, *Prince Consort*, 2: 179.

33. Arnstein, 'Queen Victoria's Other Island,' p. 55.
34. Cited in Joanna Richardson, *Victoria and Albert* (London, 1970), p. 142. See also Sidney Lee, *Queen Victoria: A Biography*, new and revised edn (London, 1904), p. 202. The baby was baptised at Buckingham Palace on June 22, 1850, with both the Duke of Wellington and the future German Emperor present as sponsors.
35. See James, *Prince Albert*, pp. 146, 172–7.
36. Ibid., p. 181.
37. For the quotations, see Christopher Hibbert (ed.), *Queen Victoria in Her Letters and Journals* (London, 1984), p. 84 and *Letters*, 1st. ser., 2: 17. For the broader context, see Jeffrey A. Auerbach, *The Great Exhibition of 1851: A Nation on Display* (New Haven, CT, 1999), and Hermione Hobhouse, *Prince Albert: His Life and Work* (London, 1983), ch. 7.

Notes to Chapter 6: Britain's Champion

1. *Regina vs. Palmerston: The Correspondence of Queen Victoria and Her Foreign and Prime Minister, 1837–1865*, ed. Brian Connell (Garden City, NY, 1961), p. 36.
2. Cited in ibid., p. 66.
3. Cited in ibid., p. 130.
4. Cited in ibid., p. 139.
5. The sentiments are those of William Ewart Gladstone. See Peter Stansky, *Gladstone: A Progress in Politics* (New York, 1979), ch. 3, 'Foreign Policy.'
6. See Jasper Ridley, *Lord Palmerston* (London, 1971), chs 26 and 27.
7. Cited in *Regina vs. Palmerston*, pp. 143–4.
8. Queen Victoria's reaction to 'Papal Aggression' is recounted in Walter L. Arnstein, 'Queen Victoria and the Challenge of Roman Catholicism,' *The Historian* (US), 58:2 (Winter 1996), pp. 301–4. The sources of the next few quotations are provided in the article.
9. *Letters*, 1st ser., 2: 279.
10. Ibid., 2: 281.
11. Ibid., 2: 277.
12. Cited in Connell, p. 158.
13. Cited in ibid., p. 160
14. Cited in Kingsley Martin, *The Triumph of Lord Palmerston* (London, 1924).
15. The fullest account of the criticism of Albert in 1853–4 may be found in Richard Williams, *The Contentious Crown: Public Discussion of the British Monarchy in the Reign of Queen Victoria* (Aldershot, 1997), pp. 99–107.

16. An account of Queen Victoria's involvement with the Crimean War (and sources for all quotations in the next several pages of this chapter) may be found in Walter L. Arnstein, 'The Warrior Queen: Reflections on Victoria and Her World,' *Albion*, 30:1 (Spring 1998), pp. 8–13.

17. *Further Letters from the Archives of the House of Brandenburg-Prussia*, ed. Hector Bolitho (London, 1938), p. 51.

18. *Letters* [1st ser.], 3: 139.

19. Cecil Woodham-Smith, *Queen Victoria: From Her Birth to the Death of the Prince Consort* (London, 1972), pp. 464–5; Christopher Hibbert, *The Royal Victorians: King Edward VII, His Family and Friends* (Philadelphia, 1976), p. 20.

20. Cited in Arnstein, 'Warrior Queen,' p. 11.

21. *Letters*, 1st ser., 3: 127.

22. Sir Edward Cook, *The Life of Florence Nightingale*, 2 vols (London, 1913), vol. 1, p. 307.

23. Bolitho (ed.), *Further Letters*, p. 75.

24. Ibid., 3: 185.

25. Cited in Arnstein, 'Warrior Queen,' pp. 7–8.

26. Cited in Herbert Maxwell, *Life of the 4th Earl of Clarendon*, 2 vols. (London, 1913) 2: 164.

27. Cited in *Regina vs. Palmerston*, p. 219.

28. *Letters*, 1st ser., 3: 186–7.

29. Ibid., 3: 127; cited in *Regina vs. Palmerston*, pp. 223–4.

30. *Letters*, 1st ser., 3: 298.

31. Ibid., 3: 304, note 2.

32. *Letters*, 1st ser., 3: 304. and Robert Rhodes James, *Prince Albert: A Biography* (London, 1983), pp. 260–1.

33. *Letters*, 1st ser., 3: 253.

34. For the details see Hannah Pakula, *An Uncommon Woman: The Empress Frederick* (London, 1996).

35. *Letters*, 1st ser., 3: 399.

36. Sir Theodore Martin, *Life of the Prince Consort*, 5 vols (London, 1875–80), 5: 117–18.

37. Ibid., 5: 119–20.

38. Cited in C. T. McIntire, *England Against the Papacy, 1858–1861* (Cambridge, 1983), p. 125.

39. Cited in ibid., p. 217.

40. *Letters*, 1st ser., 3: 388.

41. Philip Schreiner Klein, *President James Buchanan: A Biography* (University Park, PA, 1962), p. 320.

42. Daphne Bennett, *King Without a Crown: Albert, Prince Consort of England, 1819–1861* (London and Philadelphia, 1977), p. 328.

43. The best brief account may be found in Dana Bentley-Cranch, *Edward VII: Image of an Era, 1841–1910* (London, 1910), pp. 20–34.

44. Cited in Bennett, *King Without a Crown*, p. 328.

45. Klein, *President James Buchanan*, p. 350.

46. *Dearest Child: Correspondence of Queen Victoria and the Crown Princess of Prussia, 1858–1861*, ed. Roger Fulford (London, 1964), p. 279.

47. Bennett, *King Without a Crown*, p. 328, and Klein, *Buchanan*, p. 350.

48. *Letters of Queen Victoria 1862–1885*, 2nd ser., ed. G. E. Buckle, 3 vols (London, 1926–8), 1: 9–10; Sidney Lee, *Queen Victoria: A Biography*, new and revised edn (London, 1904), pp. 316–19; Norman B. Ferris, 'The Prince Consort, *The Times*, and the *Trent* Affair,' *Civil War History* (1960), pp. 152–6. For the broader context, see Walter L. Arnstein, 'Queen Victoria and the United States,' in Fred M. Leventhal and Roland Quinault (eds), *Anglo-American Attitudes: From Revolution to Partnership* (Aldershot, 2000), pp. 91–106.

49. Cited in James, *Prince Albert*, pp. 264–9. Doctors at the time attributed the death to typhoid. Medical historians of our own day suspect that the disease that had come to afflict the Prince over time was stomach cancer. See Stanley Weintraub, *Victoria: An Intimate Biography* (New York, 1987), pp. 299–300.

Notes to Chapter 7: The Reclusive Widow

1. Queen Victoria to Lord Derby Feb. 17, 1862, in the *Letters of Queen Victoria, 1862–1885*, 2nd ser., ed. G. E. Buckle, 3 vols (London, 1926–8), 1: 20.

2. Elisabeth Darby and Nicola Smith, *The Cult of the Prince Consort* (New Haven, CT, 1983), p. 3. This is a reliable illustrated survey of the manner in which Victoria reacted to Albert's death and of the manner in which he was memorialised – in prose, poetry, portraiture, sculpture, and architecture.

3. Daphne Bennett, *King without a Crown: Albert Prince Consort of England, 1819–1861* (London and Philadelphia, 1977), p. 375. Darby and Smith, *Cult of the Prince Consort*, p. 20.

4. Cited in Hannah Pakula, *An Uncommon Woman: The Empress Frederick* (London, 1996), p. 179.

5. *Dearest Mama: Private Correspondence of Queen Victoria and the Crown Princess of Prussia, 1861–1864*, ed. Roger Fulford (London, 1968), p. 34.

6. *Letters*, 2nd ser., 1: 36.

7. Cited in Elizabeth Longford, *Victoria R.I.* (London, 1964), pp. 383–4.

8. *The Later Correspondence of Lord John Russell, 1840–1878*, ed. G. P. Gooch, 2 vols (1925), 2: 323.

9. Cited in Bennett, *King without a Crown*, p. 376.
10. See, e.g., the examples provided by Roger Fulford in his introduction to *Dearest Mama*, pp. 8–11.
11. Darby and Smith, *Cult of the Prince Consort*, p. 30.
12. *Dearest Mama*, pp. 27, 154–5. See also Darby and Smith, *Cult of the Prince Consort*, ch. 2.
13. The London *Morning Post* of Dec. 2, 1875, cited in Darby and Smith, *Cult of the Prince Consort*, p. 40.
14. See Darby and Smith, *Cult of the Prince Consort*, ch. 3, and Chris Brooks (ed.), *The Albert Memorial* (New Haven, CT, 2001).
15. Cited in Darby and Smith, *Cult of the Prince Consort*, pp. 59, 13. The latter words are those of the Rev. Norman Macleod, the queen's favorite Scottish preacher.
16. *Dearest Mama*, pp. 85–6.
17. See Pakula, *An Uncommon Women*, pp. 144–5. See also Georgina Battiscombe, *Queen Alexandra* (Boston, 1969), ch. 1.
18. King Frederick VII of Denmark had divorced his first two wives before contracting a morganatic marriage with a one-time milliner whom he created a countess.
19. Cited in Pakula, *An Uncommon Women*, p. 145.
20. *Dearest Mama*, p. 127.
21. Cited in Battiscombe, *Queen Alexandra*, p. 43.
22. Ibid., pp. 44–50; *Dearest Mama*, p. 180.
23. *Your Dear Letter: Private Correspondence of Queen Victoria and the Crown Princess of Prussia, 1865–1871*, ed. Roger Fulford (London, 1971), pp. 165, 166.
24. Cited in Battiscombe, *Queen Alexandra*, p. 70.
25. Cited in Stanley Weintraub, *Queen Victoria: An Intimate Biography* (New York, 1987), p. 330.
26. *Letters*, 2nd ser., 1: 244.
27. Ibid., 1: 10, 28, 30, 102.
28. She did draft quite a few, however. See, e.g., ibid., 1: 48–50.
29. *Dearest Mama*, pp. 231, 241 and *passim*.
30. *Your Dear Letter*, p. 217.
31. *Letters*, 2nd ser., 1: 143–4.
32. Ibid., 1: 271.
33. Cited in Pakula, *An Uncommon Woman*, pp. 234–5.
34. *Your Dear Letter*, p. 79.
35. Ibid., pp. 286, 287, 310, 312, 315.
36. *Letters*, 2nd ser., 1: 32, 38–50.

37. Ibid., 1: 9–10; Sidney Lee, *Queen Victoria: A Biography*, new and revised edn (London, 1904), pp. 316–19.
38. Cited in Arthur Ponsonby, *Henry Ponsonby, Queen Victoria's Private Secretary: His Life from His Letters* (New York, 1944), p. 326.
39. *Hansard's Parliament Debates*, 3rd Series, 181: 22.
40. *Letters*, 2nd ser., 1: 265.
41. Ibid., 1: 266.
42. Walter Bagehot, *The English Constitution* (Ithaca: Cornell University Press, 1966), p. 86. First published in London in 1867.
43. *Your Dear Letter*, p. 320.
44. *Letters*, 2nd ser., 1: 255.
45. *Your Dear Letter*, p. 22.
46. Ibid., p. 48.
47. Cited in Longford, *Victoria R.I.*, p. 574.
48. Dorothy Thompson, *Queen Victoria: The Woman, the Monarchy, and the People* (New York, 1990), pp. 60, 68 and *passim*. The fullest account of the relationship may be found in Tom Cullen, *The Empress Brown: The Story of a Royal Friendship* (London, 1969). The film *Mrs. Brown* (1999) starring Dame Judy Dench and Billy Connolly is inaccurate on points of detail, and it unfairly caricatures several of the queen's English private secretaries, but its portrayal of the relation between Queen Victoria and John Brown is persuasive.
49. Cited in Longford, *Victoria R.I.*, p. 567.
50. *Your Dear Letter*, pp. 169, 172, 173.
51. *Letters*, 2nd ser., 1: 296. For the broader context, see Walter L. Arnstein, 'Queen Victoria Opens Parliament: The Disinvention of Tradition,' *Historical Research*, 63 (June 1990), pp. 178–94.
52. *Letters*, 1st ser., 1: 213.
53. *Letters*, 2nd ser., 1: 390–1; *Your Dear Letter*, p. 120.
54. On the subject of Victoria and the army, see Walter L. Arnstein, 'The Warrior Queen: Reflections on Victoria and Her World,' *Albion*, 30:1 (Spring 1998), pp. 1–28. See also Giles St Aubyn, *The Royal George: The Life of H.R.H. Prince George Duke of Cambridge, 1819–1904* (New York, 1964).
55. Sir Theodore Martin, *Queen Victoria as I Knew Her* (Edinburgh, 1908), pp. 119–20.
56. *Queen Victoria at Windsor and Balmoral: Letters from Her Grand-Daughter Princess Victoria of Prussia – June 1889*, ed. James Pope-Hennessy (London, 1959), p. 36.
57. Cited in Bennett, *King Without a Crown*, p. 144.
58. Cited in Longford, *Victoria R.I.*, p. 286.

59. *Your Dear Letter*, pp. 174, 176; Longford, *Victoria R.I.*, p. 442.
60. *Your Dear Letter*, pp. 180, 222.
61. Cited in David Tribe, *President Charles Bradlaugh, M.P.* (London, 1971), p. 131.
62. Cited in Philip Magnus, *Gladstone* (London, 1954), p. 200.
63. Philip Guedalla, *The Queen and Mr Gladstone* (Garden City, NY, 1934), p. 305.
64. Cited in Theo Aronson, *Victoria and Disraeli: the Making of a Romantic Partnership* (London, 1977), p. 117.
65. *Darling Child: Private Correspondence of Queen Victoria and the German Crown Princess, 1871–1878*, ed. Roger Fulford (London, 1976), p. 29.
66. Cited in Magnus, *Gladstone*, p. 218.
67. The republican impulse never faded entirely. See Richard Williams, *The Contentious Crown: Public Discussion of the British Monarchy in the Reign of Victoria* (Aldershot, 1997).
68. William M. Kuhn, *Democratic Royalism: The Transformation of the British Monarchy, 1861–1914* (London, 1996), p. 40. The chapter on Gladstone and Victoria constitutes the most acute recent reappraisal of that difficult relationship. See also *Darling Child*, pp. 31–2.
69. *Letters*, 2nd ser., 2: 194, 196.

Notes to Chapter 8: The Guardian of the Constitution

1. Cited in W. F. Monypenny and G. E. Buckle, *The Life of Benjamin Disraeli, Earl of Beaconsfield*, new and revised edition in 2 volumes (London, 1929), 2: 997.
2. *Darling Child: Private Correspondence of Queen Victoria and the German Crown Princess, 1871–1878*, ed. Roger Fulford (London, 1976), p. 47.
3. *Letters of Queen Victoria, 1862–1885*, 2nd series, ed. G. E. Buckle, 3 vols (London, 1926–8), 3: 222.
4. Ibid., 2: 315. On her accession, she contended in 1894, 'the Constitution was delivered into her keeping,' *Letters of Queen Victoria, 1886–1901*, 3rd ser., ed. G. E. Buckle, 3 vols (London 1950–2), 2: 450.
5. For details of the citations on this topic, see Walter L. Arnstein, 'Queen Victoria and the Challenge of Roman Catholicism,' *The Historian* (US), 58:2 (Winter 1996), pp. 295–314.
6. *Darling Child*, p. 178.
7. Philip Guedalla, *The Queen and Mr Gladstone* (Garden City, NY, 1934), p. 250.
8. *Letters*, 2nd ser., 1: 377.
9. *Darling Child*, p. 104.

10. *Letters*, 2nd ser., 2: 290, and citations in Arthur Ponsonby, *Henry Ponsonby, Queen Victoria's Private Secretary* (London, 1942), pp. 158, 177.
11. *Darling Child*, pp. 80–1.
12. Ibid., pp. 128, 129.
13. *Letters*, 2nd ser., 2: 321–2.
14. Ibid., 2: 333–4.
15. Ibid., 2: 414.
16. Ibid., 2: 428. See also Monypenny and Buckle, *Life of Benjamin Disraeli*, 2: 783–91.
17. Cited in Stanley Weintraub, *Edward the Caresser: The Playboy Prince Who Became Edward VII* (New York, 2001), p. 212.
18. Cited in ibid., p. 212.
19. *Darling Child*, p. 204.
20. Cited in Weintraub, *Edward the Caresser*, p. 222.
21. *Darling Child*, p. 211.
22. Cited in Monypenny and Buckle, *Life of Benjamin Disraeli*, 2: 808–9
23. In the pages that follow, for the sake of convenience, Beaconsfield will continue to be referred to as Disraeli.
24. *Letters*, 2nd ser., 2: 468.
25. See Bernard S. Cohn, 'Representing Authority in Victorian India,' in Eric Hobsbawm and Terence Ranger (eds), *The Invention of Tradition* (Cambridge, 1983), p. 206 and *passim*.
26. The subject of the queen's connection with the 'Eastern Question' of 1876–8 and the sources of all the quotations in the next several pages may be found in Walter L. Arnstein, 'The Warrior Queen: Reflections on Victoria and Her World,' *Albion*, 30:1 (Spring 1998), pp. 22–3.
27. Cited in Monypenny and Buckle, *Life of Benjamin Disraeli*, 2: 1089.
28. Cited in ibid., 2: 1194, 1196.
29. Cited in ibid., 2: 1219.
30. Cited in Theo Aronson, *Heart of a Queen: Queen Victoria's Romantic Attachments* (London, 1991), p. 189.
31. *Beloved Mama: Private Correspondence of Queen Victoria and the German Crown Princess, 1878–1885*, ed. Roger Fulford (London, 1981), p. 131.
32. Ibid., p. 93.
33. Cited in Monypenny and Buckle, *Life of Benjamin Disraeli*, 2: 550f.
34. Cited in ibid., 2: 674.
35. *Letters*, 2nd ser., 2: 424–5.
36. Ibid., 3: 16; Elizabeth Longford, *Victoria R.I.* (London, 1964) p. 546.
37. *Letters*, 2nd ser., 2: 131.
38. Ibid., 3: 114.

39. *Darling Child*, p. 185.
40. *Beloved Mama*, p. 87.
41. Longford, *Victoria R.I.*, p. 510.
42. *The Letters of Disraeli to Lady Chesterfield and Lady Bradford*, ed. Marquess of Zetland, 2 vols. (New York, 1929), 2: 326.
43. *Your Dear Letter: Private Correspondence of Queen Victoria and the Crown Princess of Prussia, 1865–1871*, ed. Roger Fulford (London, 1971), p. 263.
44. *Darling Child*, p. 209.
45. *Letters*, 2nd ser., 3: 18.
46. Her Highness Princess Marie Louise, *My Memories of Six Reigns* (New York, 1957), p. 19.
47. Cited in Stanley Weintraub, *Victoria: An Intimate Biography* (New York, 1987), p. 365.
48. Cited in Ponsonby, *Henry Ponsonby*, p. 85.
49. Cited in *Darling Loosy: Letters to Princess Louise*, ed. Elizabeth Longford (London, 1991), p. 31.
50. Longford, *Victoria R.I.*, pp. 464–6, 484; Giles St Aubyn, *Queen Victoria* (London, 1991), pp. 410–11. Also *Your Dear Letter*, pp. 142, 192.
51. St Aubyn, *Queen Victoria*, pp. 411, 479, 578.
52. *Letters*, 2nd ser., 3: 4.
53. See *Advice to a Grand-Daughter: Letters from Queen Victoria to Princess Victoria of Hesse*, ed. Richard Hough (London, 1975), pp. xix and *passim*.
54. Charlotte Zeepvat, *Prince Leopold: The Untold Story of Queen Victoria's Youngest Son* (Thrupp, Stroud, 1998), pp. 70, 65, and *passim*. In 1872, one of Leopold's doctors, John William Legg, published the first important treatise on hemophilia in English.
55. Cited in Ponsonby, *Henry Ponsonby*, p. 90.
56. *Beloved Mama*, p. 162.
57. Ibid., p. 137.
58. See Michaela Reid, *Ask Sir James: Sir James Reid, Personal Physician to Queen Victoria and Physician-in-Ordinary to Three Monarchs* (London, 1987), pp. 56–7.
59. Cited in Dorothy Thompson, *Queen Victoria: Gender and Power* (London, 1990), p. 57. See also Longford, *Victoria R.I.*, pp. 569–71 and *passim*.
60. *Beloved Mama*, pp. 159–60.
61. *Letters*, 2nd ser., 3: 37–8.
62. Cited in Robert Blake, *Disraeli* (London, 1966), p. 620; and in *Letters of Disraeli*, 2: 330.
63. Cited in Monypenny and Buckle, *Life of Benjamin Disraeli*, 2: 1397.
64. *Letters*, 2nd ser., 3: 48.

65. His title was an honourary one. He was the heir to the Dukedom of Devonshire, but he had been legally elected to the House of Commons.
66. Cited in Monypenny and Buckle, *Life of Benjamin Disraeli*, 2: 1411.
67. Cited in Guedalla, *Queen and Mr Gladstone*, p. 514.
68. *Letters*, 2nd ser., 3: 250.
69. Cited in Walter L. Arnstein, 'Queen Victoria's Speeches from the Throne: A New Look,' in Alan O'Day (ed.), *Government and Institutions in the Post-1832 United Kingdom* (Lewiston/Queenstown/Lampeter, 1995), pp. 145–6.
70. Cited in Guedalla, *Queen and Mr Gladstone*, pp. 505–08.
71. Cited in Longford, *Victoria, R.I.*, p. 582.
72. For Prince Arthur and the Egyptian campaign, see Walter Arnstein, 'The Warrior Queen,' pp. 20–1, and Noble Frankland, *Witness of a Century: The Life and Times of Prince Arthur Duke of Connaught, 1850–1942* (London, 1993), *passim*.
73. Cited in Guedalla, *Queen and Mr Gladstone*, p. 637.
74. *Beloved Mama*, pp. 90, 148, 182.
75. Cited in Guedalla, *Queen and Mr Gladstone*, pp. 511, 531–2.
76. *Letters*, 2nd ser., 3: 517, 519–20.
77. Cited in Guedalla, *Queen and Mr Gladstone*, pp. 625–6.
78. Cited in ibid., pp. 673–4.

Notes to Chapter 9: The Imperial Matriarch

1. *Letters of Queen Victoria, 1886–1901*, 3rd series, ed. George Earle Buckle, 3 vols (London, 1930–2), 1: 55.
2. Ibid., 1: v.
3. The eighty-sixth Irish Home Rule MP was elected for the English city of Liverpool.
4. *Letters*, 3rd ser., 1: 33, 78–9.
5. Ibid., 1: 10, 121.
6. See Walter L. Arnstein, 'Queen Victoria and the Challenge of Roman Catholicism,' *The Historian* (US), 58:2 (Winter 1996), pp. 309–11.
7. *Advice to a Grand-daughter: Letters from Queen Victoria to Princess Victoria of Hesse*, ed. Richard Hough (London, 1975), p. 81.
8. *Letters*, 3rd ser., 1: 172–3.
9. Ibid., 1: 31.
10. Ibid., 1: 166, 374.
11. *Darling Child: Private Correspondence of Queen Victoria and the German Crown Princess, 1871–1878*, ed. Roger Fulford (London, 1976), pp. 209, 86, 112.

12. *Beloved Mama: Private Correspondence of Queen Victoria and the German Crown Princess, 1878–1885*, ed. Roger Fulford (London, 1981), p. 177.

13. Cited in *Dear and Honoured Lady: The Correspondence between Queen Victoria and Alfred Tennyson*, ed. Hope Dyson and Charles Tennyson (London, 1969), p. 117.

14. *Beloved Mama*, p. 177.

15. For the fullest account of the Golden Jubilee, see Jeffrey L. Lant, *Insubstantial Pageant: Ceremony and Confusion at Queen Victoria's Court* (New York, 1980), pp. 52, 61–3, and *passim*. See also Stanley Weintraub, *Victoria: An Intimate Biography* (New York, 1987), ch. I.

16. Cited in Lant, *Insubstantial Pageant*, pp. 52, 155, 103.

17. Cited in ibid., p. 152.

18. Cited in ibid., p. 156.

19. *Letters*, 3rd ser., 1: 148.

20. See Lant, *Insubstantial Pageant*, pp. 136, 147–9.

21. See ibid., pp. 92, 156.

22. See Thomas Richards, 'The Image of Victoria in the Year of Jubilee,' *Victorian Studies*, 31: 1 (Autumn 1987), pp. 7–32.

23. Weintraub, *Victoria: An Intimate Biography*, p. 3; *Vanity Fair*, June 25, 1887.

24. *Letters*, 3rd ser., 3: 350.

25. Cited in Lant, *Insubstantial Pageant*, pp. 12–13.

26. Frank Prochaska, *Royal Bounty: The Making of the Welfare Monarchy* (London, 1995), pp. 69, 110. Most of the material on this and the next several pages is drawn from chapters 3 and 4 of that highly important book.

27. Ibid., pp. 96–7.

28. Cited in ibid., p. 111.

29. See Olive Checkland, *Philanthropy in Victorian Scotland* (Edinburgh, 1980), pp. 226–28.

30. Cited in Prochaska, *Royal Bounty*, p. 135.

31. Sidney Lee, *Queen Victoria: A Biography*, new and revised edn (London, 1904), pp. 267, 290, 534.

32. *Letters*, 3rd ser., 1: 390,

33. Ibid., 1: 404–6.

34. Ibid., 1: 417.

35. Cited in Giles St Aubyn, *Queen Victoria: A Portrait* (New York, 1992), p. 536. One part of William's statement was altogether untrue inasmuch as a German doctor had attended his birth.

36. Cf. *Letters*, 3rd ser., 1: 425. I[mperator] = Emperor; R[ex] = King.

37. Ibid., 1: 440–1; St Aubyn, *Queen Victoria: A Portrait*, p. 540.

38. Hannah Pakula, *An Uncommon Woman: The Empress Frederick* (London, 1996), p. 441; *Letters*, 3rd ser., 2: 51.

39. *Beloved and Darling Child: Last Letters between Queen Victoria and Her Eldest Daughter, 1886–1901*, ed. Agatha Ramm (London, 1990), p. 196.

40. *Advice to a Grand-daughter*, p. 110.

41. *Beloved and Darling Child*, p. 195; St Aubyn, *Queen Victoria: A Portrait*, p. 577.

42. *Letters of Queen Victoria, 1837–1861*, 1st series, ed. A. C. Benson and Viscount Esher, 3 vols (London: John Murray, 1908), 3: 296.

43. *Letters*, 3rd ser., 1: 377.

44. Ibid., 1: 377, 668.

45. Ibid., 2: 13.

46. See Neil Parsons, *King Khama, Emperor Joe, and the Great White Queen: Victorian Britain through African Eyes* (Chicago, 1998).

47. *Letters of Queen Victoria, 1862–1885*, 2nd ser., ed. G. E. Buckle, 3 vols (London, 1926–8), 2: 361.

48. Cited in Robin W. Winks (ed.), *British Imperialism: Gold, God, Glory* (New York, 1963), p. 78.

49. *Letters*, 3rd ser., 2: 26.

50. Cf. ibid., 1: 103–4; 305, 317, 334.

51. Ibid., 1: 277,

52. David Cannadine, *Ornamentalism: How the British Saw their Empire* (London, 2001).

53. *Letters*, 3rd ser., 2: 67.

54. A persuasive account of the relationship may be found in chapters 19 and 20 of Theo Aronson, *Heart of a Queen: Queen Victoria's Romantic Attachments* (London, 1991). See also Michaela Reid, *Ask Sir James: Sir James Reid, Personal Physician to Queen Victoria and Physician-in-Ordinary to Three Monarchs* (London, 1989). After the queen's death, King Edward VII soon saw to it that his mother's personal letters to the Munshi were burned and that the latter was shipped back to India.

55. *Beloved and Darling Child*, p. 32; *Letters*, 3rd ser., 2: 48.

56. Ibid., p. 161.

57. Herbert Sullivan and Newman Flower, *Sir Arthur Sullivan: His Life, Letters, and Diaries* (London, 1927), pp. 71, 11n., 133.

58. *Martyn Green's Treasury of Gilbert & Sullivan* (New York, 1941), pp. 649, 650, 630.

59. Queen Victoria's journal for May 11, 1887 is cited in Frances Dimond and Roger Taylor, *Crown and Camera: The Royal Family and Photography, 1842–1910* (Harmondsworth, 1987), p. 180.

60. Weintraub, *Victoria: An Intimate Biography*, pp. 493, 179–80.
61. *Beloved and Darling Child*, pp. 144–6; the 'defect . . . Constitution' letter is cited in Elizabeth Longford, *Victoria R.I.* (London, 1964), p. 650.
62. Robert Rhodes James, *Rosebery* (London, 1963), pp. 335–6.
63. Cited in ibid., p. 339n.
64. *Letters*, 3rd ser., 3: 36.
65. Cited in Lant, *Insubstantial Pageant*, p. 216.
66. Cited in ibid., p. 219.
67. See William M. Kuhn, *Democratic Royalism: The Transformation of the British Monarchy, 1861–1914* (Basingstoke, 1996), p. 67.
68. *Letters*, 3 rd ser., 3: 174.
69. Cited in Stanley Weintraub, *Edward the Caresser: The Playboy Prince who Became Edward VII* (New York, 2001), p. 351.
70. *Letters*, 3rd ser., 3: 44–5.
71. Cited in Beckles Willson, *American Ambassadors to Great Britain, 1786–1929* (New York, 1929), p. 14.
72. *Beloved and Darling Child*, p. 213.
73. Ibid., p. 215.
74. Ibid., p. 235.
75. *Letters*, 3rd ser., 3: 371.
76. Ibid., 3: 362.
77. Ibid., 3: 397.
78. Cited in Longford, *Victoria R.I.*, p. 683.
79. *Letters*, 3rd ser., 3: 409.
80. Weintraub, *Victoria: An Intimate Biography*, p. 620.
81. *Letters*, 3rd ser., 3: 614.
82. Lee, *Queen Victoria: A Biography*, p. 526; Frederick Ponsonby, *Recollections of Three Reigns* (London, 1951), pp. 78–9.
83. *Letters*, 3rd ser., 3: 503–5.
84. Cited in Walter L. Arnstein, 'The Warrior Queen: Reflections on Victoria and Her World,' *Albion* 30:1 (Spring 1998), p. 25.
85. See Walter L. Arnstein, 'Queen Victoria's Other Ireland,' in *More Adventures with Britannia*, ed. Wm Roger Louis (Austin, TX, 1998), p. 59 and passim.
86. Cited in Arnstein, 'Warrior Queen', p. 25.
87. Jerrold M. Packard, *Farewell in Splendor: The Passing of Queen Victoria and Her Age* (New York, 1995), pp. 19–20.
88. Reid, *Ask Sir James*, p. 205.
89. Packard, *Farewell*, pp. 59–60.
90. Ibid., pp. 220, 238–57.

Notes to Chapter 10: The Paradoxical Monarch

1. Jerrold M. Packard, *Farewell in Splendor: The Passing of Queen Victoria and Her Age* (New York, 1995), p. 258 and *passim*.
2. *Truth*, Jan. 24, 1901, p. 178.
3. *St James's Gazette*, Jan. 22, 1901.
4. Cited in Alfred F. Havighurst, *Britain in Transition*, 4th edn (Chicago, 1985), p. 2.
5. Elizabeth Longford, *Victoria R.I.* (London, 1964), p. 707.
6. Alan Hardy explores the origins of that statement in *Queen Victoria Was Amused* (London, 1976).
7. Cited in Longford, *Victoria R.I.*, p. 498.
8. See Michael Nelson, *Queen Victoria and the Discovery of the Riviera* (London, 2001).
9. Cf. *Darling Child: Private Correspondence of Queen Victoria and the Crown Princess of Prussia, 1871–1878*, ed. Roger Fulford (London, 1976), p. 257.
10. *Letters of Queen Victoria, 1886–1901*, 3rd series, ed. G. E. Buckle, 3 vols (London, 1930–2), 1: 448.
11. *Dearest Child: Correspondence of Queen Victoria and the Crown Princess of Prussia, 1858–1861*, ed. Roger Fulford (London, 1964), pp. 184, 252, pp. 182, 254.
12. *Darling Child*, p. 159.
13. Mark Twain, *Queen Victoria's Jubilee* [New York, *c.*1900].
14. Byron Farwell, *Queen Victoria's Little Wars* (London, 1973). See also Thomas Pakenham, *The Anglo-Boer War* (London, 1979).
15. Farwell, *Queen Victoria's Little Wars*, pp. 216–17.
16. Cited in Arthur Lawrence Merrill, *Life and Times of Queen Victoria* (Chicago, 1901), p. 216.
17. Cited in Longford, *Victoria R.I.*, pp, 673, 442.
18. *The Letters of Queen Victoria, 1837–1861*, 1st series, ed. A. C. Benson and Viscount Esher, 3 vols. (London: John Murray, 1908), 3: 170.
19. Cited in Sir Theodore Martin, *Queen Victoria As I Knew Her* (London, 1908), p. 69.
20. *Dearest Child*, p. 67.
21. David Cannadine, 'The Last Hanoverian Sovereign? The Victorian Monarchy in Historical Persepective, 1688–1988,' in *The First Modern Society: Essays in English History in Honor of Lawrence Stone*, ed. James Rosenheim (New York, 1989), pp. 127–65.
22. Cited in *Beloved Mama: Private Correspondence of Queen Victoria and the German Crown Princess, 1878–1885*, ed. Roger Fulford (London. 1981), p. 10.

Select Bibliography

Primary Sources

Advice to a Grand-Daughter: Letters from Queen Victoria to Princess Victoria of Hesse, ed. Richard Hough (London, 1975).

Broughton, Lord [John Cam Hobhouse], *Recollections of a Long Life*, 6 vols (London, 1911).

Connell, Brian, *Regina vs. Palmerston: The Correspondence of Queen Victoria and Her Foreign and Prime Minister, 1837–1865* (Garden City, NY, 1961).

Darling Loosy: Letters to Princess Louise, ed. Elizabeth Longford (London, 1991).

Dear and Honoured Lady: The Correspondence between Queen Victoria and Alfred Tennyson, ed. Hope Dyson and Sir Charles Tennyson (London, 1969).

Dearest Child: Private Correspondence of Queen Victoria and the Crown Princess of Prussia, 1858–1861, ed. Roger Fulford (London, 1964).

Dearest Mama: Private Correspondence of Queen Victoria and the Crown Princess of Prussia, 1861–1864, ed. Roger Fulford (London, 1968).

Your Dear Letter: Private Correspondence of Queen Victoria and the Crown Princess of Prussia, 1865–1871, ed. Roger Fulford (London, 1971).

Darling Child: Private Correspondence of Queen Victoria and the German Crown Princess, 1871–1878, ed. Roger Fulford (London, 1976).

Beloved Mama: Private Correspondence of Queen Victoria and the German Crown Princess, 1878–1885, ed. Roger Fulford (London, 1981).

Beloved and Darling Child: Last Letters between Queen Victoria and Her Eldest Daughter, 1886–1901, ed. Agatha Ramm (London, 1990).

Further Letters from the Archives of the House of Brandenburg-Prussia, ed. Hector Bolitho (London, 1938).

The Girlhood of Queen Victoria: A Selection from Her Majesty's Diaries between the Years 1832 and 1840, ed. Viscount Esher (London, 1912).

Guedalla, Philip, *The Queen and Mr Gladstone* (Garden City, NY, 1934). [Includes excerpts from more than 1200 letters.]

The Later Correspondence of Lord John Russell, 1840–1878, ed. G. P. Gooch, 2 vols (London, 1925).

The Letters of Disraeli to Lady Chesterfield and Lady Bradford, ed. Marquess of Zetland, 2 vols (New York, 1929).

Letters of Queen Victoria, 1837–1861, 1st ser., ed. A. C. Benson and Viscount Esher, 3 vols (London, 1908).

Letters of Queen Victoria, 1862–1885, 2nd ser., ed. G. E. Buckle, 3 vols (London, 1926–8).

Letters of Queen Victoria, 1886–1901, 3rd ser., ed. G. E. Buckle, 3 vols (London, 1930–2).

Life with Queen Victoria: Marie Mallet's Letters from Court, 1887–1901, ed. Victor Mallet (Boston, 1968).

Her Highness Princess Marie Louise, *My Memories of Six Reigns* (New York, 1957).

Martin, Sir Theodore, *Queen Victoria As I Knew Her* (London, 1908).

My Mistress the Queen: The Letters of Frieda Arnold, Dresser to Queen Victoria, ed. Benita Stoney and Heinrich C. Weltzien, trans. Sheila de Bellaigue (London, 1994).

Queen Victoria at Windsor and Balmoral: Letters from Her Grand-Daughter Princess Victoria of Prussia – June 1889, ed. James Pope-Hennesy (London, 1959).

Queen Victoria in Her Letters and Journals, ed. Christopher Hibbert (London, 1984).

Twain, Mark, *Queen Victoria's Jubilee.* (New York, 1900).

Secondary Works

Biographies of Queen Victoria

Charlot, Monica, *Victoria the Young Queen* (Oxford, 1991).

Corelli, Marie, *The Passing of the Great Queen: A Tribute to the Noble Life of Victoria Regina* (New York, 1901).

Duff, David, *Victoria and Albert* (New York, 1972).

Erickson, Carolly, *Her Little Majesty: The Life of Queen Victoria* (London, 1997).

Hibbert, Christopher, *Queen Victoria: A Personal History* (London, 2000).

Gernsheim, Helmut and Alison, *Victoria R: A Biography with 400 Illustrations based on Her Personal Photograph Albums* (London, 1959).

Lee, Sidney, *Queen Victoria: A Biography*, new and revised edn (London, 1904).

Longford, Elizabeth, *Victoria R.I.* (London, 1964).

Marshall, Dorothy, *The Life and Times of Victoria* (London, 1972).

Merrill, Arthur Lawrence, *Life and Times of Queen Victoria* (Chicago, 1901).

Richardson, Joanna, *Victoria & Albert* (London, 1970).

St Aubyn, Giles, *Queen Victoria: A Portrait* (London, 1991).

Strachey, Lytton, *Queen Victoria* (London, 1921).

Thompson, Dorothy, *Queen Victoria, Gender and Power* (London, 1989).

Weintraub, Stanley, *Victoria: An Intimate Portrait* (New York, 1987).

Woodham-Smith, Cecil, *Queen Victoria: From Her Birth to the Death of the Prince Consort* (London, 1972).

Related biographies, monographs, and surveys

Arengo-Jones, Peter, *Queen Victoria in Switzerland* (London, 1995).

Arnstein, Walter L., *Britain Yesterday and Today: 1830 to the Present*, 8th edn (Boston, 2001).

Aronson, Theo, *Heart of a Queen: Queen Victoria's Romantic Attachments* (London, 1991).

——, *Victoria and Disraeli: The Making of a Romantic Partnership* (London, 1977).

Ashdown, Dulcie, *Queen Victoria's Mother* (London, 1974).

Auchincloss, Louis, *Persons of Consequence: Queen Victoria and Her Circle* (New York, 1979).

Auerbach, Jeffrey A., *The Great Exhibition of 1851: A Nation on Display* (New Haven, CT, 1999).

Bagehot, Walter, *The English Constitution* (London, 1867).

Battiscombe, Georgina, *Queen Alexandra* (London, 1969).

Bennett, Daphne, *King without a Crown: Albert, Prince Consort of England, 1819–1861* (London and Philadelphia, 1977).

Bentley-Cranch, Dana, *Edward VII: Image of an Era, 1841–1910* (London, 1992).

Blake, Robert, *Disraeli* (London 1966).

Bolitho, Hector, *Prince Albert* (London, 1938).

Brooke, John, *King George III* (London, 1972).

Brooks, Chris (ed.), *The Albert Memorial* (New Haven, CT, 2001).

Burn, W. L., *The Age of Equipoise: A Study of the Mid-Victorian Generation* (London, 1964).

Cannadine, David, *The Pleasures of the Past* (London, 1989).

——, *Ornamentalism: How the British Saw their Empire* (London, 2001).

Cecil, David, *Melbourne* (London, 1955).

Checkland, Olive, *Philanthropy in Victorian Scotland* (Edinburgh, 1980).

Cook, Chris, and Brendan Keith (eds), *British Historical Facts, 1830–1900* (New York, 1975).

Cullen, Tom, *The Empress Brown: The True Story of a Victorian Scandal* (Boston, 1969).

Darby, Elisabeth, and Nicola Smith, *The Cult of the Prince Consort* (New Haven, CT, 1983).

Dimond, Frances, and Roger Taylor, *Crown and Camera: The Royal Family and Photography, 1842–1910* (Harmondsworth, 1987).

Duff, David, *Victoria Travels* (New York, 1971).

Farwell, Byron, *Queen Victoria's Little Wars* (London, 1973).

Finlayson, Geoffrey, *Decade of Reform: England in the Eighteen-Thirties* (New York, 1970).

Frankland, Noble, *Witness of a Century: The Life and Times of Prince Arthur Duke of Connaught, 1850–1942* (London, 1993).

Frothingham, Paul Revere, *Edward Everett, Orator and Statesman* (Boston, 1925).

Hardie, Frank, *The Political Influence of the British Monarchy, 1868–1952* (London, 1970).

——, *The Political Influence of Queen Victoria, 1861–1901* (London, 1935).

Hardy, Alan, *Queen Victoria was Amused* (London, 1976).

Hibbert, Christopher, *George IV: Regent and King* (Newton Abbot, 1975).

——, *The Royal Victorians: King Edward VII, His Family and Friends* (Philadelphia, 1976).

Hobhouse, Hermione, *Prince Albert: His Life and Work* (London, 1983).

Homans, Margaret, *Royal Representations: Queen Victoria and British Culture, 1837–1876* (Chicago, 1998).

——, and Adrienne Munich (eds), *Remaking Queen Victoria* (Cambridge, 1997).

Hudson, Katherine, *A Royal Conflict: Sir John Conroy and the Young Victoria* (London, 1994).

James, Robert Rhodes, *Prince Albert* (London, 1983).

——, *Rosebery* (London, 1963).

Klein, Philip Schreiner, *President James Buchanan: A Biography* (University Park, PA, 1962).

Kuhn, William, *Democratic Royalism: The Transformation of the British Monarchy, 1861–1914* (London, 1996).

——, *Henry and Mary Ponsonby: Life at the Court of Queen Victoria* (London, 2002).

Lant, Jeffrey L., *Insubstantial Pageant: Ceremony and Confusion at Queen Victoria's Court* (New York, 1980).

Le May, G. H. L., *The Victorian Constitution: Conventions, Usages and Contingencies* (New York, 1979).

McIntire, C. T., *England Against the Papacy, 1858–1861* (Cambridge, 1983).

Magnus, Philip, *Gladstone* (London, 1954).

Marek, George R., *Gentle Genius: The Story of Felix Mendelssohn* (New York, 1972).

Martin, Kingsley, *The Triumph of Lord Palmerston* (London, 1924).

Martin, Sir Theodore, *The Life of His Royal Highness, the Prince Consort*, 5 vols (London, 1875–80).

Matthew, H. C. G., *Leslie Stephen and the New Dictionary of National Biography* (Cambridge, 1995).

Monypenny, W. G., and G. E. Buckle, *The Life of Benjamin Disraeli, Earl of Beaconsfield*, 2-vol. edition (London, 1929).

Munich, Adrienne, *Queen Victoria's Secrets* (New York, 1997).

Nelson, Michael, *Queen Victoria and the Discovery of the Riviera* (London, 2001).

Packard, Jerrold M., *Farewell in Splendor: The Passing of Queen Victoria and Her Age* (New York, 1995).

Pakenham, Thomas, *The Anglo-Boer War* (London, 1979).

Pakula, Hannah, *An Uncommon Woman: The Empress Frederick* (London, 1996).

Parsons, Neil, *King Khama, Emperor Joe, and the Great White Queen: Victorian Britain through African Eyes* (Chicago, 1998).

Ponsonby, Arthur, *Henry Ponsonby, Queen Victoria's Private Secretary: His Life from His Letters* (New York, 1944).

Ponsonby, Frederick, *Recollections of Three Reigns* (London, 1951).

Porter, Andrew (ed.), *The Nineteenth Century*, vol. III of the *Oxford History of the British Empire* (Oxford, 1999).

Prochaska, Frank, *Royal Bounty: The Making of the Welfare Monarchy* (New Haven, CT, 1995).

Reid, Michaela, *Ask Sir James: Sir James Reid, Personal Physician to Queen Victoria and Physician-in-Ordinary to Three Monarchs* (London, 1987).

Ridley, Jasper, *Lord Palmerston* (London, 1971).

Rose, Kenneth, *King George V* (London, 1983).

Rowell, George, *Queen Victoria at the Theatre* (London, 1977).

St Aubyn, Giles, *Edward VII: Prince and King* (London, 1979).

——, *The Royal George: The Life of H.R.H. Prince George Duke of Cambridge, 1819–1904* (London, 1964).

Staniland, Kay, *In Royal Fashion: The Clothes of Princess Charlotte of Wales and Queen Victoria, 1796–1901* (London, 1997).

Stansky, Peter, *Gladstone: A Progress in Politics* (New York, 1979).

Strachey, Lytton, *Eminent Victorians* (London, 1918).

Sullivan, Herbert, and Newman Flower, *Sir Arthur Sullivan: His Life, Letters, and Diaries* (London, 1927).

Tribe, David, *President Charles Bradlaugh, M.P.* (London, 1971).

Triton, Paul, *The Lost Voice of Queen Victoria: The Search for the First Royal Recording* (London, 1991).

Twain, Mark, *Queen Victoria's Jubilee* [New York, c. 1900].

Vallone, Lynne, *Becoming Victoria* (New Haven, CT, 2001).

Van der Kiste, John, *Children at Court, 1819–1914* (Stroud, 1995).

Victorian Britain: An Encyclopedia, ed. Sally Mitchell (New York, 1988).

Walpole, Sir Spencer, *Life of Lord John Russell*, 2 vols (London, 1889).

Warner, Marina, *Queen Victoria's Sketchbook* (London, 1979).

Weintraub, Stanley, *Edward the Caresser: The Playboy Prince who Became Edward VII* (New York, 2001).

——, *Uncrowned King: The Life of Prince Albert* (New York, 1997).

Williams, Richard, *The Contentious Crown: Public Discussion of the British Monarchy in the Reign of Queen Victoria* (Aldershot, 1997).

Willson, Beckles, *American Ambassadors to Great Britain, 1786–1929* (New York, 1929).

Wilson, A. N., *The Victorians* (London, 2002).

Winks, Robin W. (ed), *British Imperialism: Gold, God, Glory* (New York, 1963).

Woodham-Smith, Cecil, *The Great Hunger: Ireland, 1845–1849* (London, 1962).

Zeepvat, Charlotte, *Prince Leopold: The Untold Story of Queen Victoria's Youngest Son* (Thrupp, Stroud 1998).

Articles, essays, and unpublished dissertations

Arnstein, Walter L., 'Queen Victoria Opens Parliament: The Disinvention of Tradition,' *Historical Research*, 63 (June 1990).

——, 'Queen Victoria and the Challenge of Roman Catholicism,' *The Historian* [US], 58:2 (Winter 1996).

——, 'Queen Victoria and Religion,' in Gail Malmgreen (ed.), *Religion in the Lives of English Women, 1760–1930* (London, 1986).

——, 'Queen Victoria and the United States,' in Fred M. Leventhal and Roland Quinault (eds), *Anglo-American Attitudes: From Revolution to Partnership* (London, 2000).

——, 'Queen Victoria's Diamond Jubilee,' *The American Scholar*, 66:4 (Autumn 1997).

——, 'Queen Victoria's Other Island,' in Wm Roger Louis (ed.), *More Adventures with Britannia: Personalities, Politics, and Culture in Britain* (Austin, TX, 1998).

——, 'Queen Victoria's Speeches from the Throne: A New Look,' in Alan O'Day (ed.), *Government and Institutions in the Post-1832 United Kingdom* (Lewiston/Queenstown/Lampeter, 1995).

——,'The Warrior Queen: Reflections on Victoria and Her World,' *Albion*, 30:1 (Spring 1998).

Budds, Michael Joe, 'Music at the Court of Queen Victoria: A Study of Music in the Life of the Queen and Her Participation in the Musical Life of Her Time' (unpublished PhD dissertation, University of Iowa, 1987).

Cannadine, David, 'The Context, Performance and Meaning of Ritual: The British Monarchy and the "Invention of Tradition" *c.* 1820–1977,' in Eric Hobsbawm and Terence Ranger (eds), *The Invention of Tradition* (Cambridge, 1983).

Cannadine, David, 'The Last Hanoverian Sovereign? The Victorian Monarchy in Historical Perspective, 1688–1988,' in James Rosenheim (ed.), *The First Modern Society: Essays in English History in Honor of Lawrence Stone* (New York, 1989).

Cohn, Bernard S., 'Representing Authority in Victorian India,' in Eric Hobsbawm and Terence Ranger (eds), *The Invention of Tradition* (Cambridge, 1983).

Ferris, Norman B., 'The Prince Consort, *The Times*, and the *Trent* Affair,' *Civil War History* (1960).

Millar, Delia, 'Royal Patronage and Influence,' in John M. MacKenzie (ed.), *The Victorian Vision: Inventing New Britain* (London, 2001).

Nash, David, 'Stability in a Distracted Age? The Recent Historiography of the Victorian Monarchy', *Nineteenth-Century Studies*, 12 (1998), 135–51.

Richards, Thomas, 'The Image of Victoria in the Year of Jubilee,' *Victorian Studies*, 31:1 (Autumn 1987).

Schama, Simon, 'Balmorality,' *The New Yorker*, August 11, 1997.

——, 'The Domestication of Majesty: Royal Family Portraiture, 1500–1850,' *Journal of Interdisciplinary History*, 17:1 (Summer 1986).

Spall, Richard, Jr, 'The Bedchamber Crisis and the Hastings Scandal: Morals, Politics, and the Press at the Beginning of Victoria's Reign,' *Canadian Journal of History*, 12:1 (April 1987).

Tyrell, Alex, and Yvonne Ward, ' "God Bless Her Little Majesty:" The Popularising of Monarchy in the 1840s,' *National Identities*, 2:3 (2000).

Ward, Yvonne M., 'The Womanly Garb of Queen Victoria's Early Motherhood, 1840–42,' *Women's History Review*, 8: 2 (1999).

Index